The St Andrews Railway

by
Andrew Hajducki, Michael Jodeluk,
& Alan Simpson

THE OAKWOOD PRESS

© Oakwood Press & Andrew Hajducki, M. Jodeluk & A. Simpson 2008

British Library Cataloguing in Publication Data
A Record for this book is available from the British Library
ISBN 978 0 85361 673 3

Typeset by Oakwood Graphics.
Repro by PKmediaworks, Cranborne, Dorset.
Printed by Cambrian Printers, Aberystwyth, Ceredigion.

Ex-NBR 'Scott' class 4-4-0 No. 62438 *Peter Poundtext* dwarfs a very young Hamish Stevenson at St Andrews engine shed, 19th April, 1953. *J.L. Stevenson*

Title page: 'B1' No. 61292 on a branch train of Gresley stock leaving St Andrews for Leuchars - note the tablet exchanger on the cab-side. *NBRSG Collection*

Front cover: Thompson 'B1' class 4-6-0 No. 61180 waits to depart with a weedkiller train - the last steam-hauled train from St Andrews, 17th April, 1967. *Mike Jodeluk*

Rear cover, top: A Railway Clearing House map showing the railways around East Fife and St Andrews.

Rear cover, bottom: Metro-Cammell dmu on a St Andrews branch working at Leuchars Junction, 1968. *S. Rankin*

Published by The Oakwood Press (Usk), P.O. Box 13, Usk, Mon., NP15 1YS.
E-mail: sales@oakwoodpress.co.uk
Website: www.oakwoodpress.co.uk

Contents

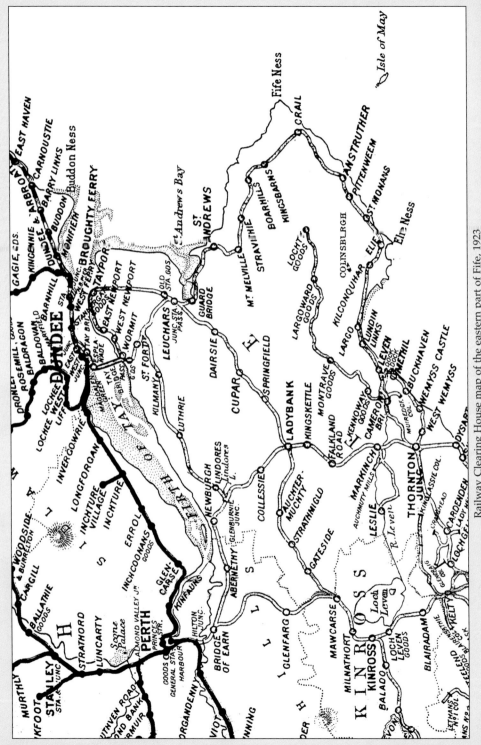

Railway Clearing House map of the eastern part of Fife, 1923

Preface

The five mile branch line from Leuchars Junction, situated on the main line from Edinburgh to Aberdeen a short distance south of the Tay Bridge, to the ancient university city and home of golf, St Andrews, was but the first link of the coastal railway that eventually encircled East Fife. Built entirely by local interests and with local capital, the small and independent St Andrews Railway was a pioneer of the cheap railway movement, a reaction against spiralling costs, over-elaborate engineering and rapacious landowners. It prospered as its eponymous terminus attracted an increasing amount of traffic and eventually was absorbed by Scotland's largest company, the North British. Carrying goods to St Andrews and the substantial traffic associated with the Guardbridge papermill, this single track branch line also carried considerable numbers of passengers, including joyful holidaymakers, expectant golfers, distracted academics, demure schoolgirls and reluctant servicemen. Surviving Grouping, Nationalisation, and, in its last years, dieselisation, the Leuchars to St Andrews branch finally succumbed to closure in an era of hollow promises and unfulfilled hopes; even now, more than a generation later, there are still those who hope to resurrect the line and restore its fortunes.

Subsequent volumes in this series will cover the rich and complex story, from inception to extinction, of the Anstruther & St Andrews Railway, The Leven & East of Fife Railway and the three goods-only branches that served Lochty, Muiredge and Leven Dock. Together they will form a comprehensive history of the 40 mile-long coastal railway line that linked Leuchars to Thornton via St Andrews, the picturesque burghs and seaports of the East Neuk, the industrial areas around Leven and the quiet farmlands that lay between. Each book will, so far as is possible, be self-contained and with only such minimal degree of repetition and overlap as will achieve this purpose.

The East Fife railways are worthy of remembrance, and for the sake of the generation who waited at the level crossings for the passing of the trains and for those born too late to have known them, the authors sincerely hope that they have achieved the simple aim of telling their tale. If we have made mistakes, and indeed we are bound to have done so, then we trust that our readers will forgive and correct us – we genuinely welcome any comments or additional information via our publishers and will endeavour to answer personally all correspondence so received.

Accordingly we now invite all of those who share our affectionate interest for this very distinctive part of our country to join us in climbing aboard and revisting the slow, but much loved, East Neuk trains of our childhood and, please, remember to have your tickets ready for inspection!

A.H., M.J. & A.S.
Cellardyke, Edinburgh, Stirling and Kirkcaldy
St Andrew's Day, 2007

St Andrews harbour with the ruins of the cathedral in the background. In this Victorian view the local fishing boats all bear Dundee registration numbers.
A.W. Brotchie Collection

Chapter One

Fields of Eden:
From Leuchars to St Andrews

'From the shores of its tidal waters, St Andrews looks, in different lights,
now close at hand, now unattainably remote.'
John Geddie, 'The Fringes of Fife'

Kingdom, County and East Neuk

Fife, a county comprising of some 320,000 acres or so and, at its greatest extent, 40 miles long and 20 in breadth, forms a long peninsula which juts out into the cold North Sea. It is bounded, to the south and the north, by the two great firths of Forth and Tay that eat into the coastline of Eastern Scotland, while its western boundary is formed by the steep ramparts of the Ochils and Cleish Hills. And yet such a description does not do justice to this proud and distinctive part of Scotland which has survived as an entity for more than a millennium and, even today, is referred to by its inhabitants as the Kingdom of Fife, although the days when Dunfermline was the seat of the Scottish kings are now long past.

A county of many contrasts, Fife includes a wide variety of landscapes from farmlands scarred with the remains of a vanished industrial past, towns both picturesque and functional, ancient harbours surrounded by once prestigious burghs and a rolling countryside which, although not spectacular, is often pleasing to the eye. In its medieval past the trading links with the Netherlands and communities bordering the Baltic led to a plentiful interchange of ideas and accounted for the red pantiles and crow-stepped gables found throughout the county. In more modern times coal mining, fishing and a diverse range of manufacturing industries led to a new prosperity which was crowned with the opening of the two great railway bridges which formed the principal entries to the Kingdom. The 20th century saw the rise of modern technologies that defeated the old, a flood of holidaymakers to the strands of the 'beggar's mantle fringed with gold' and new problems and opportunities which faced, but did little to defeat, the indomitable spirit of both natives and incomers. When all is said and done and whatever changes befall them, Fifers are still justifiably proud of their independence of mind and strength of character and the oft-repeated maxim that 'you need a lang spin tae sup wi' a Fifer', far from being an insult, is widely regarded as a badge of honour to those who live between the Forth and Tay.

The Kingdom flourishes and no more so than in its most easterly part, the East Neuk, which contains the handful of prettily-set parishes between Leuchars and Largo. Predominantly rural, this area of undulating sandstone hills intersected by burns running from west to east, is ringed by a band of rich and productive arable farmland where root crops and grain are grown and sheep and cattle are grazed. At the beginning of Victoria's reign, small craft

7

ventured out from the diminutive harbours to catch the herring and even smaller boats kept close to the often inhospitable shoreline to bring in crabs and lobsters while all of the trades associated with the fishing industry, such as curers and coopers, net repairers and fisher lassies, were all found locally to a greater or lesser extent. The area was largely self-sufficient, a self-sufficiency caused in the main by the fact that the inhabitants were poor and the roads in and out of the area were such that journeys to anywhere else were long, hard and, above all else, expensive.

Place of the Rushes

The most northerly parish served by the St Andrews railways was Leuchars, centred on its eponymous village and aptly deriving its name from the Gaelic *Leachair* meaning 'the place of the rushes' in view of its marshy and, formerly at any rate, ill-drained situation. The village of the same name, later to gain significance as the junction for the St Andrews line, was until recent times, a small and insignificant place dominated by its castle and parish church, both of which dated from the 12th century with the latter surviving to the present day and thought to contain the finest extant example of Romanesque architecture in Fife. In the 17th century there were only four villages in the whole county that could fund a parish school and Leuchars was one of them. By the end of the following century Leuchars was not only the site of two annual fairs but also, in the words of Robert Heron in his *Scotland Delineated* of 1796, 'a rising village, having a considerable number of inhabitants, mostly manufacturers'. The manufacturers in question were weavers producing on their wooden handlooms coarse and fine linens which they supplied to the merchants of Dundee and Cupar, but with the rise of power-driven machinery the weavers started to fall on hard times and the economy of the village began to suffer accordingly. By 1840 there was a penny post office in Leuchars but the inhabitants of the village had to resort to Cupar, St Andrews and even Dundee for their more important purchases and the fairs, which dealt respectively in the sale of cattle and small wares were 'but like those in many other towns and villages, they are now but little attended'; in time Leuchars would achieve a new notoriety by becoming an important railway junction and the site of an important RAF station.

Galliots, Schooners and Sloops

A mile or so south of Leuchars village, and situated in the parish of that name, lay the small settlement of Guardbridge,* otherwise known as Gair or Guar Bridge, *gair* being the Scots word for a strip of fine or green grass which presumably must have been a feature of the area worthy of note. Here was the lowest crossing point on the River Eden, one of the principal rivers of the county which rises close to the Kinross-shire border and flows for nearly 30 miles through its verdant strath, passing right through the county town of

---

* This version, adopted by the railway, is used throughout this book except when reference is made to the Guard Bridge Paper Company, who used the alternative two-word form.

The mouth of the Eden.   *Farnie's Handbook to St Andrews, 1860*

Cupar and its junction with the smaller Motray Water.* Close by was the ford which was superseded in the early 15th century by a six-arch stone bridge which owed its inception to the influential and enterprising churchman, Bishop Wardlaw of St Andrews. The Bishop's bridge did away with the need to wade through the strong currents and cross the dangerous alluvial flats and it was built to such a high standard that it survives to the present day, although motor traffic is now carried over its parallel 1937 ferro-concrete replacement.

By the time that the railway arrived there, Guardbridge had become the scene of two main industries, namely a brick and tile works which relied on the fine clay deposits found locally and a distillery which was situated next to the mudflats between the Eden and Motray. The distillery was described in an 1860 guidebook to St Andrews as 'looming large and ghostly from the near bank of the Eden estuary'. As part of a growing trend to build large licensed whisky distilleries to replace the smaller home stills once common in Scotland, the plant at Seggie (from the Scots word meaning sedgy or overgrown with reeds) was opened in 1810 by William Haig, a local man whose family owned two barley-growing farms in the vicinity. The Seggie Distillery flourished and eventually extended to three stills with a total capacity of some 18,000 gallons. In the words of John Leighton, in his 1840 *History of the County of Fife*:

> For purity and excellence of quality, the plain patent spirit manufactured here stands unsurpassed and is highly esteemed both in Scotland and England. The quantity of spirits annually made here is from 400,000 to 500,000 gallons - a large proportion of which is sent to the English markets for the purpose of being converted into gin ... There is a still increasing quantity of the spirits used in Scotland both for making compounds and for family consumption - many persons preferring it to the finest malt spirits.

The mashing process was performed by steam-driven machinery and two engines, one a Boulton & Watt of 25 horsepower erected in 1820 and the other an old engine formerly in use at the closed distillery at Kincaple. William Haig subsequently expanded his interests to include the Seggie Brick and Tile Works and became Provost of St Andrews where it was said that he 'raised the financial affairs of the city ... to a flourishing condition'. He died in 1847 and control of Seggie passed to Robert and John, his sons. Robert was later to become a Director of the St Andrews Railway while John, who founded the famous Cameron Bridge Distillery, was the first and only Chairman of the Leven Railway and had the added distinction of being the father of Field Marshall Douglas Haig who commanded the British forces during the major part of World War I.

* The Motray is also known as the Moultrie Burn, although in modern times this latter name is rarely used.

Guardbridge was, by virtue of its situation, a small but busy port with three piers on the riverbank, namely the Cupar and Leuchars Piers, close to the confluence of the Motray Burn and the Eden and a third pier, subsequently known as the Railway Pier, situated close to the road bridge. From the Leuchars and Cupar Piers small vessels conveyed supplies of Tyneside coal and East Anglian grain to the distillery, wood from Scandinavia bound for a timber merchant in St Andrews, and cargoes of bones which were destined for a bone mill in Ceres where fertiliser was made. Outward traffic was, principally, casks of whisky from the Seggie Distillery which were mainly bound for the London market and some local crops, mainly potatoes, for Edinburgh and Dundee. In addition a small number of fishing vessels were based at Guardbridge and they usually landed haddock, cod, ling, skate, halibut and flounders for what was described as the home market with any unsold surplus being sent to Cupar; during the season these same boats were employed in the herring fisheries off Caithness. Some indication of the traffic which formerly used the quays at Guardbridge in the immediate pre-railway era can be found in a colourful report which appeared in the *Fifeshire Journal* of 18th April, 1839:

The tiny harbour here, formerly used alone for the exportation of grain and potatoes, or the importation of coal or stone, has all at once sprung up into the dignity of an ample shipping port. The vessels from the domains of none fewer than four European potentates have in the course of a single week come alongside. The following are the arrivals in the past week:

Galliot *Ikinawilimina*	Captain H.I. Topps, with bones from Holland. King William I's domain.
Galliot *Fortuna*	Captain Johan, with bones from Hanover. King Ernest Augustus's domain.
Galliot *Enigheden*	Captain Frederick Frederischen, with timber from Norway. King Charles XIV's domain (and who is to take home potatoes).
Schooner *Margery*	Captain D. Pringle with coals from Newcastle, and to reload with potatoes.
Sloop *Eagle*	Captain John Morrison from Clackmannan with coals and to be reload with grain.

The last two vessels are, of course, subject to Queen Victoria.

By way of explanation a galliot was a swift Dutch cargo boat (from Dutch *galjoot*, derived from Latin *galea*); a schooner was a small sea-going fore and aft-rigged vessel with between two and four masts; a sloop was a small one-masted fore and aft-rigged vessel.

Merrily Down the Stream

The road and railway from Guardbridge to St Andrews, four miles distant, followed closely the south bank of the Eden estuary, passing over the wind-blown sand of the links close to the wide and muddy tidal flats. On the north bank lay the edge of Tentsmuir, a wild and lonely tract of land intersected with dykes and water-filled ditches. It was said that, even as late as the 19th century, this place was inhabited by a race apart, descendants of shipwrecked Scandinavian sailors who indulged, or so it was claimed by locals, in wrecking, smuggling, poaching and other unlawful activities and they were said to live in a land into which few respectable folk would venture. Of this stretch of river which John Geddie in his evocative work *The Fringes of Fife* described, somewhat poetically, as flowing through 'these 'Elysian fields beyond Eden', he also commented that:

> ... impressions must vary greatly with the weather, the time of the year, and most of all, the state of the tide. They may be cheerful and inspiring in bright sunshine and with a heaving and clumping flood of sea-water filling the whole space, a mile or more in breadth between us and the sands of Tents Moor they can be depressing enough under a heavy sky and at half-tide, when sand banks and mud banks, and stretches of black mussel scalp and dull coloured sea marsh, rise out of the shallow waters that were once the port of St Andrews, and fill nearly the whole space from shore to shore.

Shellfish, in particular mussels (which were used as bait), were collected from the shore and exported further up the coast as far north as Caithness and until recent times the remains of the granite ballast carried by the small vessels used in this trade were scattered along the shoreline and used as a building material in the vicinity. Another local coastal industry was the collection of a bright green sea-weed (known as sea-sleek) which was used as manure for arable crops. At Coble Shore, a sand spit ran out for the shore and blocked more than half of the estuary's width a mile or so east of Guardbridge while at St Andrews another spit of blown sand reached out for a good mile or so in a northerly direction and terminated at Out Head, where the Eden estuary reached the sea.

The road route into St Andrews, as it approaches the city,* runs eastwards away from the shore, traversing, according to John Leighton, an area of low flat land 'which is in tillage, though the larger portion forms links or downs, which afford pasture for sheep, and are also useful as a place of pleasant recreation for the inhabitants of the city'. The route then skirts the Pilmour Links and estate of Strathtyrum before entering the built-up environment via North Street; while the railway ran to the north of the road bisecting the famous links and Old Course before terminating at the very edge of the town.

Saints, Scholars and Setbacks

St Andrews is a name which conjures up many images - a market town and Royal Burgh of great charm, a harbour giving shelter from the often stormy and dangerous bay of the same name, the romantic ruins of a once great cathedral and ecclesiastical centre, a holiday resort with two great sweeps of sand, the oldest of all of Scotland's universities, second only in age in Britain to the universities of Oxford and Cambridge. Perhaps most famously of all it is known throughout the world as the site of The Royal and Ancient and the undisputed original home of golf - and all of these crammed into such a small city.

The first settlements here dated from neolithic times, the promontory of St Andrews being originally known in Gaelic as *Muckross*, 'the swine headland'. In 370 AD a Greek monk, Regulus or St Rule, was said to have come ashore at this

---

*   City, Burgh or Town? Since in St Andrews the nomenclature seems to be interchangeable, the present authors have used all three indiscriminately to reflect this!

point, bringing with him the bones of the apostle St Andrew, and as a result the Culdee Christians then knew the place as *Kilrule*, the Church of Rule - another theory, however, is that Regulus was an Irish missionary of the 6th century. In or about the year 550 the Ulsterman Cainneach, or Kenny, founded the priory of Kirkheugh in honour of St Andrew and in 736 the site had become the seat of a Bishop. By the beginning of the 10th century *Kilrule* or *Kinrimund* ('the hill of the high kings') had become the seat of the Bishop of Alba (Scotland) and by the end of the century King Kenneth III had renamed the place as St Andrews, after the newly-adopted patron saint of the united nation. This was followed by the expansion of the town, the building of a great cathedral and castle, and a period of prosperity with local merchants trading with their counterparts in Northern Europe. St Andrews duly became a place of church government and a centre of pilgrimage. In 1411 Bishop Wardlaw founded Scotland's first university in the town and this was joined in 1450 by Bishop Kennedy's temporal College of St Salvator. By the beginning of the 16th century the population of the town had risen to nearly 14,000 and 60 ships were based at the harbour. At the time of the great annual Senzie fair, which lasted 15 days, no fewer than 300 vessels, many of them foreign, cast anchor in the bay.

During the Reformation the town saw much change with the abandonment and eventual destruction of its cathedral and the secularisation of many of its institutions, including the university which became so demoralised and run-down that it was in real danger of being moved away to the distant city of Perth. By the 18th century it could be truly said that the fortunes of St Andrews were still on the wane and that great observer and diarist, James Boswell, on visiting St Andrews with Dr Johnson, commented that 'it was somewhat dispiriting, to see this ancient arch-episcopal city now sadly deserted', adding that no guidebook to the antiquities of the town seemed to be available at the present time. Fifty years later Robert Chalmers described the place as being, 'a highly genteel town, the ghost of a fine city now only remarkable as the seat of the least prosperous University in Scotland; the number of students seldom exceeds 140 and its harbour boasts of little trade. There still persists an almost monastic quiet', although another contemporary commentator added, on a more upbeat note, that St Andrews was also 'a great resort of families of limited income who have nothing to do, and who can enjoy its elegant and literary society at comparatively little expense'.

The Home of Golf

Slowly the city began to recover, and new roads were built to Kennoway, Crail and Largo, the storm-damaged harbour was repaired and there was a small revival of local trade but the city remained something of a rural backwater, largely bypassed by commerce and industry and still living on its illustrious past. But a new dawn was coming and this was largely due to the fact that St Andrews enjoyed a great natural asset in the large area of grassy links which lay to the north of the town and which were ideally suited to the playing of golf. Though the true origins of that game are obscure and, to some at least, contentious, golf had become a sufficiently popular pastime in Scotland that, in 1457, King James II was forced to ban it because it was seen to be a serious interference with the practice of archery and thus an endangerment to the defence of the country against the English. The ban, happily, did not last long and in 1552 the Charter of Archbishop Hamilton reserved the rights of the townspeople of St Andrews to use the links for 'golff, football, schuteing and all gamis'.

With time the playing of golf became more and more popular and no more so than in St Andrews where, by the end of the 17th century, it was being referred to as 'the metropolis of golfing' and where, in 1754, the Society of St Andrews Golfers was founded. Ten years later the Old Course, the world's first 18-hole golf course, was in full use and although there were some early setbacks concerning incompatible uses of the links, the game flourished so much so that the Society of Golfers received the patronage in 1834 of the eccentric sailor king William IV, and thus received, rather self-consciously, its modern name of The Royal and Ancient. By the time that the railway arrived in St Andrews, the town was already placed quite firmly on the golfing map of Britain and, within time and fuelled by the new-found accessibility of the city and the concomitant rise of the game and the middle classes, was destined to surpass all rivals to become the undisputed home of the game throughout the world.

The City Awakens

Golf may have been in the ascendancy but all was still not yet well in St Andrews. A rather unrestrained account published in the *Ordnance Gazetteer for Scotland* concluded that in the early years of the 19th century:

> There was not a foot of side-pavement in any of the streets; filth and squalor abounded unchecked; cows and pigs grazed in front of the colleges; the venerable ruins were fast going, by neglect, to decay, and were littered with rubbish; the lines of the public streets were continually broken by awkward abutments of ungainly houses; there were few visitors of any distinction, even to the splendid links, which lay with all their vast capabilities almost untrodden; and generally St Andrews, considering the prestige of its antiquity as an ecclesiastical city, and its rank as a seat of learning, was at the lowest pitch of miserable neglect and decay.

However all of this was about to change. By the late 1830s and with the help of a substantial legacy from Dr Andrew Bell of Cheltenham, a new building programme for the university was underway and a grammar school conducted on the advanced principles of the Madras or monitor system of education had been opened. Trade was reviving and by this time there was a weekly corn market and the twice-yearly hiring fairs for farm servants. The most famous of all these fairs was the Lammas Fair* held on the second Monday of August. This had, like many such events throughout the country, managed to evolve into a venue of amusement, traders and hucksters and other exotic attractions having the power to draw people in from all over Fife and has survived to the present day as a busy funfair noisily taking over the main streets of the town at the height of the tourist season.

---

* The festival of Lammas or Loaf Mass dated from pre-Christian times and was a celebration of thanksgiving for the bread made from the first corn of the new harvest.

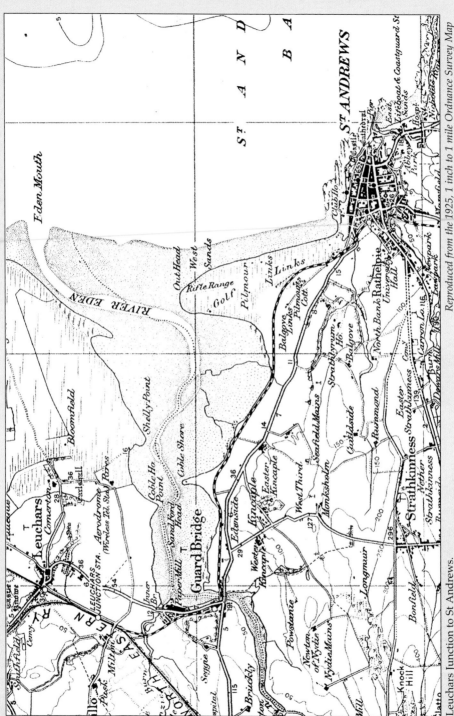

Reproduced from the 1925, 1 inch to 1 mile Ordnance Survey Map

Leuchars Junction to St Andrews.

At the beginning of the Victorian era the only real industries that St Andrews possessed were a limited amount of linen weaving 'for the manufacturies of Dundee' and a golf ball works where some 10,000 or so items were produced every year. In 1843 a local man, Robert Paterson, was reputed to have made the first rubber or gutta percha golf balls, an invention which rapidly replaced the old leather balls filled with feathers and this development undoubtedly revolutionised the game. For the rest, the local economy depended upon agriculture, the making of golf clubs and other accessories for the game, a brewery of purely local interest, a small ironworks which made and repaired agricultural machinery and on the more genteel pursuits of servicing the needs of the scholars and professors of the university. However, in the ascendancy was another even-greater source of revenue and, according to John Leighton:

Blessed with pure air, a comparatively mild and equal climate, easy access to the sea and secure and sheltered bathing places, St Andrews has deservedly become a place of great resort for persons desirous of or requiring sea bathing; and from the necessary literary nature of its society, the excellent opportunities of a superior education which it affords, the attraction of the game of golf, and the cheapness of its markets, it has been selected as a desirable place of residence by numerous persons of moderate fortune, and military gentlemen who have retired from active life. But desirable on all of these grounds as it may be as a place of residence, or of the occasional resort to the invalid, it has another, and to the intelligent tourist, highly pleasing class of attractions To the artist, its numerous ruins and ancient buildings afford picturesque objects for his pencil; to the antiquary, of research and investigation; and all who love their country, or have read its annals, must feel that they are on hallowed ground, every spot of which calls up some reverend history, some inspiring recollection.

A charming Victorian print of North Street, St Andrews showing gas lamps, horse-drawn cabs and a workman passing the time of day.   *Authors' Collection*

Such comments boded well for any potential railway line that could bring tourists cheaply, and in large numbers, to St Andrews.

In 1842, using the words of the author of the entry in the *Ordnance Gazetteer*, 'both the hour came, and the man, in the person of Hugh Lyon Playfair', a retired Major in the East India Company, who settled in the town, was elected Provost of St Andrews in that year and 'at once set to work on the new reformation on which his heart was set, and during his provostship revolutionised the town'. Old streets were widened, levelled, causewayed and provided with side paths, a new quay and seawalls built and public buildings planned under his direction.* Perhaps most importantly of all, Playfair possessed a healthy degree of foresight and was one of the first to understand that, if St Andrews was truly to flourish, it would need to be connected at an early date to the ever-expanding Scottish railway network for he knew where the real key to future prosperity was to be found.

The harbour at St Andrews, nestling next to the perilous cliffs beside the castle, was small but busy being used by a small fleet of resident fishing boats and visiting coasters. A graphic description of the general traffic using it in the immediate pre-railway era is provided by a random entry in the *Fifeshire Journal* of 27th July, 1848 when the vessels listed as using their harbour, along with their masters, are:

Arrivals:	July 21	*Perseverance*	(Philp)	Bo'ness	(coals)
	July 21	*Janet*	(Sime)	Newcastle	(coals and goods)
	July 21	*Lady Gowens*	(Foreman)	Perth	(ballast)
	July 22	*Vine*	(Conacher)	Newcastle	(coals)
	July 22	*Hero*	(Melville)	Leith	(goods)
Sailings:	July 21	*True Blue*	(Sime)	Alloa	(ballast)
	July 26	*Dolphin*	(Wilson)	Newcastle	(iron ore)
	July 26	*Vine*	(Conacher)	Newcastle	(iron ore)

Throughout the first half of the 19th century a weekly goods and passenger packet sailed directly from St Andrews harbour to the port of Leith but the passage was long and frequently rough, while the rocky coast and treacherous sands of Abertay were not a great inducement to the further development of passenger traffic from St Andrews.

Travel by road was, however, a different matter and, prior to the railway era, a regular network of horse-drawn coaches operated from the town. From starting points at the Black Bull and Star inns a daily service for Anstruther left every day at 3 pm, while a twice-weekly coach left for Cupar each Thursday and Saturday morning at 9.30. A service to the north connected with the ferry to Dundee every Tuesday and Friday morning at 8.30 and there was,

> ... a coach to Largo, whence there is a steam boat to Edinburgh, leaves St Andrews every lawful morning during Spring, Summer and Autumn, returning after the arrival of the steam boat from Edinburgh, and passing through all of the towns on the coast. There are carriers weekly to Cupar, Edinburgh and Dundee, by which goods may be brought from, or forwarded to, any part of the Kingdom ... [and] there are carriers who go regularly to the neighbouring towns on the south coast of the county.

The time for better connections by rail was clearly drawing near.

---

* Not all of these 'improvements' were, apparently, appreciated: 'Playfair was the worst offender against the ancient charm of St Andrews, though he thought he was beautifying them' - Russel Kirk, *St Andrews*.

Chapter Two

A Great Advantage:
Proposals for a Line to St Andrews

*'The short branch will obviously be of great advantage to its
Citizens and the public generally.'*
Edinburgh & Northern Railway Prospectus

Crossing Fife

When railways were still in their infancy, plans were drawn up by Robert Stevenson for a trunk line which was to cross Fife and which would provide a link between the growing commercial centres of Edinburgh, Perth and Dundee. Stevenson was a noted lighthouse engineer who came from a distinguished family of the same and who was responsible, amongst other feats, for the installation of the Bell Rock light; he was also the grandfather of the celebrated novelist and poet Robert Louis Stevenson. His survey, completed in 1819, was sound but the main drawback was that at that time the steam engine insufficiently capable of drawing a train over such an extended distance and the scheme remained effectively stillborn. Within the space of a few years, however, the position had radically altered and projects such as the building of the Stockton & Darlington and Liverpool & Manchester railways had shown that such dreams could become a reality, a prospect greatly enhanced when the Rainhill trials proved that the steam locomotive was a viable proposition. Therefore it was not surprising that a plethora of proposed railway schemes relating to both local and trunk lines throughout Scotland began to emerge after 1830 and, although some of the schemes were based on sound principles, others were little more than extravagant fantasies which were dismissed as such by the innately cautious businessmen of that era.

In 1835 John Geddes, better known for his skills as a mining and engineer who had been commissioned by the Earl of Rothes, put forward a plan to build a line across Fife which was to run from Burntisland to Ladybank where it would divide with one branch to Perth and the other to Tayport. In the following year Stevenson once again advanced a similar proposal to his first, being followed by a broadly similar plan which emerged from the engineering partnership of Thomas Grainger and John Miller who put forward yet another scheme for a line striding through the county. By this time Grainger already had a good track record of involvement in several successful schemes such as the Monkland and Kirkintilloch and Paisley & Renfrew lines while Miller was an Edinburgh lawyer turned civil engineer and whose star was definitely in the ascendancy. Between the two of them they would shortly be responsible for the construction of almost one-half by mileage of the Scottish railway system and their most prestigious work was probably that which they carried out on the Edinburgh & Glasgow Railway.

One thing that all of these early schemes for a line through the eastern part of Fife had in common was that there was no question of the great Firths of Forth and Tay being anything other than too formidable a barrier to be bridged or tunnelled. In consequence connecting ferries were to be provided from the proposed southern terminus of the line at Burntisland to Granton near Edinburgh and from the proposed northern terminus at Newport (a small but thriving port on the southern bank of the Tay) to Broughty Ferry, three miles from Dundee. Although the distance travelled by train was to be only 38 miles, the railway and its associated ferries would, it was estimated, have speeded up the London mails to the North by as much as 10 hours. A striking example of the local importance of the scheme was that, for the first time, it would be possible for a Dundee mill owner to have breakfast at home, visit Edinburgh to conduct his business, and return home for a late supper, although it would have to be admitted that the majority of his day would have been spent on the train. Of all of these early proposals the Grainger and Miller scheme was technically the most feasible but it was, nevertheless, still ahead of its time and, given that the initial enthusiasm for investing money in railways in the country had passed, it was hardly surprising that insufficient funding was likely to be advanced to enable any of these railways to reach fruition.

Railway Mania

In 1840, the line surveyed by Grainger and Miller was revived under the name of the Eastern Fife Railway. However, this proposal met with much opposition, both from the promoters of potentially rival schemes including a projected line to Perth and Dundee via Dunfermline, Lochgelly and Glenfarg and also from local landowners who objected to the line crossing their properties. As a result the Bill for the by-now renamed Edinburgh, Dundee & Northern Railway was rejected by Parliament in 1842. Another similar Bill failed in the following year, an occurrence which John Gibson, an Edinburgh law agent [solicitor] attributed to the fact that 'the Fife proprietors have as usual been cold and indifferent to this proposed great improvement in their county'.

However, times were changing and as the economic outlook improved, the promoters of the Edinburgh, Dundee & Northern (ED&N) found themselves with some powerful allies including John Learmonth, an Edinburgh businessman who was Chairman of the nascent North British Railway, the Duke of Buccleuch whose extensive landowning interests included the harbour at Granton and the Liverpool businessman John Gladstone, father of the then President of the Board of Trade and future Prime Minister. There was still, however, the perennial problem of attracting local capital to finance new railways in the country. But the reluctance of Scottish investors to put their money into railway schemes to serve their own land was being more than matched by the enthusiasm of English speculators, especially from London, Lancashire and Yorkshire, to subscribe for shares in the mushrooming Scottish railway companies that often projected a romantic image that their potential traffic did not always justify. By 1844 it was clear that sufficient impetus had been gained to allow the ED&N scheme to be resurrected and a final, this time successful, attempt was made to seek authorization to build what was by now known under the shorter title of the Edinburgh and Northern Railway.

The early 1840s were, however, a period of wild financial speculation, afterwards known as the Railway Mania, when suddenly it seemed as though an endless series of rival lines were being promoted across the whole country and Fife was no exception. Amongst the schemes proposed was the Glasgow and Dundee Direct Railway (also resurrected as the Glasgow and Dundee Junction Railway), which was to leave the Scottish Central line near Larbert, cross the Forth at Alloa and run via Kinross, Auchtermuchty and Kilmany to Newport, with a proposed floating bridge across the Tay from that point. In addition a loop leaving the main line at Monimail and proceeding by way of Cupar and Guardbridge to join the original line at Newport was planned together with a separate connecting branch line from Guardbridge to the harbour at St Andrews. Another proposal was for a grandly-named Scottish Direct Northern Junction Railway which was to run northwards from Elie, where it was to connect with a ferry from North Berwick, and then run via a circuitous line via St Andrews to Dundee while a Fife Central Junction Railway scheme was also proposed, this line also having a connection with a ferry link at Elie. To a greater or lesser extent the citizens of St Andrews were interested in each of these schemes and indeed Provost Playfair and other St Andrews bailies,* councillors and a university official were amongst the promoters of the Fife Central proposal.

The Edinburgh & Northern

Amongst such speculation, the Grainger and Miller† scheme was triumphant and, on 31st July, 1845, the Edinburgh & Northern Railway Act (8 & 9 Vict., cap. clviii) was passed, but not without considerable delay and the enormous cost of £65,177 being incurred in legal and Parliamentary costs - a sum which the impecunious company could barely afford. The 1845 Act provided for the construction of a line from the low water pier at Burntisland which would then follow the coast to Kirkcaldy and then turn inland via Markinch to reach the small and relatively unimportant village of Ladybank in the Howe of Fife. At this point the line was to divide, one branch continuing to Perth via Newburgh while the other would run directly to the county town of Cupar. In addition to these lines provision was also made for a short spur from the main line at Kirkcaldy to serve the busy harbour there. John Learmonth was appointed Chairman of the company, a significance not lost upon potential shareholders since it was clear from the very beginning that the line was destined to become an essential link in the projected East Coast main line that would eventually stretch from the smoky expanding metropolis of London to the granite city of Aberdeen, some 523 miles distant. Within a few weeks of the passing of the Act

---

* A municipal magistrate akin to an English alderman; the position has been obsolete since local government reorganization in 1975 although some councils subsequently revived the title on an honorary basis.

† Grainger later became Engineer to the Leeds & Northern Railway and died as a result of a collision on that line while Miller eventually retired from railway work and became both a country gentleman and Liberal MP for an Edinburgh constituency.

the Newburgh to Perth line was dropped from the company's agenda and a bridge over the Tay, to be built several miles upstream from Perth, was proposed in its place. The bridge was subsequently deleted when the Admiralty objected to it as being a potential hazard to shipping and as a result of this the present route from Ladybank to Hilton Junction near Perth was substituted.

Soon proposals were put forward for an extension of the Edinburgh & Northern from Cupar to Newport, where it was proposed that a two-mile-long bridge would be constructed over the Tay to Dundee, by now a busy trade and manufacturing centre. This bridge, which if built would have been the longest bridge in the world, once again met objection from the Admiralty and the plan was abandoned. The scheme was then modified so that the line was now to terminate at Ferryport-on-Craig, a small fishing and ferry port whose chief attraction was that it was situated at the narrowest part of the Firth of Tay, the length of the crossing from there being only seven-eighths of a mile across to Broughty Ferry, by then linked by a short railway link via the Dundee & Arbroath line to Dundee. Fast steam packet boats would be able to complete the crossing in a matter of minutes and thus provide onward connections to the North and thus Ferryport-on-Craig was an ideal terminus for the line through Fife. In the course of these changes some discussions also took place between the Edinburgh & Northern and a number of merchants from Cupar who were in favour of a minor diversion of the Ferryport line to the south so that it could also serve the small harbour at Guardbridge on the River Eden. The merchants' suggestion was not followed, apparently on the grounds that the 'extra heavy expense' of diverting the line could not be justified on the basis of the modest additional revenue which, it was thought, might accrue.

The Edinburgh & Northern was opened in four stages. On 20th September, 1847 services commenced between Burntisland, Kirkcaldy, Ladybank and Cupar with a connecting service provided from Edinburgh to Granton via the former Edinburgh, Leith & Granton Railway, which had merged with the Edinburgh & Northern in the previous year. On the same day the first part of the Ladybank to Perth line was also opened, although only as far as Lindores, where a temporary terminus at Glenburnie was provided; a road link was provided from there to Perth. Eight months later, on 17th May, 1848, trains were extended on the main line from Cupar to a temporary terminus at Leuchars, then 'an insignificant village of some 500 or so inhabitants, mainly poor weavers' and situated some five miles north-west of St Andrews on the main road from that city to Cupar. A total of four (later increased to five) trains per day were provided in each direction and a connecting omnibus service was provided from Leuchars to the centre of St Andrews. The line was an immediate success, nearly 200,000 passengers travelling over it between May and August 1848 and *Tullis's Guide to the Edinburgh & Northern Railway*, published in Cupar shortly afterwards, commented in a somewhat partisan way that:

> It stands as one of the leading lines in the country. In regard to capital, cost and general importance, it stands proportionally high. In respect to the prospect of remuneration to the proprietors, it is second to no railway in Great Britain ... The [passenger] carriages of every class are of the best construction of their kind - the first class carriages being splendid and comfortable in the highest degree.

No doubt that this was a considerable improvement over the existing direct steamship service to Leith which was often rough and unpleasant (although there was also a coach service which connected with a shorter passage from Elie to Leith) but the dignity of the city and the ambitions of its provost were not easily assuaged by the absence of a direct railway to St Andrews. On 18th July, 1848 the Edinburgh & Northern opened the third section of its line, that from Glenburnie to Hilton Junction and Perth.

A Branch for St Andrews?

In the original Edinburgh & Northern Prospectus mention was made of a proposed branch line to St Andrews, this proposal being mentioned in a report issued by the Directors of the company in July 1845, in the following terms:

> As the extension railway to Newport passes within 4½ miles of St Andrews, the Directors instructed their engineer to examine the country and report on the cost of a branch line which could be made to connect that city with the trunk line. They have received his report on the line selected, which is nearly level, and he has furnished them also with an estimate of cost which, for a single line, will be very moderate. The Directors would not have felt themselves justified in recommending a very great expenditure to secure a [direct] connection with St Andrews, where there is no seat of manufacturing enterprise - but it being the seat of one of the Universities, and containing, as it does, a population of 6,000 with a populous district surrounding it - and as it is a place much resorted to in the summer months by the inhabitants of Edinburgh and the Western parts of the country for sea-bathing quarters - and there being a considerable intercourse between it and Dundee, they have no hesitation in giving it as their opinion, that the traffic will fully remunerate the Shareholders for the cost of the branch.

The proposed branch line was later omitted from the Edinburgh & Northern Bill, the reason being given that it would have been 'as laid down, of considerable cost, and open to objection from certain of the landowners'. The omission, however, did not stop lobbying taking place on behalf of local interests anxious to see some progress in the building of a branch to the city, in particular the St Andrews Town Council who, at a meeting in December 1845, urged the Edinburgh & Northern to build the branch, and reminded them of the interest that had been recently shown in the area by the aborted Glasgow and Dundee Junction and rival Fife Central Junction schemes. A barely disguised warning was also given that, if the Edinburgh & Northern did not serve St Andrews then other companies would step into the breach.

This broadside may have had some effect for in March of the following year the Edinburgh & Northern issued a public notice stating that it was intending to build 'a branch railway diverging from or out of the Newport branch ... at a point at, in or near to Seggiehill in the parish of Leuchars and terminating in, or near, the City of St Andrews'. In the accompanying statement issued by the company on behalf of the promoters it was said that:

> It seems hardly necessary to make any statement respecting the objects of this Branch, as these are obvious, and attended with comparatively little outlay of Capital. The

Branch, in length only 4 miles and 6 furlongs, diverges out of the [Tayport] Extension line referred to, about midway, and reaches the City of St Andrews with little injury to property. The City is well known as the seat of one of the Universities, and is much resorted to for its educational inducements, and during summer, as affording pleasant Sea-Bathing quarters. Its situation is very isolated and difficult of access, and the short branch will obviously be of great advantage to its Citizens and the public generally.

Shortly thereafter the *Fifeshire Journal* gave its readers further details of the scheme, stating that the branch railway would leave the Edinburgh & Northern main line 'about 400 feet south east of Seggie Hill steading and curve gracefully north and east until it came to Seggie' to cross the main road at Guardbridge 'between the toll-house and wharf and cross the river Eden by a bridge with 30 foot wide arches at an average height of 32 feet'. The line was then 'to run east along the low ground by the riverside', cross the turnpike or high road and terminate near to the place known as Argyle, an old settlement outwith the burgh boundary and whose name probably derives from *Erra ghaidheal*, 'the limit of the gaels' but had no geographical connection with the county of Argyll. On 19th November of that year the *Journal* reported that 'the engineers for the Edinburgh and Northern Railway Company were here a few days ago, and have, we understand, finally determined on the line and terminus of the branch to St Andrews'. According to that paper, the line was to 'cross the high road near the Swilken Burn Bridge, by a viaduct above 30 feet high, and terminate east of Mr Ireland's brewery and near the West Port'.

Second thoughts

In November 1846 the Edinburgh & Northern shareholders were assured by their Directors that they considered that it was time to advance with the Bill for a branch line to St Andrews and that it would be a 'useful accessory' to their business. Accordingly efforts were made to obtain Parliamentary sanction for the line and, on 22nd July, 1847, before any trains had actually commenced to run on the main line, the cumbrously named Edinburgh & Northern Railway (Saint Andrews and Newburgh Harbour Branch and Road Crossings, Newport Railway Extension) Act (10 & 11 Vict., cap. cclxxvii) received the Royal Assent. It provided *inter alia*, for 'a branch railway from the Newport Branch of the Edinburgh & Northern Railway at a point thereon at, in or near to, Seggie Hall in the parish of Leuchars, in and through the Parish of Leuchars, St Andrews and St Leonard and the Royal Burgh of St Andrews to the City of St Andrews, all in the County of Fife ...' But all was, apparently, not well for by September of that same year the Edinburgh & Northern shareholders were being advised that the proposed branches to St Andrews and Newburgh Harbour 'will prove, when executed, of decided utility; but your Directors desire authority to postpone their execution, until several of the more pressing Works now on hand are nearer to completion'. And postpone their execution they did for nothing further happened despite the continual reappearance in the Directors' statements to the shareholders at the half-yearly meetings 'of their earnest wishes of their desire to construct the branch railway to St Andrews'.

The railway from Leuchars to Tayport (the name subsequently officially adopted by the railway company in preference to the original name of Ferryport-on-Craig) was opened to the public on 17th May, 1850 and the Edinburgh & Northern settled down to develop its freight and passenger services and connecting ferries. Any references to the St Andrews branch in the company's minutes became sparse and, eventually, the matter was dropped altogether. The reasons for the apparent disinterest were all too obvious. The Edinburgh & Northern, which in an attempt to better reflect the names of the principal cities served soon became the Edinburgh, Perth & Dundee Railway (EP&D), had already spent much of its capital in promoting and building its main lines and was now engaged in a potentially destructive battle with the Scottish Central Railway for a share of the traffic to the potentially lucrative markets of the north-east and accordingly was hardly in a position to add anything to its already over-extended network. There was another reason, too - the growing contemporary awareness amongst railway companies in general that the building of branch lines was no longer the financial panacea that it once had seemed and was that this now something to be avoided.

Cheap Railways

Far from adding traffic to existing lines, branch lines were now seen as tending to drain away capital which, with the marked financial downturn after 1846 (a direct response to the wild era of speculation afterwards contemptuously known as the Railway Mania) was increasingly difficult and expensive to raise. A further consideration was undoubtedly the fact that the running costs of such branch lines that had been built were typically in excess of any profits which those lines might reasonably have been expected to generate. An early example of the disillusion of a major company with one of its branches can be found in the dismay of the North British when a Committee of Investigation reported to the shareholders at a special meeting that 'the Committee regret that the Directors should ever have undertaken the formation of the North Berwick branch'. This short line, which was to run from Drem Junction to North Berwick, was of an equivalent length to the St Andrews branch and was costed at a total of £50,846 15s. 5d. before certain economies were carried out to try to reduce this figure to a more manageable sum.*

The reasons for this contemporary and almost universal lack of enthusiasm amongst the larger companies towards the institution of the branch line were many, but included the fact that many such lines were constructed in a manner which was vastly over-engineered and built to the standards which had been prevalent and necessary for main lines in the 1830s when steam locomotives were too weak and underpowered to negotiate anything other than easily graded and gently curved routes. In addition, double track was often specified where there was little possibility that the traffic forecast would ever justify this provision. It was often said, with much justification, that too much money was spent on ornamental 'fripperies' such as castellated tunnel mouths, monumental bridges and elaborate stone-built stations. Perhaps most

* See further A. Hajducki, *The North Berwick and Gullane Branch Lines*, Oakwood Press, 1992.

importantly of all, the cost of acquiring land was resulting in crippling initial costs which could never be recouped. Here the blame was laid, fairly and squarely, at the feet of local landowners who, throughout Scotland, were attempting to maximise their assets at the expense of the railway companies who were seen as having limitless purses. In March 1849 John Learmonth commented in the influential *Herepath's Railway Journal* that when it came to buying land 'every advantage is taken of the unfortunate promoters of a railway'. A graphic example of this could be found in the construction of the North Berwick branch where the original estimate for the purchase of the land required had been £7,083 15s. 0d. but the eventual sum which the company had to outlay for this was £18,949 7s. 0d., an increase of some 167 per cent over the estimate. The position in relation to land acquisition was certainly not helped by the attitude of juries summoned by the sheriff under the Land Clauses Consolidation (Scotland) and Railway Clauses Consolidation (Scotland) Acts of 1845 to assess the amount of compensation payable for the purchase and severance of compulsorily acquired land where agreement could not be reached. Such juries, comprised of 13 local persons who were either landowners or professional gentlemen themselves, tended to side with the owners of the properties which were sought to be acquired and, like their contemporaries throughout the country, seemed to regard the larger railway companies as the milch cows, which, if they ever had been, was certainly no longer the case.

In response to many of these criticisms, however, a movement was growing up whose adherents subscribed to the view that branch railways could, and indeed should, be built much more cheaply than existing lines. This 'cheap railway movement', expounded by the redoubtable Herepath and others, advocated the construction and maintenance of rural branch lines to a lesser standard than had previously been the case and held that this could be done by avoiding unnecessary earthworks, making a trackbed that would support light locomotives and short trains moving at relatively slow speeds and saving money by providing a cheaper infrastructure such as lighter rails and simple wooden bridges and stations. The slow speeds envisaged were in the order of between 12 and 15 mph and operation of such lines was proposed on the 'one engine in steam principle' (i.e. only one engine at a time allowed on the line), so that there would be no need for signalling or other expensive regulation. Staff could largely be dispensed with and booking agents were deemed unnecessary since what was later referred to as 'conductor-guard working' could be employed whereby a single employee would act not only as the train guard but would also sell tickets to passengers on board the train.

These 'cheap railways' were designed to serve local communities at a price which could be regarded as affordable, although it was realised that if such branch lines were to have any real prospect of success not only would they have to be locally promoted but also locally funded. In other words the inhabitants of the area which it was proposed to serve would have to bear the expense of constructing the line and that there was no point in looking to the impoverished main line companies for cash. By an accident of history, St Andrews was destined to have the very first of these 'cheap railways' and to provide a role model for many such branch lines in later years.

Chapter Three

The Train Now Arriving:
The St Andrews Railway 1849-1852

'Now the ship is afloat, we hope to make a prosperous voyage of it.'
William Smith, Chairman, St Andrews Railway

All Those Friendly

By the autumn of 1849 it was becoming obvious to all that the Edinburgh & Northern was not in a position to build a line to St Andrews, whether or not it still even wished to do so. Fuelled by the cheap railway movement and, in November of that year a group of influential local persons began to make it known that they were prepared to go ahead with such a line on their own. They made no secret of the fact that this was to be a local concern to benefit the area through which it was to run rather than provide a notional lining of the pockets of rich investors who lived elsewhere. Learning from previous mistakes they entered into negotiations with landowners who, with one exception, were reasonably sympathetic and made sure that local businesses and other interests in the area were all brought on board so that when they were ready to go public they would have a general support in the area.

On Thursday 19th December, 1850 a meeting was held in St Andrews Town Hall in order that the proposal to build an independently-owned railway to the city could be aired. The public intimation of the meeting had requested the presence 'of all those friendly to the new railway'. The meeting was chaired by Provost Playfair and resulted in the formation of the St Andrews Railway Company. On the following day, the publication of its Prospectus made the claim that:

> St Andrews, a locality so deeply interesting from historical and antiquarian associations and famous as the seat of the most ancient Scottish university as well as possessing other educational institutions not to be excelled either in the efficiency of instruction or in the moderate charges of education, and holding out so many inducements from sea bathing, golfing and otherwise as a residence, has felt the disadvantage of being hitherto to a very great extent … out of the line of railway communication.

In the Prospectus it was noted that the total number of passengers who travelled from St Andrews and fed into the Edinburgh, Perth and Dundee at Leuchars station was, in the year ending 26th October, 1850, 42,420, i.e. an average of over 110 per day and it was reasonably thought that this annual figure could be increased, if the branch line were built, to a number in excess of 63,500 which would bring in a projected annual revenue of some £1,843 6s. 6d. from passengers. The Prospectus also embraced detailed estimates of freight revenue from businesses along the route and included the following list of prospective annual revenue from a number of sources:

	£
Conveyance of mails	40
Coals and general merchandise	300
Parcels	75
Lime	40
Pavement and other hard stone from Forfarshire	15
Freestone to the Tay, etc.	175
Guardbridge pier and tilework traffic	80
Kincaple tilework traffic	100
Farm produce, cattle and manure	100
Seggie distillery traffic	130
	£1,055

As was not uncommon for such estimates, there seems to have been an overestimate of the amount of revenue that the proposed line would have diverted away from road and sea routes already in operation. It was confidently predicted in the Prospectus that the total annual revenue of the line would exceed £3,000 but that, even if revenue was down to that figure, the annual maintenance costs would not exceed £50 per mile and that the total annual expenditure including wages and taxes would not exceed £700 which, after the payment of dividends, would still leave an annual surplus of some £1,175. The probable annual expenses of the company were given as follows:

	£	s.	d.
Maintenance of Way, Buildings and Works @ £50 per mile	225	0	0
Taxes	125	0	0
Station clerks	140	0	0
Signalman at Milton Junction	40	0	0
Gate keeper at Guardbridge	31	4	0
Two porters (total)	54	12	0
Stationery	25	0	0
Sundries	30	0	0
	670	16	0

As one of the promoters, William Smith, a druggist [i.e. chemist] in the town, went on to point out that not only was the line likely to pay but that one of the great advantages of seeking to build a railway at that particular time was that contractors were desperately eager to obtain work since 'the existing contracts on the great lines' were all finished. Consequently the contractors wished to keep their staff and labour force together and thus would provide low quotes for any new work. This was borne out by the fact that although 306¾ miles of new line had been opened in Scotland during 1848, by 1851 the mileage of new lines opened annually had declined to a mere 5¾ miles. In addition, and almost certainly in consequence of the sharp fall in new mileage, the cost of labour and materials used in railway building had also fallen sharply during the same period.

A Permanent Pecuniary Investment

A week after the public meeting, the St Andrews Town Council met on the Christmas Eve in order to discuss how council-owned property would be affected by the new railway. It was resolved unanimously that intimation be given of the Council's assent to the proposed line. Dr Adamson,* a local medical doctor and later a Director of the company, then proposed that the Town Council give 'a more decided testimony of its approval of the undertaking in consideration of the advantages that the railway would confer upon the city' by applying for 10 shares in the new concern; this motion also was also carried unanimously.

What was unusual about the St Andrews Railway proposal, so far as its promoters were concerned, was their concern that its capital should be subscribed locally so as to avoid the company falling into outside hands - in other words it was hoped that it would be a local company serving local needs and not part of a great financial monolith as contemporary railway companies were often quite rightly suspiciously regarded. The company promptly applied for Parliamentary approval of its scheme and, with little real opposition, was incorporated on 3rd July, 1851 by the St Andrews Railway Act (14 & 15 Vict., cap. liv) with an authorized capital of £21,000 in the unusually small denomination of £10 shares and with authority to borrow a further £7,000. The first Directors of the company, none of whom had any previous railway experience, were the Chairman, William Smith, Provost Playfair, Alexander Meldrum of Kincaple, a local landowner and brickworks proprietor, Andrew Aikman, a St Andrews grocer and wine merchant, Robert Haig, proprietor of the distillery at Guardbridge and John Brown, a local merchant and clothier. The Company Secretary was Walter Ireland, and the Head Office of the company was situated at Albert Buildings, St Andrews. As the *Fifeshire Journal* reported at the opening of the line:

> From first to last there has been a degree of earnestness and personal responsibility pervading the Management altogether unusual ... The line has been got up not as a speculation, but as an urgent requirement of the city and neighbourhood and, as such and conducted with the economy of a private undertaking, is sure to prosper [and] ... we see no reason to change our conviction of the safety of this branch even as a permanent pecuniary investment.

A similar local pattern emerged in terms of the shareholdings. Within one week of them being advertised for subscription 75 per cent of the 2,100 paid-up shares in the company had been taken up, the major shareholders including the two MPs for, respectively, the County of Fife and the St Andrews Burghs, both of whom held 100 shares each and Robert Haig who also held the same number; the St Andrews Town Council subscribed to the 10 shares (worth £100) previously agreed upon. By way of a postscript, as late as 1868 it was estimated that 1,567 of these shares were still held by persons living in or around St Andrews while only 13 were owned by persons who lived outwith the area of influence of the North British Railway which eventually absorbed the company.

---

* John Adamson, (1809-1870) was born at Boarhills and qualified in medicine at Edinburgh University. Master of Madras College, he was an innovator in public health and photography and his medical practice became one of the largest in Fife.

Bouch and Mathieson

The enterprise would not have been possible without the enthusiastic support of the young consulting engineer, Thomas Bouch, an ambitious young man of 28 who had started out his career as an assistant engineer on the Lancaster & Carlisle Railway and, in 1849, had become the Resident Engineer of the Edinburgh, Perth & Dundee. Now working on his own account, Bouch was an enthusiastic exponent of the 'cheap railway' principle and had made his views clear when he had stated that

> The failure in railways was the excessive waste in capital in their construction. The best paying lines were not those that got the most traffic, but those which had been constructed at least expense.

The St Andrews Railway was Bouch's first such commission so that it was perhaps not surprising that as one of the carrots offered to the Board he agreed to act at a fee set at a nominal £100 per mile rather than the then more usual charge of £500 per mile. In all the circumstances the Board were apparently pleased with their choice of Engineer, especially as Bouch believed that the line could be constructed for something in the region of £4,740 per mile, a fraction of the £32,133 average cost per mile of a Scottish railway at this time. Whether all of the economies which he practised were, in the longer term, wise was to be brought home to the Directors at a later stage when expensive remedial works had to be undertaken, but as Bouch told them subsequently in connection with criticisms of the sub-standard track used 'with this slight road, it was arranged that light engines only should be used and run at moderate speed'. He then commented that the line had been built with 'a very limited capital' adding that 'every economy consistent with obtaining actual safety' had been practised. From the St Andrews Railway Bouch went on to become the Engineer responsible for numerous other lines such as the Leven, East Fife and Peebles Railways and, notably, the first train ferry in the world. The culmination of his career was the boldly conceived but parsimoniously constructed Tay Bridge, for which he was knighted. The subsequent fall of that bridge in 1879 brought about his personal downfall.

The contractor chosen to build the St Andrews line was Kenneth Mathieson, an experienced contractor who was later to be involved in constructing other lines in Britain including the Aboyne to Ballater railway and the Bridport branch in Dorset;* his career was crowned by his election as Provost in his home town of Dunfermline. Mathieson had already worked on the Edinburgh, Perth and Dundee line and the Board were duly impressed by the fact that not only had he given evidence in favour of a branch line to St Andrews during the Parliamentary hearings on the 1847 Act but also that he was willing to take up some £6,000 worth of shares in the St Andrews Railway in lieu of payment in cash.

The *Fifeshire Advertiser* of 16th August, 1851 reported that:

> We understand that the contract with Mr Mathieson for the construction of this line was formally signed on Monday [i.e. 11th August] and that operations will be commenced in the following week. Mr Mathieson undertakes to complete the line, erect stations and otherwise render the entire works fit for that for the sum of £15,000, this sum being exclusive of certain contingencies which, if they arise, are to be borne by the Company. It is expected that four to five months will be sufficient to construct the undertaking.

* See *The Bridport Railway* by B.L. Jackson and M.J. Tattershall, (Oakwood Press).

The St Andrews Railway Directors and officers, 1851. This early photograph shows (*from left to right*) Andrew Meldrum, Andrew Aikman, John Brown, Robert Haig, William Smith (Chairman), Andrew Briggs, Walter Foggo Ireland (Secretary) and Provost Sir Hugh Playfair. *Authors' Collection*

The company minutes thereafter duly record that, without any tender being put out, Mathieson agreed to construct the line

> … as shown on the plans and sections and as detailed in the schedule, and in terms of the specifications as to the quality of the work, for the sum of fourteen thousand pounds sterling inclusive of sidings to Seggie Distillery, Spence's Pier and Mr Meldrum's tile works, these sidings together being twelve hundred yards in length … The said Kenneth Mathieson, junior, hereby agrees to take up six hundred shares [i.e. £6,000 worth] of the capital stock of the St Andrews Railway Company and to pay up the calls as made upon the stock …

Acquisition and agreement

Most of the land required for the St Andrews Railway had been cannily acquired by the promoters prior to the Bill being published and thus the twin evils of greedy landowners and sympathetic jurors deciding on compulsory purchase sums had been avoided. At the first general meeting of the new company, held in the Town Hall of St Andrews in August 1851, William Smith informed the shareholders that:

> An amicable settlement with the proprietors of land along the proposed line is now being proceeded with, and they [the Directors] fully anticipate that the line will be formed without one single law plea – not a very common result in the history of railways.

Leuchars (Old) not long after the discontinuation of passenger services.   *NBRSG Collection*

Leuchars (Old) looking north in 1956 and showing the signal box, level crossing and footbridge and the line to Tayport which was abandoned six months earlier. The curiously gabled public house on the left survives to the present day and provides a convenient reference point.

W. Hennigan Collection

It was afterwards calculated that the eventual cost of the acquisition of the land required for the railway (including all sums necessary for both purchase and severance, i.e. diminution in value of lands cut through) amounted to £5,824, a figure remarkably similar to the earlier fair price valuation for lands required by the Edinburgh & Northern's original proposal for a St Andrews branch of £5,443. Apart from opposition expressed by the factor of the Strathtyrum Estate near to St Andrews (principally on the basis that he did not wish to see Sunday trains operating on the line) there was no real opposition to the line and amongst landowners there was either a complete disinterest or a lukewarm desire to co-operate in land sales, perhaps due to the fact that it was well-known that the railway was to be built on a shoestring and that it had no real capital behind it. An early proposal to feu (lease) the land rather than buy it outright was not proceeded with in view of the cheap purchase costs which had been negotiated but even so the company procrastinated in paying out the agreed sums in exchange for the land which they had acquired.

Leuchars to Eden

There were few physical obstacles encountered in the construction works due to the fact that the terrain was mostly flat. The station at Leuchars was to be provided with allegedly suitable accommodation for the branch trains and from here trains were to run over the EP&D main line to a point called Milton, where the physical junction was to be made with the St Andrews Railway, about one mile north of the junction at Seggiehill at which point the line authorized by the 1847 Act had been projected to leave the main line. This meant that the St Andrews branch trains required to share the half-mile or so from Leuchars to Milton with the main line trains of the EP&D - a situation which was thought, from the very beginning, to be rather less than satisfactory. In 1853 it was said that the Directors of the St Andrews Railway had it in their contemplation

> … to carry a separate line of rail from the junction at Milton to Leuchars station. Various circumstances, especially the high price of iron, had as yet prevented the Directors taking the subject into their more serious consideration. They had, however, every hope of giving even this - if it be deemed expedient - without going beyond the original capital.

However, the separate line of rails was not laid.

From Milton Junction the line headed in a south-easterly direction and crossed over the Motray Water (Moultrie Burn) on a wooden viaduct which was provided for in Section 29 of the 1851 Act in terms that:

> … the said railway shall be carried across the tidal water of *Moultrie Burn* near to *Milton* and about 530 yards above the bridge on the turnpike road leading from *St Andrews* to *Leuchars*, on a timber bridge or viaduct, 49 yards in length, consisting of five arches, each 20 feet 4 inches of span and 16 feet in height from the bed of the said *Moultrie Burn,* or in such other way as shall be previously approved of by the Lord High Admiral of the United Kingdom of Great Britain and Ireland …

Leuchars (Old) looking south *c.*1925 with Edinburgh, Perth & Dundee Railway buildings on left - note the original canopy, the wooden structure for tablet exchange (*right*) and the very obvious difference in heights evidencing the lengthening of both platforms.   *NBRSG Collection*

Leuchars (Old), 22nd August, 1956 with LNER pattern non-corridor stock stabled in the former St Andrews bay platform.   *A.G. Ellis Collection*

An early post-Grouping view of Leuchars (Old) taken from the footbridge and looking south. Note in the background the Edinburgh-bound train approaching Leuchars Junction on the up main line.   *NBRSG Collection*

Soon the only intermediate station, Guardbridge, was reached. The village lay on the left (or western) bank of the tidal River Eden, about 4 miles WNW of St Andrews and was of little significance, having a population of less than 70, and was not destined to grow until the paper mill was established there a decade or so later.

The Act provided, in Section 30, that the railway would be carried

> … across the tidal *Eden* near the *Guardbridge*, above the *Guardbridge* Quay or Wharf on a timber bridge or viaduct, 106 yards in length, consisting of 9 arches, each of 32 feet in span, and 16 feet in height from the bed of the said *River Eden*, or in such other way as shall be previously approved by the Lord High Admiral …

Section 31 stated that during the construction of both viaducts or bridges, and then after construction was complete

> … the said Company shall cause to be hung out or exhibit on each of the said Bridges every Night, from Sunset to Sunrise, a Light, to be kept burning by at the Expense of the Company, for the Navigation and safe Guidance of Vessels: and for ever after the Completion of the said Bridges, the said Company shall cause to be hung out or exhibited , upon or near the Centre of each of the said Bridges, every Night, from Sunset to Sunrise, a good and sufficient Light, to be kept burning by and at the Expense of the Company, for the Navigation and safe Guidance of Vessels: and which Lights shall be subject to the Provisions in that Behalf contained in the Harbour, Docks and Piers Clauses Act 1847: and in case the said Company shall neglect to exhibit and keep either of such Lights burning as aforesaid, they shall forfeit and pay for every such Neglect the Sum of Ten Pounds.

ANNO DECIMO QUARTO & DECIMO QUINTO

VICTORIÆ REGINÆ.

✱✱

Cap. liv.

An Act for making a Railway from the *Edinburgh, Perth, and Dundee* Railway at or near to *Milton* in the Parish of *Leuchars* to the City of *St. Andrews,* to be called "The *St. Andrews* Railway."

[3d *July* 1851.]

WHEREAS the making of a Railway, leading from the *Edinburgh, Perth, and Dundee* Railway at a Point at or near to *Milton* in the Parish of *Leuchars* in the County of *Fife* to a Point near to the City of *Saint Andrews* in the Parish of *Saint Andrews* and County aforesaid, would be of great public Advantage, by opening an additional, certain, and expeditious Means of Communication between the said Places, and by facilitating Communication with more distant Towns and Places : And whereas the Persons herein-after named are willing, at their own Expense, to carry such Undertaking into execution : And where as it is expedient that the Company hereby to be incorporated shall be enabled to enter into Agreements, as after mentioned, with the *Edinburgh, Perth, and Dundee* Railway Company, incorporated by the several Acts following ; that is to say, the Acts (Local and Personal) of the Sixth and Seventh *William* the Fourth, Chapter One hundred and thirty-one ;

There was a further provision, contained in Section 35 of the Act, that reflected the fact that the line ran beside tidal waters and that there was a danger of shipping being led into difficulties by the possible confusion of signal lamps with navigation lights:

> That all the stationary Lights on the said Railway near the Sea Coast, or which could otherwise be seen at Sea, shall at all Times be sufficiently and properly shaded by the Company, with good and sufficient Shades, so that such Lights shall not be visible from the Sea; and for every Default herein the Company shall forfeit and pay a Penalty not exceeding Ten Pounds.

These provisions, which were inserted in order to assuage the fears of the Lords of Admiralty, in consequence of which they did not oppose the Bill, were later regretted by the company and within a short time the St Andrews Railway attempted without success to have the permanent lighting provisions annulled.

A Most Suitable Location

From the wooden railway bridge there was a level run along the banks and links on the south side of the Eden to St Andrews itself, roughly paralleling the turnpike road but a hundred yards or so to the north of it. Passing a projecting spit known as the Coble Shore, the railway then passed within half a mile of the Seafield Brick and Tile Works and the adjacent clay pit owned by Alexander Meldrum of Kincaple, another Director of the St Andrews company; these works were connected to the new railway by a tramway. A short distance from Seafield the line diverted from its generally eastwards course and turned south, crossing the Balgove Links, skirting the adjacent Pilmour Links close to Pilmour Cottage before coming to a halt next to the main road at 'a field in the sheep parks of the farm of Balgove', a place inconveniently situated outside of the city walls just beyond the 17th hole on the Old Course and a good half-mile or so from the middle of St Andrews itself. Opposition to the extension to a more central location had been advanced by, amongst others, the committee of the Royal and Ancient and although those who used the line regularly would bemoan the long walk into town, the Directors of the line felt that their outlying station was 'most suitable' since it was built in accordance with their desire to save money and to avoid the costly climb that would be necessary if the terminus was to be brought further into the town. This station, referred to latterly as St Andrews Links, was to remain the terminus of the St Andrews Railway until 1887 when it was to be replaced by the new station serving the line from Anstruther but would remain in use for goods traffic until the eventual closure of the railway in the 1960s.

Some Doubts Expressed

There was, however, some local scepticism both of the course of the line and of its likely profitability. In response to this the *Fifeshire Journal* on 31st July, 1851 commented that:

Several correspondents, with whose remarks it is unnecessary to occupy our space, have questioned the possibility of completing the line with the capital authorised by the Company's Act. The statutory capital, as formerly mentioned, is £21,000 and power is taken to raise an additional £7,000 if required. The Directors are confident, however, that for the ordinary capital they will be able to meet all the ordinary outlay and place the line in fair working order. The sum may appear small, compared with the railway outlays in 1845, '46 and '47, but then it will be remembered that experience has brought wisdom, and that the undertaking as a whole, is placed in unusually favourable circumstances. The length is somewhat short of five miles; the district is remarkably flat and level; what cuttings there may be are entirely through clay and sand; there is not a single embankment worth noticing; and scarcely two hundred yards of retaining walls are required throughout the entire course of the line. Besides there is to be only one line of rails, the ground for which has been easily acquired; no expensive stations are to be erected; and the most difficult part of the undertaking – the bridges over the Moultrie and Eden - are to be constructed of wood, and will last for twenty-five or thirty years without any additional expense for repairs. In fact from a careful study of the plans and sections with which we have been favoured there seems nothing to prevent the whole being put in working order for even less than the stipulated capital. Indeed we have reason to know that the estimated contracts are considerably below this figure; but as incidental expenses will ever arise under the most skilfully and carefully conducted operations, it is well to give the contractors the benefit of the doubt, and say at one in round numbers the £21,000. On the contrary, it were better rather to exceed the authorised capital than to permit any portion of the works to be finished in a temporary and unsatisfactory manner. And here we may be allowed a few remarks on what may be considered imperfections or rather omissions in the project.

The line - and those acquainted with the locality will readily follow us - is proposed to start from a point on the Edinburgh and Northern near to Milton farm to cross the Moultrie between two and three hundred yards above the present stone bridge, to cut through the clay height north of Seggie distillery, to cross the Eden at Mr Spence's wharf, thence by a rather sudden curve by the back of Eden cottage, and along the back of the firth outside of Seafield embankment, and round to the east of Pilmuir Cottage, terminating at the corner of Strathtyrum sheep park. The only level crossing is at Guard Bridge, where there will also be a station; and the only sidings or branches are those in connection with Seggie Distillery, Mr Spence's new wharf, Guard Bridge tile works and Mr Meldrum's new brick and tile works at Kincaple. Now the first imperfection that must present itself is that the proposal to start from Milton, instead of running from that point parallel to the main-line, and starting from the already established station at Leuchars. In fact, cheapness, convenience, accommodation and risk of accidents, all point out the indispensable necessity of adopting this course.

Again the sheep-park terminus appears to be another blunder. If it must be there in the meantime, let it be erected in the most temporary manner, and let every effort be made to induce the Golfers and the Strathtyrum Trustees to allow it to be carried forward at least to the vacant feu beside the Life-Boat house. At this point a permanent and commodious station might be erected, and that without any detriment either to the Swilken bleaching-green or the much-cherished golfing course; but to think of establishing anything like permanent erections at the sheep-park were little short of absurdity. A third and dangerous-looking imperfection is the sudden curve in crossing the Eden. Surely it was or is still possible to remedy this defect. The navigation of the river at this point is now of little value, and once the line were completed would be of no value whatever, and should therefore not be permitted to stand at all in the way of the public safety. Another point before we close is the vexatious imposition by the Admiralty; compelling sealights to be burned on the bridges over the Eden and Moultrie. Every one acquainted with these rivers must see at once the folly of this precaution; and the needlessness of the permanent expense which it must cause to the company. Every exertion should be made to get the enforcement annulled as wholly unnecessary and vexatious; and if the Admiralty must occasionally show work for its money, we presume the Directors will have no great difficulty in suggesting a few much better jobs than protecting the navigation of two tidal duck-dubs like the Eden and Moultrie.

So much for the plans and expense of construction; the question Will it pay? And the data upon which the Company have founded their estimates, we reserve for another occasion.

In the following month the *Fife Herald* expressed some optimistic doubts in relation to the proposed traffic which the line might carry as outlined in the company's Prospectus:

There can be no doubt that the passenger traffic is under estimated, when we consider not only the general tendency of the public to avail themselves of railway facilities, but also the absolute certainty of many excursion trains to St Andrews. Again, the third item appears to be understated, as there can be little doubt of coals being largely carried to St Andrews and the East of Fife from the western coal fields, and also the main traffic in merchandise will then be by rail and not as now by packet, which is very slow, hazardous, and, we may add, unprofitable to the packet company, who have not for several years paid one farthing of dividend. Further, the free-stone traffic is evidently under the mark, considering the vast fields of Strathkinness, Nydie and Kincaple, and the demand not only for stone in Dundee, but also in Perth, in various towns in Fife, and even in Leith and Edinburgh. Moreover there is nothing set down for the carrying of fish to inland markets and nothing is to be reckoned upon the ironstone of Denhead, which may yet find its way to the foundries of the west of Fife, instead of as present, to the furnaces of Newcastle.

Proceeding Favourably

On 18th September, 1851 the *Fifeshire Journal* reported that 'the contractor commenced operations on this line in the beginning of last week by making a cutting in a field at Guardbridge, on the west side of the turnpike road', there having been a small ceremony to mark the cutting of the first sod 10 days before on which occasion it was said by the Directors that 'the experience of observing construction of many similar railways has brought wisdom to the enterprise'. Barely two months later the *Journal* of 13th November, 1851 stated that 'satisfactory progress was being made and that no difficulties had been encountered' and a week later mentioned that 'the formation of the railway is progressing rapidly. The piles have been driven for the bridges and the levelling is almost complete between the junction with the trunk line and the sea wall or Salt Grass Dyke in the Seafield Estate, being about three-fifths of the whole'. On 29th January, 1852 the same paper reported that 'Our railway proceeds favourably to completion - the bridges across the Eden and Moultrie now being well advanced, the sea wall at Seafield being nearly finished, and a portion of the permanent rails being laid down in the middle of the line'. By March it was being reported to the shareholders that progress on the line was so rapid that it could well be finished ahead of schedule and, in a somewhat optimistic note it was forecast that the railway might even be completed for less than the scheduled sum, an event which would prove 'that the shareholders have been particularly fortunate in their choice of Directors to whose judicious management the success of the undertaking up to this point may be fairly ascribed'. It was also said that the line was now complete between St Andrews and Guardbridge and that the section between Guardbridge and the junction at Milton would be completed soon and that the station at St Andrews was also nearly finished. Then, after Easter, it was announced that the expected opening date for the line would be Thursday 10th June, 1852.

Avoiding the Shillings

However despite the general satisfaction with the progress of the line, relations between the Directors and Kenneth Mathieson were on occasions far from harmonious. The not unusual arguments between a railway and its contractor in relation to the amounts of money payable, including those due for disputed 'extras' and the timing of payments due, led on one occasion to the Board seeking to have a firm of Edinburgh lawyers act as mediators and on another to seek the intercession of Thomas Bouch to find a mutually agreeable solution. The company minutes in May 1852 record that the Directors 'were to abandon any further attempt at an amicable arrangement with Mr Mathieson', notwithstanding the proud boast of William Smith to the shareholders that 'we are carrying on our operations with the utmost economy and not spending one shilling where it can be avoided'. In the same month a notice was published to the effect that 'The St Andrews Railway Company wants to borrow on Debenture in one or more sums, £7,000. Interest 4 Per Cent' while shortly thereafter Mathieson and Bouch agreed between them that the final cost of constructing the line was to be fixed at £15,141. Mathieson then agreed that he would forego taking £2,500 of the money due to him and take the same amount in debentures instead. Peace was thus restored and, after he had handed the line over to the Directors, Mathieson joined them on the Board and remained a Director until 1858, by which time he had disposed of all of his shares in the company.

It had never been the intention of the Directors of the St Andrews Railway that they should operate the trains themselves as not only did they possess no locomotives or rolling stock or, indeed, the considerable capital with which to buy the same but also, more importantly, they had between them no practical experience whatsoever of railway operations. However, due to both local geography and economic considerations the service over the branch had, in any event, never been intended to be a true 'stand alone' one but, rather, had been intended to operate solely as a feeder line to the EP&D line at Leuchars. Accordingly, and after considerable bargaining between them, the St Andrews and the Edinburgh, Perth & Dundee companies entered into an operating agreement which, it was thought, was bound to bring benefit to both parties. The EP&D agreed that, for a 25 year period from 1st July, 1852, they would work the line by providing locomotives and stock at a cost of one shilling per mile for passenger trains of not more than five carriages, mixed trains of not less than eight vehicles and mineral trains of up to 10 wagons, additional vehicles being charged proportionately. In return for the whole of the receipts obtained by them, the EP&D would pay the interest on all borrowings and meet the costs of running trains and maintaining the line and of employing staff - William Smith somewhat picturesquely described this latter provision as 'the paying for all necessary enginemen, stokers, guards, brakesmen and every necessary servant for working the locomotive power'. Most importantly, from the point of view of the St Andrews shareholders, the EP&D would pay a guaranteed dividend of 4½ per cent per annum on the St Andrews Railway shares, a not ungenerous and safe capital return in what were uncertain times for railway investors. Any surplus which remained after the deduction of all of these costs was to be shared equally between the Edinburgh, Perth & Dundee and the St Andrews companies. To enable the agreement to be given effect to a Joint Committee was formed, comprising of the Chairman and two Directors from each company, the Chairman of the smaller concern to serve as the Chairman of the 'St Andrews Railway Joint Committee'. The agreement between the companies subsisted until 31st July, 1877, despite the later absorption of the former company by the North British Railway.

An Inspector Calls

On 24th June, 1852 the *Journal* was able to report that:

On Tuesday afternoon a locomotive engine came along the line for the first time from the junction to the St Andrews terminus. It appeared to be an engineer's trip for the examination of the Government Inspector's visit, which is expected to be on Thursday. The engine went off again in the evening. The novelty of such an arrival here brought a number of people to the terminus. The day for opening is we believe still involved in doubt.

In those days all passenger-carrying railways were required to be inspected by a member of the Railway Inspectorate, part of the Board of Trade in London. The Inspectorate consisted of military officers from the Royal Engineers and, on the same day that the report of the light engine appeared in the *Journal*, Captain Laffan inspected the newly completed St Andrews Railway and, after declaring himself highly satisfied with the 'substantial and workmanlike manner' in which the works were executed, submitted the following report:

Perth, June 24th 1852.
I have the honour to report to you for the information of the lords that I this day inspected the St Andrews Railway from its junction with the Edinburgh, Perth and Dundee Railway at Leuchars to its terminus at St Andrews, a distance of 4 miles and 45 chains.
The St Andrews is a single line. It is to be worked by the Edinburgh, Perth and Dundee Company. A single tank engine is to work exclusively on the single line, and no other has at any time to be allowed to pass the junction points. The line has been executed in accordance with the Parliamentary plans. The works are extremely slight - as the country through which it passes consists for the most part of level downs.

Saint Andrews.

Captain Laffan's report
of inspection of line from its
junction with the Edinburgh
Perth and Dundee Railway at
~~Leuchars~~ Dundee to its terminus at
St Andrews.

Perth June 24th 1852

No 1484
PM

Sir

I have the honor to report to you for the
information of the Lords &c that I this day inspected the
St Andrews Railway from its junction with the Edinburgh
Perth and Dundee Railway at Leuchars to its terminus
at St Andrews, a distance of 4 miles and 45 chains.

The St Andrews is a single line: it is to be
worked by the Edinburgh, Perth and Dundee Company;
A single tank engine is to be told off to work exclusively
on the single line, and no other is at any time to be
allowed to pass the junction points.

The line has been executed in accordance with the
Parliamentary plans. The works are extremely sleight — as
the county through which it passes consists for the most
part of level downs. the line crosses but one public road
it is a level crossing; the gates closing across both
railway and road, and a gatekeeper is appointed. —
There are no road bridges. — There are two timber
viaducts, one of 5 spans crossing the Moultree Burn
the other of 9 spans over the Eden River, both are
constructed of timber and in each the openings are of
moderate span — I believe both these structures to be
sufficiently strong.

The

Board of Trade Inspection Report, 24th June, 1852.   *Authors' Collection*

The line crosses but one public road - it is a level crossing; the gates closing across both railway and road, and a gatekeeper is appointed. There are two timber viaducts, one of 5 spans crossing the Moultrie Burn, the other of 9 spans over the Eden River, both are constructed of timber and in each the openings are of moderate span - I believe both the structures to be sufficiently strong.

The rail used weighs 60 lbs to the yard. It is of the ordinary double 'T' form, in lengths of 16 feet and laid to bearings 4 feet apart. This forms a light permanent way, but the traffic is never likely to be heavy.

Switches are laid for sidings, to be constructed hereafter, to accommodate several manufacturing establishments along the line, but at present they are not to be used and the switches are locked. Previous to their being used, the Company's engineer has engaged to send me a certificate to the effect that proper chock blocks are fixed to prevent anything on the sidings interfering with the traffic upon the main line, and the chock blocks and switches are always to be kept locked and their key to be entrusted to no one but the guard of the train which works the line.

I believe this line to be in a fit state to receive public traffic and beg to recommend that permission be given to the Company to open it.

I have the honour to be, viz. Your most obedient servant,
(signed) R.M.Laffan   (Capt. R E)

The final cost of building the line, according to the figures presented to the shareholders in 1852, amounted to some £21,565 which, apart from the monies paid to the contractor and in acquiring land, also included £546 in Parliamentary costs and £526 in 'other preliminary expenses'. However, this was not the true final figure since not all the land compensation payments had yet been made and both the stations and certain of the subsidiary works had still to be executed - for instance as late as 1854 it was reported that the St Andrews station master's house was 'nearly finished' - so that a more accurate figure was arrived at in the 1855 company accounts when it was shown that the total cost of the works was £25,314; this amended figure did not, of course, include the substantial costs which were subsequently incurred in attempting to remedy the initial economies effected when building the line. However, the shareholders appear to have been satisfied and, shortly before the opening of the line, the *Fifeshire Journal* commented that:

... very little more than the authorised sum will be required to meet all liabilities... On the whole, the undertaking is a pattern and model to other districts similarly situated, and its success will no doubt materially influence the adoption of many such branches.

Cheering Loudly

On Tuesday 29th June, 1852 the St Andrews Railway was officially opened to all traffic when, according to the *Scotsman*:

This event, highly important not only for the town of St Andrews but for the whole of Fife, took place on Tuesday at mid-day. Strangers, especially those belonging to the chief towns in the county, had been invited by the Directors to be present. A number of additional first-class carriages had been provided to conduct them along the main-line to Leuchars. When the Leuchars station was reached, the Directors, Mr Ellice,* and a large number of

* Edward Ellice was the Liberal MP for the St Andrews Burghs, a constituency covering St Andrews, Crail and Anstruther; in addition he was a Director of the EP&D.

the inhabitants were there to receive the strangers and accompany them along the new line to St Andrews. After a short delay, incident on the exchange of courtesies, all took their seats. They filled some 8 or 10 first-class carriages. On starting the Leuchars folks, crowds of whom had gathered at the station, cheered loudly and lustily.

According to the *Fifeshire Journal*, the Directors and their friends left St Andrews between eleven and twelve noon in order to meet the self-same strangers who had come from as far away as Cupar, Kirkcaldy and Dunfermline and, as the paper takes up the story:

These deputations arrived at about half-past twelve and after a few minutes spent in congratulations, took their seats along with the Directors for St Andrews. The drive was easily accomplished in fifteen minutes, including a partial halt at Guard Bridge station, and all expressed themselves highly satisfied with the smoothness and steadiness of the motion. The day, with the exception of a brief sunny shower, was delightful, and being high water at the time, the full tide of the Eden close on the left and the green corn fields on the right, with the grey towers of the old cathedral city rising in bold-relief in the distance, presented a picture such as those who saw St Andrews for the first time are not likely soon to forget. After arriving at the station, the party marched with banners and music to the Provost's residence and gardens, where after enjoying themselves for a while they dispersed in groups to visit the ruins of the cathedral and castle, the buildings of the University and other sights of the city.

At three o'clock the parties reassembled in the Town Hall where 100 invited guests including the Directors, the Provosts of St Andrews and other Fife local authorities and a selection of 'other important personages' sat down for a celebration meal. 'The dinner and wine were by Mr Christie, of the Royal Hotel, and more than sustained the well-known character of that establishment'. Lengthy speeches and loyal toasts followed with much rejoicing and ponderous punning and other toasts to divers persons as the Provost of Kirkcaldy and the Directors of the Leven Railway were made. William Smith, as Chairman, made a long and humorous speech during which, alluding to the fact that this was a local line and that none of those involved were professional railwaymen, he said that when the Directors embarked on the enterprise they thought that chairs were not things that supported the rails but were easy chairs in which to sit and that they thought that sleepers were the Directors themselves, all of which produced much laughter. He then likened his fellow Directors to being 'just like a company of young officers who had undertaken to convey a ship to a port and had a rather rum sort of crew' and, after thanking both Thomas Bouch and Kenneth Mathieson and alluding to the disagreements which the Directors had had with them, went on to pronounce that 'We are again very good friends. Now the ship is afloat, we hope to make a prosperous voyage of it', Lastly, and probably to the relief of his audience, he concluded by proposing a toast to the Leven Railway, 'a company which is only at the beginning of its difficulties, but would surmount its problems just as the St Andrews Railway had done and prove very beneficial to the railway's promoters and the country through which it would pass'.

The considerable satisfaction and pride with which the citizens of St Andrews regarded their railway was obvious and there could be little doubt that the whole proceedings were sincere and well-meant.

At six o'clock all returned to the terminus of the railway where the St Andrews men took good-bye of the different deputations. In a few minutes the train was once more at Leuchars, this time passing along the shores of the Eden at low water, which produced a striking contrast to the morning's scenery.

On the following day, Wednesday 30th June, the shareholders of the company and 50 citizens of St Andrews were treated to a cheap excursion to Dunfermline in order that they could enjoy the delights of the new railway although it was said locally that if the train had been better advertised there would have been a greater number of passengers. In any event, shortly before nine in the morning the special train left St Andrews, arriving at its destination some 30 miles away, at 11. The majority of the party visited Dunfermline's famed Abbey and Palace and the pleasure grounds at Pittencrieff, although the local press made the somewhat acerbic comment that some persons 'preferred enjoyment of a less intellectual kind'. The return journey commenced at seven in the evening but by the time that the train reached St Andrews, at about 9.30, there was an anxious crowd of almost 1,000 persons awaiting its arrival, many of whom had been waiting for several hours in order to see the great novelty of a steam train arriving at the city:

At last the smoke of a train was perceived nearing Leuchars ... soon it was seen coming citywards and sweeping along Edenside it came southwards over the links and entered the station, amidst the enthusiastic applause of the assembled multitude, many of whom in their eagerness to get a full sight of such novelties as an engine and carriage, gave the police constables much cause to keep the rails clear.

The St Andrews railway was now, at last, ready for business and on the following day, Thursday 1st July, 1852, the line was opened to traffic.

EDINBURGH, PERTH, AND DUNDEE RAILWAY.

OPENING OF ST ANDREWS RAILWAY.

The ST ANDREWS RAILWAY will be OPENED, for Passenger and Goods Traffic, On THURSDAY FIRST the 1st of July.

TRAINS will run as follow :—

To St Andrews—	A.M.	A.M.	P.M.	P.M.
From Edinburgh, at	6.30	9.45	12.30	3. 0
From Dundee, at	—	8.50	2.50	5.45
From Perth, at	6.45	10.45	3.30	—
From St Andrews—				
To Edinburgh, at	6.25	8.50	3.10	6. 0
To Dundee, at	8.50	11.55	2.20	5. 0
To Perth, at	6.25	8.50	3.10	6. 0

For FARES, &c., see Time Bills for July.

By order.

Notice from the *Scotsman*, 30th June, 1852.

Chapter Four

The Finest Watering Place:
The St Andrews Railway 1852-1862

'The best remuneration to the Directors was the good done to St Andrews
and the dividends yielded to the shareholders'
William Smith, Chairman, St Andrews Railway

Travelling Cheaply

The public service over the St Andrews railway commenced on Thursday 1st July, 1852 with the departure of the 6.25 am from the terminus which took a leisurely 25 minutes or so to complete the 4¾ mile journey to the junction at Leuchars. Here a connection was made with an up main line train bound for Burntisland where passengers could change on to the ferry for Granton and proceed by the former Edinburgh, Leith and Granton line to the centrally situated Canal Street station of the Edinburgh, Perth & Dundee Railway and adjacent to the Edinburgh & Glasgow Railway terminus; should passengers have alighted at Ladybank they would have found a connection for Newburgh and Perth. Thereafter there were trains from St Andrews which left at 8.50 am, 3.10 and 6 pm all of which made up main line connections at Leuchars for Burntisland and Perth. The 8.50 am and a further three services leaving St Andrews at 11.55 am, 2.20 and 5.00 pm, each made down main line connections at Leuchars for Tayport where passengers could proceed to Dundee via the Broughty Ferry crossing and the Dundee & Arbroath line. A similar pattern of weekday services was run in the other direction with a total of seven trains providing connections from four Burntisland, three Perth and three Tayport services. Coach services were provided to give early-morning connections at St Andrews station from Crail, Anstruther and Pittenweem. In the best Presbyterian tradition, and for more practical reasons of economy, there was no Sunday service on the line.

Passenger trains normally consisted of a rake of the rather primitive four-wheeled wooden carriages provided by the EP&D for its own passengers. Usually each train had one coach each respectively for first, second and third class passengers with a separate guard's van and, if the train was a mixed one, a small number of four-wheeled goods wagons were also attached. The usual motive power, in view of the light nature of the trackwork and bridge structures, was a small four-coupled engine which was stabled overnight at St Andrews. The passenger fares charged were, according to the *Scotsman*, 'extremely moderate - the railway has been made very cheaply and is to be travelled very cheaply'. As an example of how cheap the travel offered was, the St Andrews Railway Directors arranged for monthly season tickets to be issued between Cupar and St Andrews at greatly reduced rates for first class passengers of £2 6s. 8d. for one month and £4 for two months, the respective equivalents for third class passengers being £2 and £3 10s., or little more than

Edwardian families enjoying their holidays on the West Sands at St Andrews.
A. Brotchie Collection

one half of the amount of daily tickets for the same periods. As the *Fifeshire Journal* put it 'this boon must be specially acceptable to professional gentlemen and others, at least during the summer and autumn months; giving them all the advantages of St Andrews, which is now the finest watering place on our coasts'.

Alarms and Excursions

The line seems to have been a success from the very outset and in the first week of the service there were a number of special excursions to St Andrews including that of 84 boys from George Watson's Hospital* in Edinburgh who came to visit the city. The *Journal* reported on 22nd July that:

> Now that the railway has brought us within reasonable reach of the rest of the world, pleasure excursions to our Ancient City are quite the order of the day. This week we had a monster party from Glasgow; next week we are to have one from Perth and another from Arbroath; in the week following we are to have parties from Kirkcaldy and Dysart and on the 12th of August another from Stirling. How many may be concocting in the interim we cannot tell, but this we know, that our authorities have made every place of interest available to sight-seers, and have taken care that they still have any facility for shelter and refreshment in the event of unfavourable weather. Go a-head old St Rule!

The city was, evidently, ready to welcome visitors and a Civic Association was formed in St Andrews to promote the town to all and sundry, providing 'that large excursion trains shall with ease and little expense see the sights of the

---

* George Watson's was a school rather than a hospital in the modern sense and is now the largest co-educational private school in Edinburgh.

place'. One of its aims was, providing that 'timeous notification was given', to meet the excursionists at the station and have them conducted around the principal places of interest and beauty. The Association had Walter Ireland, the St Andrews Railway Secretary, as its own Chairman and three other Board members also served on its committee, so the Association was well geared towards achieving its goals. Soon, however, complaints were being made that such timeous intimation was not being given to the Association, particularly on the part of the Edinburgh, Perth & Dundee company, and that excursion trains were arriving unannounced or with such short notice that they could not be met by members of the Association's committee. However another problem was also being encountered, this time very much a reflection on the downside of tourism - the tourists themselves - and it was being claimed that 'great evils that have risen from the excursion trains to St Andrews' with 'many of the excursionists often being in a state of intoxication'. Ironically one of the worse examples of this intoxication was provided by certain intemperate travellers who had arrived on a Perth temperance excursion train and whose subsequent conduct in the town quite clearly failed to live up to the lofty ideals of the promoters of the excursion. The dawn of the age of tourism clearly had its drawbacks!

There seems, however, also to have been a certain laxity in the way that additional excursion trains were operated by the EP&D, and on 26th August, 1852 the *Journal* reported that on the previous Saturday there had been an accident which showed 'the necessity of the utmost care being taken that the numerous pleasure trips should not be allowed to interfere with the ordinary traffic'. It appeared that the return working of an excursion train from Edinburgh left St Andrews combined with the 6 pm service train to Leuchars and on arriving at Guardbridge station, a banking engine which was intended to assist the train up the incline at that part of the line [and probably not in accordance with the 'one engine in steam' Regulations], followed so closely upon it that 'before it could be stopped, it came with considerable force upon the last carriage causing a severe shock to the passengers, three or four of whom sustained slight cuts and bruises'.

On 11th November, 1852 the same paper carried a letter which was signed 'T.D.' and which highlighted another potential danger on the line.

SIR – A dozen lines, if you please, of the *Journal* to draw the attention of the Directors and the Public to what appears, if not positively dangerous, at least very dangerous like, and not at all agreeable to a man of my nerve. I refer to the unprotected state of the railway embankment where it skirts the estuary of the Eden near to the Kincaple siding. During the late storm, the waves seem to have been breaking over the very rails, or at all events, have undermined the sandy embankment close under the sleepers - giving two and separate portions of the line anything but a safe appearance. A fortnight has now nearly elapsed since the storm abated, and nothing has yet been done by the Directors to fill up these breaches and render the embankment more substantial and safe. At whose door the fault lies, your humble servant knows not; but this he knows - that should any accident happen from the rails breaking down at these spots, the Directors will then learn to their cost whose duty it is not to break the heads and limbs of the Public. A hundred pounds or so would raise a substantial barrier, but ten or even twenty hundred may not cover the damage resulting from a culpable break down.

A separate complaint expressed was that the single tank locomotive allocated to work the ordinary trains on the branch appeared to have been less than reliable and in view of the parlous state of the Edinburgh, Perth & Dundee finances there was no back-up readily available. The St Andrews correspondent of the *Journal* somewhat peevishly reported on 9th December, 1852 that:

On Friday, for the second time we believe, passengers by our line were put to considerable inconvenience by something going wrong with the engine, so that it could not proceed at the appropriate hour and omnibuses had to be used, as formerly, to convey them to and from Leuchars. It may be thought economical to have but one locomotive but if for the want of another such irregularities once destroy confidence, the company may find, when too late, that they have been practising a very mistaken economy.

This does not seem to have been a one-off for on 28th April, 1853 the *Journal* informed its readers that:

On Wednesday last there was a temporary suspension of transit by rail to the city. It appears that on one engine alone rests the responsibility of conveying each and all of the trains to and from Leuchars. On the day mentioned it became unfit for work on the arrival of the first Edinburgh train at Leuchars, the axle having broken fortunately before starting. Such an emergency as this was totally unprovided for, and there was no fresh engine procurable nearer than Ladybank. The guard of the St Andrews train travelled to the city by means of Her Majesty's Mail-gig to intimate what had occurred. Immediately on his arrival the omnibuses waiting at the terminus were despatched towards the main-line above Milton where the passengers clambered up the railway embankment and over and through the fence to reach the vehicles. This is now the second interruption of the sort that has taken place.

There was a curious incident reported in the *Fifeshire Journal* of 21st July, 1853:

On Wednesday afternoon, as the second train from the south was going along betwixt Dairsie and Leuchars, a boy fell out of a first-class carriage from the door having burst open. The guard signalled the engine driver to stop but this was not accomplished till the train was at Leuchars. Thereafter the St Andrews engine was despatched south with a first-class carriage containing Dr Scott to the place where the boy had fallen out. Before this, however, he had been found by Mr Meldrum of Pittormie, who conveyed him to his house and got him attended to.

A Valuable Accessory

Notwithstanding such difficulties, passenger traffic continued to grow at a satisfactory rate and tourists and university students, as well as the merchants of the town and commercial travellers all used the line. Not long after the line opened, the Directors of the Edinburgh, Perth & Dundee Railway reported to their shareholders at the Half-Yearly Meeting held in September 1852 that, in relation to the St Andrews Railway, 'although it would be premature to pronounce an opinion as to the ultimate results, yet, judging from the amount of Traffic which has already passed over the Branch, it promises to be a valuable accessory to your Line'.

The promise appears to have been kept for in the first year that the branch was open some 1,250 people per week were reported to have travelled on the line. The half-yearly return to 31st July, 1853 showed that 11,355 train miles were run providing passenger receipts of £718, while for the same period in the following year receipts amounted to £811. It was estimated that the additional revenue gained by the main line and branch as a whole as a result of the opening of the branch amounted, in its first seven months, to some £1,000. Goods traffic was 'encouraging' but below that which had been anticipated. Perhaps this was not surprising given that during the first month of operation the company had made no proper provisions for the same and at Guardbridge there were 'no cranes, weighing machines &c. for the carrying on of such a trade'. Nevertheless the Directors 'looked for a greatly larger [sic] increase in the goods traffic'.

In September 1852 the EP&D Chairman reported to their shareholders that:

The St Andrews branch was opened on 1st July last, and has since that period been operated by you. I am one of those who conceive that if the fortunes of this company are to be retrieved at all, it will, to a great extent, be effected by giving judicious encouragement to cheaply-constructed branch lines, for the development of the local traffic, from which the parent company cannot fail to receive substantial and increasing advantages.

In March 1854 he reported that:

As was anticipated, the Traffic on the St Andrews Railway ... has continued to show a gradual increase; and, in reference to the last Half-year, it is satisfactory to remark that after payment of preferential charges, a surplus remains sufficient for the full payment of the stipulated allowance of 1s. per mile for the Locomotive Power and Use of the Plant supplied by this Company. To the Main Line the St Andrews Railway forms an important adjunct, and the benefits in this respect will now, doubtless, be realised to the full extent, without contingent loss, of the Working Agreement, in virtue of which the Branch was projected and executed.

Towards the end of the first decade tourist guides which included the railway were appearing - one of the first being the *Handbook of St Andrews* published in 1859 and written by Henry Brougham Farnie.* Other improvements to benefit tourist traffic to the city were welcomed by the St Andrews company, provided, of course, that they did not cause the parsimonious Board to expend much money - these included series of minor ameliorations to the stations on the line. An early example of such was provided by the application of John Chalmers 'for the use of the Gentleman's Room at St Andrews for the sale of aerated waters, confectionery, etc' was acceded to 'on condition that the room be kept open at all times for its lawful purpose'.

---

* Farnie was a colourful character who was a graduate journalist and son of James Farnie, shipowner and one-time Provost of Burntisland. He wrote a number of guidebooks of Fife interest and in 1861 acquired the Crieff newspaper *The Strathearn Herald*; he was later editor of the *Fifeshire Journal*. He lived, somewhat controversially for the time, with a lady to whom he was not married and died in Paris in 1889, having achieved a not inconsiderable success in the music publishing world.

An Ill-provided Junction

Although it may have originally been the intention to build a new junction station at Milton where the St Andrews branch made a physical connection with the EP&D line this was never, apparently, proceeded with and the branch trains ran along the main line for ¾ mile before reaching the existing Leuchars station which was situated on the south side of the level crossing on the St Andrews to Newport road close to the village. Here minimal passenger facilities were provided, no doubt sufficient for the inhabitants of Leuchars but hardly palatial, the station having been built as a rather temporary wayside structure during a period when the EP&D was strapped for cash. Indeed, as Farnie's *Handbook* was to comment some years after the line opened 'Leuchars has always been a country village of but small size and importance; at present, even when propped up by the business consequent upon railway transit, it is mainly inhabited by weavers and farm labourers'. A small goods yard with a shed was situated on the east side of the station and dealt with a small amount of local traffic.

Within a short time of the opening of the line the St Andrews Board reported that they 'were aware of the great detention of passengers which often takes place at Leuchars and we are endeavouring to make arrangements to get this great annoyance removed'. The problem appears to have been caused by the faulty marshalling of trains on the main line and the fact that, with totally inadequate sidings accommodation, it was extremely difficult to make up the branch trains in time. This was compounded by extremely poor connections between the branch trains and the main line as the cost of providing a dedicated connection to each main line train would have a 'regretful effect' on the running costs of the branch line. The St Andrews company attempted to improve both the timetable and the station and the Board minutes comment that 'The proprietors are no doubt aware of the miserable state of Leuchars station. At that station there is no accommodation or comfort for passengers and it will require a considerable sum to do what is needed there'.

The timetable remained unchanged but much needed alterations at Leuchars were afoot. In September 1854 the St Andrews shareholders were informed that 'the new station house at Leuchars has been contracted for and will forthwith be erected, the St Andrews company having contributed £250 towards the erection'. At the beginning of 1855 the new station house and carriage shed were completed, although some subsequent commentators seem to have erroneously assumed that this 'new station house' was built on the site of the present Leuchars Junction station rather than the original Old station site. In September 1857 the EP&D shareholders were informed that 'for expediting the Trains on the St Andrews Railway [a] new siding and crossing has been constructed at Leuchars station'. In the following year the timber platforms at Leuchars, which were 'much decayed' were removed and a stone and gravel platform substituted in its place and in 1859 the footbridge at the station underwent reconstruction. Leuchars station was, however, still open to criticism and in February 1864 the *Dundee Courier* in an editorial commented that:

A more ill-provided junction does not exist on the line. The waiting room for First and Second Class passengers is a small, circumscribed compartment, or rather box, with three wooden chairs and a small fire, minus a poker, in a grate scarcely fit for a ploughman's bothy. What we have said of the compartment for gentlemen applies equally for the room for ladies. Both rooms are simply despicable. The fact is that the station was never meant for a junction at all, being originally built for the village of Leuchars alone, and no additional accommodation has been provided after the construction of the St Andrews branch.

However Leuchars station remained largely unimproved until, in the North British era, a new station was built nearer to the physical junction when the Tay Bridge line was opened whilst the old station imaginatively soldiered on to serve the Tayport line.

Merchandise, General and Otherwise

The revenue earned by goods traffic was rather less than that earned from passenger traffic and, given the fact that St Andrews was not an industrial centre and that such industries as there were tended to be of a local nature such as the St Andrews Foundry ('manufacturers of cast iron goods of every description - boilers, cattle troughs and plough metal') and four golf ball and club makers situated appropriately in Pilmuir Links and Golf Place, this is hardly surprising. The carriage of coal, chiefly for household use, would have been an important and regular source of freight and most of this tended to come from the Fife and Clackmannan pits; it should be noted that St Andrews also continued to receive coal and other goods by sea for many years after the railway opened, albeit on no very great scale. Other inwards traffic to the small goods yard at the terminus provided general merchandise including food, stock for local shops and other domestic items, building and agricultural requisites including brick, stone and tiles and salt for livestock, together with a number of animals, principally cattle and sheep. Fish and agricultural produce, principally grain, potatoes and barley grown in the surrounding fertile soil, comprised most of the outward traffic from the city. Notwithstanding the rural nature of the town, freight business on the line seems to have been satisfactory in the early years and, in April 1856, the Directors of the St Andrews company reported that 'in answer to a question by Mr Purvis of Kinaldy, it was stated that the goods traffic for the half-year from the two stations on the line [i.e. Guardbridge and St Andrews] amounted to about 20,000 tons'.

Although the coming of the railway might have been thought to have had an adverse effect on the trade of local carriers, there still seems to have been sufficient traffic for them; in 1866 these carriers included R. Bisset ('from Anstruther every Thursday'), James Braid of 110 Market Street ('to Dundee every Tuesday and Friday'), Allan McIntyre of 113 South Street ('to Dundee every Thursday and Friday, to Anstruther, Crail and Kingsbarns every Thursday and Saturday') and Mrs R. Scott ('to Cupar every Tuesday').

The coal yard at St Andrews station had a number of stances for coal merchants including David Balsillie, William Berwick, Edward Sang and David Pringle. It is likely that they were supplied with their coal in this era by some of the Fife coal owners such as the Earl of Rosslyn's Colleries, C.J. Balfour & Co. of Balgonie and the Lochgelly Iron & Coal Co. Coal was also delivered to the town by sea, probably from the small Fife ports such as Dysart, Charlestown, Limekilns, Inverkeithing and Kirkcaldy, from the Lothian ports of Leith, Cockenzie and Prestonpans, from Alloa and from the Tyne.

One unusual cargo which was dispatched both by sea from the small harbour at St Andrews and also by rail was what was described as 'iron ore' but was more correctly Denhead Blackband ironstone carted to the harbour and station from the small ironstone mines west of the town at Denhead, near Strathkinness. The ironstone, mined until about 1868, was originally shipped to ironworks in the north-east of England for smelting but was also dispatched by rail to the iron industry of West Fife which was situated, principally, in Lochgelly and Oakley. The Joint Committee minutes list quoted rates for this traffic as well as rates for the conveyance of ironstone from St Andrews and Guardbridge to Tayport from where it would, presumably, have been shipped to smelting centres such as the Carron ironworks at Falkirk or to the busy industries of Tyneside. As a measure of the importance of this trade, the St Andrews company minutes reveal that, in the summer of 1854, in consequence of the opening of new workings at Cairn Hill and Mount Melville, the Board was 'about to get the loading bank raised so as to give facility for the loading of ironstone' at the terminus.

The coastal trade from the harbour had never, in modern times at least, been great and in 1859 it was said that 'the tonnage of the port is 101 tons (2 vessels) and the chief trade lies in (exports); grain, potatoes and iron ore and (imports) English coal, timber, guano, salt and slates. There are thirteen fishing boats belonging to the port, manned by 70 men and employed in taking white fish'. The potato traffic, at least, seems to have survived the coming of the branch line and in March 1860 the *Fifeshire Journal* reported that 'there are a good many vessels loading at the harbour for London and the English provincial markets'.

There were a number of commercial premises situated at the harbour including Gibson's sawmill and timber merchants and a branch of Robert Hutchison & Co, flour and provender merchants of Kirkcaldy but it was not long before the ironstone traffic ceased and 'the port sank again to the position of a sub port, and the shipping trade particularly since the opening of the railway has been very small, and is confined to the export of grain and potatoes and import of coal, timber, guano, salt and slates'. Throughout the first half of the century a weekly goods and passenger vessel sailed direct from St Andrews to Leith, and this service appears to have been sufficient for the potential sea traffic so that when an attempt was made in the 1860s to institute a daily Leith to St Andrews service via Anstruther this did not prove a financial success and was soon discontinued.

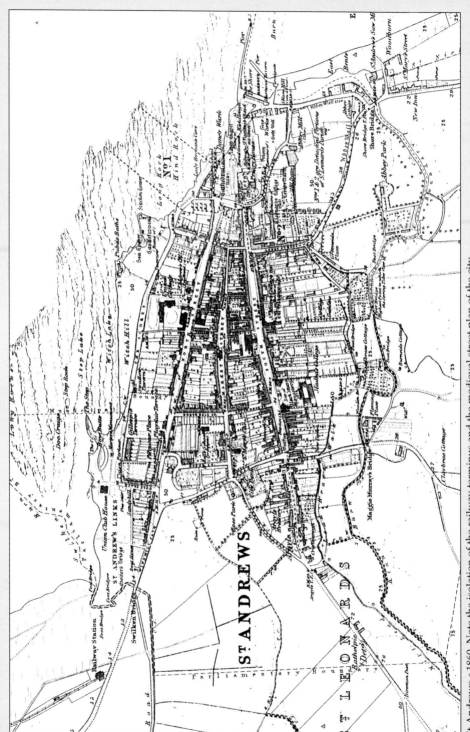

St Andrews c.1860. Note the isolation of the railway terminus and the medieval street plan of the city.

Whisky Galore

At Guardbridge two of the most important local industries were situated. The most imposing of these was the Seggie Distillery, which gave employment to 100 or so men and provided grain (as opposed to malt) whisky principally for the London and Glasgow markets. Some idea of the importance of the distillery to the local economy can be gained from the fact that it was the largest single customer of the Bank of Scotland branch in St Andrews. In 1847 William Haig died and control of the Seggie distillery passed to his sons Robert Haig and John Haig, the latter already having established his own distillery at Cameron Bridge near Leven. Prior to the advent of the railway the tidal river wharves were used by vessels bringing in the raw materials of coal and grain and for shipping out the whisky, the bulk of that product being sent by sea, using vessels owned by a Peter Robertson of St Andrews, to an agent in London. Robert Haig was quick to realise the potential of using rail transport. Not only was Haig a shareholder and Director of the St Andrews Railway but, as manager of the Seggie Distillery, was quick to take steps to secure a connection from his works on to the branch line. On 8th April, 1852 at the meeting of the Road Trustees for Fife 'an application was read from Mr Haig of Seggie Distillery, applying for authority to cross the Turnpike road on the level in making a branch line from the St Andrews railway to his works' and the trustees agreed to permit the crossing to be made 'at right angles with the road and not in a slanting direction as proposed in the plan'. The Inspector's report makes it clear that the points for this siding were installed prior to the opening of the line but there seems to have been no particular urgency applied for it is only on 11th April, 1853 that the railway company minutes record that 'An estimate from D. Pitkethly for making Seggie Siding, amounting to £149, was read and accepted'.

Seggie Distillery seems to have provided a considerable traffic for the line, both inward and outward, and concessionary rates were offered by the company in order to secure a monopoly for transport, even after Robert Haig's departure from the Board. An example is given in the Joint Committee minutes of 1858 when it was agreed that coal to the distillery would be carried at the reduced rate of 3s. 0d. per ton and that grain from Leith would be taken at 6s. 6d. per ton provided, in both cases, that Haig promised to convey all such traffic by rail. The distillery nevertheless ceased production in or about 1860, after which the siding appears to have been lifted, causing a decrease in the line's goods receipts of £460 in the following year. Then, as the *Journal* reported on 5th December, 1867:

... the railway lye from Guardbridge to the Seggie distillery has been relaid at considerable expense. The inference is that the extensive buildings are to be again occupied, to the revival of trade and the consequent prosperity of the neighbourhood. We are as yet ignorant of the kind of business which is to be prosecuted.

In July 1869 the distillery buildings underwent 'extensive alteration and repair' and by the end of the harvest season of that year they were being used as a maltings and brewery owned by Haig, Sons and Laing. Presumably the siding was still in use but the brewery did not prosper and within a short period the siding was, once again, out of use. However, its fortunes were about to change and the manner in which Seggie Siding was to become the single largest source of goods traffic on the whole line is related in a later chapter.

Brick, Tile and Stone

The other important industry at Guardbridge was brick and tile making. In the early and mid years of the 19th century the government encouraged farmers to improve their land by draining their fields using cheap labour and locally made tile drains and pipework. In the vicinity of Guardbridge there were two such works both of which relied on clay dug from immediately adjacent pits. At Guardbridge, situated on the south side of the Cupar to St Andrews road, was the Seggie Brick and Tile works and the railway company minute book for 31st March, 1851 records that 'the committee unanimously agree to make a siding from the station at Guardbridge to the north side of the turnpike road immediately at the back of the toll house, for the use of Colonel Lindsay's Tile Works'.

A short distance from Guardbridge towards St Andrews was located the premises of the Seafield Brick and Tile Works owned by Alexander Meldrum of Kincaple, a Director of the railway company. Although the works was situated south of the main road and at some distance from the railway the same entry in the minute book records that 'Mr Meldrum stated that with regard to the siding to his tile works he is quite satisfied with the siding being brought to the north side of the turnpike road' and it was eventually constructed thus. From the 'loading bench' at this siding a narrow-gauge tramway was constructed which ran southwards to the brickworks. The works and tramway were taken over by David Meldrum, Alexander Meldrum's son, in or about 1860 and the site employed 28 labourers on a seasonal basis. The siding and tramway were noted as having been removed by 10th August, 1898 although the works, now owned by Thomas Wilson & Son, continued to produce a wide variety of goods including chimney heads, firebricks, flower pots, vases, hyacinth and bulb bowls and milk coolers until they eventually closed in 1942.

A later brickworks, also served by a private siding, was that of the Eden Brick and Tile Works of Messrs P. & C. Cunningham, situated on the landward side of the railway between Guardbridge and Seafield. In May 1873 the North British Works Committee approved of an application made in the name of McLean & Co of Dundee to construct a siding alongside the works 'provided that the parties pay £380, and the St Andrews Railway Company the balance of the cost'. They did and the Brickworks Siding (otherwise the Eden Brickworks Siding) was opened for traffic on 27th September of that year. The firm was later known as McLean & Cunningham but the rail traffic does not seem to have lived up to expectation for within a few years the siding was disused and severed from the main line. The fortunes of the Brickworks Siding were revived when it was reinstated by the North British at the expense of R. Patterson and re-opened on 5th July, 1897; once again the siding did not prosper and it was again lifted in July 1906, the North British paying George Bruce of St Andrews, who was by now the proprietor of the brickworks, the sum of £50 for the materials used.

Other industries in the locality included a number of quarries which principally produced basalt for road metal and paving slabs, mainly for local use. Sandstone for building was worked at nearby Strathkinness and at Knock Hill and Nydie Quarry but there was no direct railway communication to any of these works and any product exported from them would have had to be carted to Guardbridge where ships would have been in competition with the railway. In about 1872 plans were lodged for a long siding from Nydie Quarry to the St Andrews railway but the line was never built. Presumably the traffic was thought insufficient to justify such expenditure or it may have been that the intended gradients ranging from 1 in 30 to 1 in 20 were considered too steep! There is no evidence of any St Andrews or Guardbridge traders ever operating their own private railway wagons throughout the independent life of the St Andrews Railway Company.

Strained Relations

On the whole the relationship between the St Andrews Railway and the Edinburgh, Perth and Dundee was a satisfactory one and, when the EP&D was taken over by the North British in 1862, the St Andrews Directors stated that they 'have to say that as a Board our intercourse with the Directors of the former line have been of the most friendly nature, and we hope that the dealings with the new and enlarged board will not be less so'. This was, perhaps, an over-statement and although the Joint Committee, set up to oversee the operation of the working agreement between the two companies, managed to sort out matters concerning rates, traffic and other minor matters, there were other more contentious issues which, with the passage of time, began to fester.

There were continual complaints about connections at Leuchars and the state of the station there was much discussed but the real problem with these and other complaints, including the frequent breakdown of the branch locomotive, was that the Edinburgh, Perth & Dundee invariably had the upper hand. That company was responsible not only for the running of the trains but also for maintaining the bridges, stations and trackwork and, contentiously when a popular St Andrews station agent was dismissed, for the hiring and firing of the staff. Many of the disagreements arose out of the need to finance necessary improvements and repairs which required the St Andrews company to raise extra capital and it could be said that Bouch and Mathieson's cheese-paring during the construction of the line caused problems within a very short time. The trackwork gave trouble almost from the very beginning with the twin evils of the economy effected by spacing the sleepers at four feet rather than the usual three feet intervals and the widespread use of treenails and sub-standard spikes becoming progressively more apparent. As a result of the first of these defects, the rails began to splay and give way on curves and in 1853, despite the Directors being 'totally unable for such a large extra outlay', extra capital was found to pay for inserting additional sleepers where necessary. The problem was exacerbated in 1858 when the EP&D, wishing to use heavier motive power to move the increasingly heavy passenger and goods loadings on the line, was told by its district engineer Barrie that the bridges, stability of the line and the insufficiency of the permanent way meant that the Hawthorn tank engines used on the company's other services could not be used on the St Andrews line. When, in 1860, the EP&D again wished to introduce heavier locomotives to work the increasing traffic, a compromise was reached with an agreement that upon their replacement the sleepers would be placed at three-feet intervals throughout the whole distance of the line but, as was evidenced by the subsequent accident and inspection in 1864, the trackwork remained far from perfect.

Another long-standing problem concerned the timber trestle bridges over the Motray and Eden. It had always been envisaged that these would be purely temporary structures but that, with care, they had been expected to last for at least 30 years. The specification had called for them to be built of the best Baltic pine but it appeared that no preservative had been applied thereto. When Bouch was approached about the matter he replied that at the time that these bridges were erected, he was of the view that to tar the bridges 'would be prejudicial to do so and the bridges therefore were declared to be finished'. As a result the bridges began, literally, to fall apart and in 1856 £1,000 was spent on repairing the Motray bridge and on effecting improvements at Guardbridge and St Andrews stations. In 1860 further repairs were carried out to the Eden bridge. The company, 'for their own protection and duty to the public' employed two local wrights, Alexander Doig and David Balsillie, to oversee the bridges and to ensure that the Board had advance warning of any further potential dangers.

A Rejected Suitor

On 29th July, 1862 the Edinburgh, Perth & Dundee was amalgamated with the North British Railway as part of the latter company's expansion and consolidation programme. Section 53 of the North British (Edinburgh, Perth & Dundee and West of Fife Mineral Railway) Amalgamation Act 1862 (25 & 26 Vict., cap. clxxxix) provided that:

> Nothing here contained shall prejudicially affect any agreement which before the dissolution of the Edinburgh, Perth and Dundee Railway Company subsisted between that company and the St Andrews Railway Company ... [and] all such agreements [are] to continue.

However the laconic relations between the two companies was to undergo a change, partly because of the personality of the ebullient Chairman of the North British, Richard Hodgson, and partly because of the inevitable imbalance of power between Scotland's largest railway company and one of the country's smallest. Hodgson no doubt was aware that the finances of the St Andrews company were, at that stage, less rosy than they had been and that the Eden and Moultrie bridges were coming to an end of their useful lives.

Negotiations between the North British and the St Andrews companies in relation to a number of matters continued over the summer and on 6th September, 1862 the *Fifeshire Journal* reported that:

We understand that the Directors of the North British Railway Company, including the Chairman, Mr Hodgson, came to St Andrews on Thursday, for the purpose of conferring with the St Andrews Railway Board with respect to certain changes contemplated on this line with the amalgamated companies. The conference was private, but it is understood that Mr Hodgson is opposed to a separate side-line for the St Andrews Railway from the point of junction with the main-line to Leuchars station, being of the opinion that the present system of working is perfectly safe, and of course, much more economical. The North British Board, on the other hand, is favourable to the project of bringing the St Andrews terminus nearer the town, and a desultory conversation was held on the best way that this might be done. Nothing, however, resulted definitely from the conference.

From the St Andrews company minutes of the 18th and 27th of the same month it was clear that serious consideration was being given to the proposals of the North British to take the company over. The proposal to borrow £6,000 floated at the half-yearly meeting had, perhaps, been on the conservative side since the North British had been talking about an additional capital of between £16,000 and £20,000 being required to replace the bridges and to bring the trackwork up to acceptable modern standards. In realising that the smaller company would be unlikely to be able to raise such an amount, the St Andrews company were prepared to bow to the inevitable and either sell out to the North British or lease to them their line in perpetuity provided that they were to able to agree terms. Hodgson, 'looking to the eventuality of trains being run express from Dundee at a high rate of speed' to St Andrews, was so confident of success that he caused to be published in the press intimation of a Bill to take over the St Andrews company and authorized Bouch to examine the line and to report back to him without the knowledge of the St Andrews Board. Bouch reported that an expenditure of £12,561 was required to relay the track with 75 lb. rails and to replace the two bridges. The St Andrews Board were outraged by Hodgson and Bouch going behind their backs and ridiculed the proposed sum to be spent on the basis that heavier locomotives were not required and that 'no company indeed having regard to fitness, or to ordinary economy, would employ engines of 30 tons or upwards to work a branch 4½ miles in length - having the small trains and run at the low speed already mentioned'. Accordingly the St Andrews Board opposed the North British Bill apart from the clause allowing the former company to raise the further £6,000 that they required and the latter company, having in any event lost interest in the takeover given the aggressive attitude of the St Andrews company, abandoned their attempts for the time being.

Thereafter relations between the two companies remained distant, the Joint Committee meeting infrequently and issues of concern, such as the perceived dragging of its heels by the North British to bring the electric telegraph to the city and the 'dreadful state of the station at St Andrews' were from time to time aired in the local press. Neither company, however, could contract out of their working agreement and, however reluctantly, the uneasy relationship between the two continued.

To be let for 19 Years, from Martinmas 1865,
BRICK AND TILE WORK TO BE LET
To be LET, for such a period as may be agreed on,

THE BRICK AND TILE WORK OF SEGGIE,

Parish of Leuchars, Fife, presently tenanted by Mr Bisset. The Work has been long established, and an extensive trade has been carried on. The Clay is of very superior quality, and easily procured. The Erections belong to the Proprietor, and are in good order and condition, and well adapted for a large business. The Guardbridge Station of the St Andrews Railway is close to the Work, which also adjoins the St Andrews and Cupar Turnpike Road. Entry at Martinmas first may be arranged.

Mr BISSET, the present Tenant, will point out the Works: and further information may be obtained on application to DRUMMOND & NICHOLSON, Writers, Cupar-Fife, with whom offers may be lodged by the 1st of September next.

Cupar-Fife, 19th July 1865. **1171**

A most desirable business for sale, 1865.

NBR luggage label c.1870.

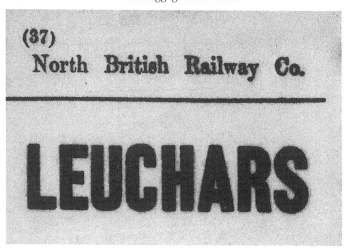

Chapter Five

Kettle on Wheels:
The St Andrews Railway 1863-1877

*'Can the local black kettle on wheels not prove equal to the occasion
or is it impossible to get a willing assistant?'*
The Fifeshire Journal, 1873

Golden Years

By 1863 many of the deficiencies of the St Andrews Railway and its services were being addressed by the Board and it was clear that the small local company was in the process of coming out of a period of depression and about to enter into an age of prosperity and contentment, even if its passengers did not always agree with that view. That such a change was necessary was undoubted, for not only had the affair with the Edinburgh, Perth & Dundee and its successor left the St Andrews company vulnerable but the goods income that the line was generating was proving to be poor due, according to the Chairman, 'to inclement weather, dullness of trade and the London exhibition' - one might have thought, however, that any notion that the Great Exhibition of 1861 had abstracted trade from the St Andrews Railway was a somewhat fanciful notion.

In June 1863 the timetable still showed seven trains per day with an additional service on Saturdays and these ran as follows:

		1	2	3	4	5	6	7	8
		am	*am*	*am*	*am*	*pm*	*pm*	*pm*	*pm*
St Andrews	*dep.*	6.10	8.30	10.10	11.50	3.00	4.15	6.30	8.50
Guardbridge	*dep.*	6.25	8.40	10.20	12.00	3.10	4.25	6.40	9.00
Leuchars	*arr.*	6.35	8.50	10.30	12.10	3.20	4.35	6.50	9.10

No. 1 - Goods and passengers - to clear the line of all loaded and empty wagons and to return Special from Leuchars to Guardbridge when required. No. 7 - To lift goods from Edinburgh, Perth & Dundee and Stations on Foreign Lines. No. 8 - Runs on Sats. only

		1	2	3	4	5	6	7	8
		am	*am*	*am*	*pm*	*pm*	*pm*	*pm*	*pm*
Leuchars	*dep.*	6.50	9.00	10.40	12.20	3.30	4.45	7.10	9.20
Guardbridge	*dep.*	7.00	9.10	10.50	12.30	3.40	4.55	7.20	9.30
St Andrews	*dep.*	7.10	9.20	11.00	12.40	3.50	5.05	7.30	9.40

No. 1 - The only train which lifts Goods and Coal for Guardbridge and St Andrews. No. 8 - Sats only.

The first two trains each way conveyed all four classes of passenger including Third or Parliamentary class, a type which had come into being as a result of the Regulation of Railways Act 1844 which required companies to operate a minimum number of 'penny-a-mile' trains for the indigent classes. Fourth class was an attempt by the North British and other companies to provide an even

59

cheaper rate of travel than Third although the accommodation was not always inferior to the Parliamentary carriages. The rigid social divisions of the mid-Victorian era still meant that a number of separate types of accommodation were conveyed by every train, leaving passengers to choose in which class they could afford to travel, notwithstanding the fact that each was, in its own way, uncomfortable and that all passengers were subject to the same delays and frustrations, however much they had paid for their ticket.

In St Andrews the number of hotels and inns available to travellers had increased to seven, namely the Cross Keys, Crown Inn, Golf Hotel, Golf Inn, Royal Hotel, Star Hotel and Lawrence's Temperance Hotel - 'an omnibus from the Royal, Cross Keys, and one from the Star Hotel awaits the arrival and attends the departure of the trains'. In addition there were connecting horse-drawn coach services from the Star Hotel to Anstruther, operated by William Donaldson, leaving at 5 pm daily, from the Royal Hotel to Crail, operated by James McIntosh, leaving at 5 pm daily and on Monday, Wednesday and Saturday only from the Royal Hotel stables at 5 pm, operated by Thomas Smith.

Trouble in Eden

On 16th May, 1864 an accident occurred near Guardbridge which was to have certain long-lasting repercussions. The official report compiled by Captain Rich of the Railway Department of the Board of Trade stated that:

A train, consisting of tender in front, engine, one guard's van, one second, one first, and one third class carriage, coupled in the order stated, left Leuchars Station at 3.30 pm on the day named. It left Guard's Bridge [sic] about 3.39 pm, being about five minutes late at each station. About 300 yards beyond the Guard's Bridge, the tender left the rails on the outside of a 30 chain curve, the engine followed, and the leading wheels of the guard's van, next to the engine, also got off the rails. All the passenger carriages remained on, and none of the passengers are reported to have been injured.

There is no turn-table at St Andrews, so that the engine always works tender first foremost in going down. It would be desirable that this line should be worked with a light tank engine. The line itself is of very light and poor construction. The rails are single-headed; in lengths of 16 feet; and weighed 65 lb. per yard lineal when laid down about 12 years since. They are considerably worn. The joint chairs weigh 22 lb. and the intermediate chairs 15 lb. each. They are weak, too narrow in the throat to admit a good key, and reported to be continually breaking. They were originally fastened to the sleepers with treenails, but a great number of spikes have now been substituted; the joints in some cases are still fastened with treenails only. All the keys are necessarily small, and many of them are loose. From the form of chair, length of bearing between the chairs (more particularly next the joints) and the consequent working of the rails; I do not think it would be possible to keep the keys tight. Many of the sleepers have been renewed; and though there are some worn out, the majority are good. Several of the points are only about seven feet long.* These, as well as the crossings, are much worn. I consider that the whole permanent way wants renewing.

---

* This measurement presumably applied to the length of the switch blades; by the end of the century the shortest switch blade length normally used on Scottish railways was nine feet in length although the Kirkcaldy Harbour branch retained until closure switch blades as short as six feet.

There are two wooden viaducts which have had considerable repairs; the cross beams on the Eden Viaduct are too weak. A 12-inch balk should be inserted between each of the present cross-beams.

There are no station signals, and the auxiliaries are too close to the station.

The North British line, from the junction with the St Andrews Railway to beyond Leuchars Station, is also indifferent and the rails, points and crossings at the station are very bad indeed.

The company have got some new rails on the ground for relaying the line, and the sooner it is done the better. The junction with the St Andrews should be formed as a double junction, and the signals and points connected. The present auxiliary signals are only about 90 and 200 yards from the point of junction. They should be removed to a much greater distance. The accident on the 16th ult was caused by the bad state of the St Andrews Railway.

Shortly after the report was released, the St Andrews company held their Half-Yearly Meeting and, after dealing with financial matters and stating that there had been a heavy outlay on additional works William Smith told the shareholders in a spirited response that:

This increased outlay has been on sleepers, fencing &c, as well as on the Moultrie Bridge, which required a thorough repair. Your Directors make this announcement with pleasure, as no doubt you will receive it, as whatever increases the strength and permanence of the line increases the public confidence and safety of both passengers and servants. You will have observed in the newspapers a report by a Government official on the inefficiency of the St Andrews Railway. It was with some surprise that your Directors learned that the official had without their knowledge gone over at least part of the line, and given what they consider a strong report. It may be necessary for the sake of those who were not original holders of the stock, to retrace part of the history of our short line. It was expected that when the Edinburgh, Perth and Dundee Company projected their line; that it would come very near St Andrews, and that our city would be connected with it by a short branch, but some of the difficulties thrown in the way of that company prevented their doing what was intended; and it seemed as if St Andrews was to be cut off from the railway system altogether. The inhabitants of St Andrews then resolved to construct such a line as would be suitable for the traffic of the place. Being entirely off the main route, they considered that a line of a lighter construction than the main-line would be quite efficient for their purpose. It was so formed because the trains and engines were to be of a light kind. The traffic and the works were to correspond. The project in that view has been most successful. The public have been satisfactorily accommodated, and, except in the person of a poor idiot who wandered on to the line, no life has been lost, nor any damage been received either by the passengers or servants during a period of thirteen years. Are we not, then, entitled to say that the line is a safe one. No doubt if the traffic of the great lines with their heavy engines were to pass over the St Andrews line, it would require to be reconstructed, but this was not intended. The Government Inspector admits that 'the majority of sleepers are good' and that 'the original treenails have been to a great extent replaced by new spikes'. The truth is, that the St Andrews line has been dealt with as other lines have been - when a sleeper is worn out; it is replaced by a new one. The chair is fastened by a spike instead of a treenail, so that treenails will shortly disappear.

You are aware, gentlemen, that the works on the line are stronger now than they were then. With creosoted sleepers of the best kind; and iron spikes over a great part of the line, it cannot miss being so; and I am assured that the weight of our rails and chairs bears as high a proportion to the plant and traffic of the line as those of the London and North-Western bear to the plant and traffic of it. You are aware, gentlemen, that your

Directors have always manifested due anxiety in regard to the strength and safety of the line; and especially to the safety and strength of the bridges; but you may not be aware that they have from time to time, independently of the watchful care of the present company and their engineer, sent men of practical skill to examine those bridges; and only a few months ago … they employed an engineer of great experience to examine the bridges. His report showed that the Guard Bridge was in good condition but that the bridge over the Moultrie Burn required to be carefully overhauled. Your Directors put themselves in communication with the North British Railway Company, who immediately did what they considered necessary in repairing and strengthening the bridge. In regard to the bridges, allow me to say that these erections were not intended to be permanent; and the time will come when they must be replaced by more permanent structures. Your Directors will therefore require to be put in such a position as to be able to accomplish this as soon as possible …

The meeting backed the Directors and carried a motion to replace the wooden bridges when circumstances allowed. There was much further discussion of Captain Rich's report and there were allegations that he had been biased against the company in producing such a 'sensational' report and that an explanation should be obtained as to why a Government official should have behaved in this way. A suggestion was made that a contrary report should be published but there was general agreement that the Directors were dealing with the matter satisfactorily. The meeting then agreed to a dividend of 4½ per cent and passed the following resolution: 'That the Directors be authorised to apply to the Government for power to borrow money to the extent of £6000, by the extension of shares, or by other means, for the purchase of land, in order to build bridges and alter the curves on the line; and to extend a separate line of rail from Milton Junction to Leuchars.'

Distant Signals

A sign of increasing sophistication can be found in the report of the *Journal* of 23rd January, 1868 when it was said that: 'We are glad to warn that the North British Railway is about to extend its telegraphic system to St Andrews and that the terminus is to be at the Post Office under Mr Murray. This will be found much more central and convenient than the Railway Station'. By the end of May the same paper was informing its readers that the posts to carry the telegraph wires had been delivered to Leuchars and to St Andrews and that the digging of the holes in which they were to stand had begun. Then on 16th July it was said that:

One of the most important acquirements which has been added to the city of late is the introduction of the telegraph. Many efforts have, by the shareholders of the St Andrews Railway, been put forth to procure this for the city and much credit is due to John Purvis, Esq of Kinaldy,* for the interest and trouble he took in the matter and whether it may have been directly or indirectly the result of his persevering effort or the result of some scheme of the North British Railway Company, the very desirable object has been acquired, and telegraphic communication has been established between St Andrews and other parts of the Kingdom.

---

* John Purvis made a trip to North America in 1851 and took a particular interest in the experimental telegraph installed between Philadelphia and Washington. He later became Chairman of the Anstruther & St Andrews Railway.

As traffic slowly increased, so did the mileage run by the trains on the St Andrews branch. These figures, which were used to calculate the operating charge made by the North British, were, in the half-years from 31st July, 1870 to 31st July, 1877 as follows:

July 1870	12,680	January 1871	12,960
July 1871	13,520	January 1872	13,520
July 1872	12,780	January 1873	14,450
July 1873	13,640	January 1874	15,203
July 1874	15,252	January 1875	15,064
July 1875	16,682	January 1876	17,118
July 1876	17,406	January 1877	17,532
July 1877	17,406		

The fact that the January figures tended to be higher than the July figures reflected the fact that not only was grain and other agricultural traffic higher in the harvest season but also that August tended to be the peak holiday month in Scotland and thus additional excursion trains were run in this period. A significant development in September 1872 was the introduction of two extra goods-only trains from Leuchars to St Andrews, thus virtually ending the practice of running mixed trains on the line. As the *Fifeshire Journal* reported of this innovation:

It is an improvement on the old system of conveying goods and passengers by the same train and it is a sign that the trade of the city is increasing. By the new system passengers will be saved an infinite amount of annoyance which they had to undergo by the shunting at the several lyes along the line.

Offensive Smells; Unrecorded Woes

Although there had been regular complaints about the state of Leuchars and St Andrews stations, it appears that the branch line terminus was a continual sore to the inhabitants of the city. This came to a head when the *Fifeshire Journal* of 15th October, 1868 commented that:

It occurs to us that the Five Per Cent to the St Andrews Railway shareholders ought to warrant the erection of a new station-house. As much is due to those who ought to have made such a dividend secure. There is no question that there is much need for it. It is a tumble-down erection which exists, neither ornamental nor adequate. There is no waiting-room which with propriety can be called one, nor is there a ticket-box which by the highest flight of fancy can be regarded as such. The thing is just a barn open at both ends to make draughts, with recesses on one side in which passengers may be squeezed, while waiting on trains or fighting their way into carriages. It is constructed so as to secure all the discomforts which incapacity for the special purpose can produce, and all coughs which the winds of heaven can generate. The arrivals and departures have to conquer their ways to their respective destinations and those succeed best who have most audacity and least temper.

The article went on at some length to complain that in 'the yawning imperfection of the cobwebbed and unpainted pile' passengers had to mingle with personal luggage and perishable goods including 'fish, flesh and flour alike' so that the only ones happy with the situation were those whose 'olifactory nerves are dull'. The tirade continued by pointing out that the increased tourist, golfing and scholastic traffic to the town was affronted by the low standard of the accommodation provided by the existing building and that it was high time that a new station was built - it was too long to wait for the replacement that would be needed if the proposed extension to Anstruther was undertaken. However, the junction station at Leuchars was also castigated:

> The North British Railway should add something to the accommodation of the Leuchars junction. Wind and weather have it all their own way here. There is, simply, no waiting accommodation, though at the week's end a month - adding half-hours and quarter-hours together - has been lost. The two companies exchange passengers who are often a sight to be seen. The constant traveller - this, by the way, is a curious being - behaves much as the Indian does who goes through the ordeal of endeavouring to get a ring out of a gallon of boiling oil without turning a hair. He simply endures and passes on. His unrecorded woes would pain even a Board who knew them not, owing to human emotions forming no part of their official care.

Nothing appears to have been done, although in 1871 representatives from the North British had a meeting with the Directors of the St Andrews Railway on the subject of additional train and station accommodation. It was therefore unsurprising that, in 1873, the state of the terminus at St Andrews was again being discussed and, as the Chairman of the company reported to the shareholders:

> Since their last meeting the Directors had met several times with the parent company in Edinburgh, and brought before them the well-grounded complaint of a want of sufficient accommodation at the St Andrews railway terminus. On calculating the probable expense of a new station, they found that it would cost more than they could be warranted in laying out. It would resolve an outlay of £2,000 or £3,000, the interest on which in three or four years would more than pay the alterations proposed to be effected on the present station. A plan of these alterations had been drawn out, and according to it the platform would be widened to double its present size, heightened and extended. This he trusted would be done before the summer season, and without incommoding passengers, in about a couple of days.

These minor alterations were carried out in the late summer and it was noted that the platform 'so far as the offices extend' had been enclosed and that 'the appearance of the station has been much enhanced and the facilities for working the passenger traffic has been greatly enhanced' but, given the relatively short time that the working agreement with the North British still had to run the badly-wanted replacements for both St Andrews and Leuchars stations had to wait until a later date.

Further expenditure on the branch line took place when a comprehensive campaign of replacing the rails on the branch with the heavier 72 lb. variety previously recommended by the Board of Trade was undertaken and other alterations authorized by the Board included increasing the size of loading banks so that heavier traffic could use them. Minor alterations to Guardbridge station were also undertaken and additional sidings provided at St Andrews so that the 'want of goods accommodation' could be remedied; in 1874 there was talk of providing new sidings should the brick works in the vicinity win any contracts to provide bricks to be used in the construction of the Tay Bridge.

The Shape of Things to Come

Although Dundee and St Andrews were barely a dozen miles apart, the journey between them was a long and hazardous one, involving a train ride to Broughty Ferry, an often stormy sea crossing followed by two further train journeys with an inconvenient and sometimes lengthy wait at Leuchars *en route*. In October 1864 the citizens of Dundee, fed up with what was regarded as the incivility of the Scottish Central Railway's servants on the circuitous route via Perth and by the inconvenience of the North British ferry service, met to discuss the building of a bridge across the Tay. Although this scheme came to nothing, the North British in November 1865 published proposals for its own bridge across the Tay, together with connecting lines from the centre of Dundee and from the proposed southern landfall at Wormit to Tayport via Newport-on-Tay and from Wormit to Leuchars via St Fort. The St Andrews Railway Chairman, William Smith, reported to the company's shareholders at the Half-Yearly Meeting held in October 1869 that:

> All our former predictions of success have been more than realised and if the proposed bridge over the Tay should be built (and I believe it will be) I think we shall see greater changes in St Andrews than any of us have seen yet. Some years ago I had occasion to be often in Dundee, and many of the leading men have said to me, give us quicker access to your city, say half an hour's ride or so, and many of us will come and reside in St Andrews, go to our places of business in the morning and return in the evening. A Dundee gentlemen, a short time ago, put it to me in this way. He said - if this bridge is built, we will then consider St Andrews as a suburb of Dundee - we will then consider Dundee a university town - (laughter) - and our lads will come over to your schools and colleges in the morning and return home in the evening. I have no doubt, gentlemen, that we shall have them in both the ways I have indicated. I am sure then, gentlemen, that with me you wish the North British Company all success with their project.

The prevailing view expressed at a subsequent public meeting in the town was also in favour of the project it being said that 'With the Tay Bridge erected, St Andrews which presented greater attractions than Helensburgh, would become to Dundee what Helensburgh had become to Glasgow'. Parliamentary powers to construct the bridge and associated lines were granted on 1st August, 1870, when the North British Railway (Tay Bridge and Railways) Act (33 & 34 Vic., cap. cxxxv) was passed, the contracts for Thomas Bouch's slender single-line bridge, the longest in the world by far, having already been awarded. The Act specifically provided for 'a railway from the North British Railway in the parish of Leuchars in the County of Fife to the turnpike road leading from Newport to Kilmany in the parish of Forgan in the same county' and, in the plans deposited, a line 'five miles, four furlongs and six chains in length' was shown, together with a new station at the point where the new line diverged from the Tayport to Cupar line, a little to the north of the junction of that line with the St Andrews branch at Milton.

An Honest Wonder

A recurrent theme, repeatedly periodically with variations, until the closure of the line nearly a century later, was the perceived (and usually justified) shortcomings in the passenger services provided to St Andrews. On 30th October, 1873 the *Fifeshire Journal* castigated the Board of the local company:

> The occasion of their half-yearly meeting may be embraced to urge upon the Directors of the St Andrews Railway the need of doing something to improve their service. No one will believe that a dividend is fairly earned who had to quit the city so early as 6.20 p.m. in order, if he is going south, to stand shivering at Leuchars ... a good half-hour. Can the local black kettle on wheels not prove equal to the occasion or is it impossible to get a willing assistant? We are quite aware that all branch lines are dependent on the trunk line, and in Fife, as we all know to our cost, a harum-scarum one it is ... It is of importance that the most favourable impression should be taken away from such a city - a city which, to a large extent since it has no manufactures, depends on its amenities, and on a smooth pleasing way of making their acquaintance. These favourable impressions are impossible in the case of those who are dragged away from the city when a third of the day is yet to run, who at Guardbridge are subject to jolts from the kettle on wheels backing over the Eden, in order with stolen momentum, to breast the despicable gradient in front and who find themselves blaspheming at Leuchars with colds to catch and nearly an hour to spare.

The newspaper went on to comment, somewhat sarcastically, that 'a reading room with, say, cards for whist' should be provided at Leuchars and ended with the comment that 'The English families who return to St Andrews, notwithstanding the non providential sorrows of the way - for the Fife line is a scheme of things by itself - are objects to us of honest wonder'.

Practical Management

The Board of the St Andrews Railway varied throughout the years. William Smith remained as Chairman until his death in 1872 when he was succeeded by one of his fellow original Directors, Andrew Aikman. The other Directors came and went and, Aikman aside, none of the founding fathers survived the company, Robert Haig and John Brown having gone by 1855 with Alan Briggs of Gordonshall, St Andrews and Kenneth Mathieson of Dunfermline, the contractor who built the line, serving in their place. By 1859 Mathieson had resigned and Dr John Adamson had been appointed while by 1864 Playfair had been replaced by the new Provost of St Andrews, Walter Thomas Milton and Alan Briggs had been replaced by Alexander Kyd Lindesay, banker, of St Andrews. By 1867 Lindesay had gone and John Purvis of Kinaldy was serving in his place. In 1870 John Orphat of Guardbridge had replaced that old stalwart Alexander Meldrum of Kincaple. The final Board of the independent company consisted of Andrew Aikman as Chairman, Purvis, Orphat, John Jamieson of Kingask, Admiral W.H. Maitland Dougall of Scotscraig and Alexander Meldrum's son, David Meldrum, W.S.* What is interesting, though, is that throughout the history of the St Andrews company, the Board remained local and free from external influence - a railway 'for the town and by the town'. The Directors were unpaid and despite shareholders attempts to introduce salaries for

---

* Writer to the Signet – a society of Scottish supreme court solicitors still extant. David Meldrum had, since 1860, been proprietor of the Seafield Brick and Tile Works.

them, turned down any money, the Chairman stating that they considered their work to be 'a labour of love' and that 'the best remuneration to the Directors was the good done to St Andrews and the dividends yielded to the shareholders'.

The Secretary of the St Andrews Railway was responsible for the routine administration of the company and some light is thrown upon his duties by a glimpse at the Minute Book of the company which, unlike those of the Leven and East of Fife companies, has survived. From the inception of the company in 1851 and for many years thereafter, a respected local solicitor, Walter Foggo Ireland, occupied that post. Ireland was also Factor for the United Colleges of St Salvator and St Leonard in the University, Factor for the City of St Andrews as well as being the local Bank Agent for the Commercial Bank of Scotland and he carried out his duties as Secretary to the company apparently to the complete satisfaction of the Board. However, the minutes of 29th June, 1868 record that Ireland had suddenly left St Andrews, 'his affairs being reported in a state of confusion and his name in the Gazette* sequestrated ...' The Directors were, understandably, seriously worried that the hapless Ireland might have absconded with the company's accounting records and cash but their fears appear to have been ill-founded and Walter Ireland's partner in the law firm of Ireland and Murray was appointed in his place. The minutes contain a description of the duties which he was to undertake:

> To keep the Minutes and the Accounts, collect the rents, summon the meetings monthly of the Directors and half yearly of the Proprietors, to keep and answer correspondence, calculate the dividends and issue warrants for the same after being signed by the Chairman or other Directors ... To calculate the interest on debentures and issue certificates of shares and debentures. To keep all the books and accounts [and] generally to do all the work connected with the office of a Secretary of a Railway.
>
> The Secretary to be elected to find security for £200. Salary to be £20 per annum, with £5 for office rent. Term of appointment to be during the pleasure of the Directors and may be terminated with 3 months notice on either side.

Mr Murray seems to have filled his post admirably on an *ad hoc* basis until he resigned and was superseded by Thomas Cochrane, described as 'Agent, Commercial Bank, Queen Street, St Andrews'. The last Secretary of the St Andrews Railway to be appointed was A.O. Spence who, in 1877, was responsible for winding-up the affairs of the company.

Money Matters

The St Andrews company published accounts, as sent to the members, are to be found in the Minute Books of the company and details were also published in the local press and an examination of these shows how a small but successful Victorian railway company functioned. The company was a sizeable local undertaking, in terms of its issued share capital and borrowings, and the majority of the shares were locally held. Revenue from both passengers and freight grew at a satisfactory rate although there were a few setbacks, principally the disastrous loss of the Seggie distillery traffic following the closing of that concern. The increase in traffic was steady and in the last six years of the company's existence the actual train miles run over the line increased

---

*   Scottish bankruptcies were then, as now, reported in the official government publication, *The Edinburgh Gazette.*

by some 29 per cent with a commensurate rise in revenue. Another source of concern was the condition of the railway itself and the state of the two deteriorating wooden bridges *en route*. In terms of the agreement with the Edinburgh, Perth & Dundee and later the North British the St Andrews shareholders received their guaranteed 4½ per cent dividend, the surplus being divided between the companies. The authorized capital was £21,000 in originally authorized shares, £6,000 in additional shares authorized by the North British Act of 1866 and authorized loans of £7,000. The issued share capital was £21,000 and £5,300 of loans at 4 per cent per annum.

In a fairly typical half-year, that ending 31st July, 1870, there was a capital balance of £88 8s. 11d. made up of received payments on the capital account of £26,300 (£21,000 in shares and £5,300 as a loan) and the expenditure on the line to date of £26,211 11s. 1d. The other accounts were as follows:

	£	s.	d.
Revenue account:			
Revenue:			
By Passenger traffic	1,268	15	9
Parcels traffic	91	15	10
Goods & Minerals	887	6	7
Livestock	29	1	3
Mail Services	19	10	0
Transfer fee	0	15	0
	2,297	4	5
Expenditure:			
To: Maintenance of way, works and station [A]	296	8	5
Locomotive power – mileage to NBR			
12,680 miles at 1s. per mile	634	0	0
Traffic expenses [D]	248	13	10
General Charges [E]	63	7	8
Rates & Taxes	46	8	11
Government Duty	41	18	6
	1,330	17	4
Balance on revenue account	966	7	1
Net Revenue account			
Interest on Mortgage & Debentures (net)	103	15	10
One-half surplus paid to NBR	200	2	4
Balance available for dividend	662	8	11
	966	7	1

Proposed Appropriation of Balance Available for Distribution:			
For distribution balance available	662	8	11
Dividend on ordinary stock at 6½%	682	16	0
Balance from reserves	20	7	1

	£	s.	d.
Abstract			
[A] Maintenance of way, works, etc.			
Wages	112	1	5
Materials	84	7	0
	296	8	5

[D] Traffic expenses			
Salaries, wages etc.	206	14	11
Stationery, clothing, coals etc	41	18	11
	248	13	10

[E] General Charges			
Clearing House Charges	23	1	2
Half maintenance of road to station	21	13	9
Salary to Secretary	10	0	0
Printing, Reports & Advertising	4	0	0
Office expenses	4	2	9
	63	7	8

In one of the last sets of accounts given to shareholders, that for the half-year ending 31st January, 1876 the gross receipts amounted to £3,508 and the expenditure to £1,769, leaving a profit of £1,739. Of this sum £134 was appropriated to the payment of debenture interest, and £540 (being one-half of the surplus profit after payment of a dividend of 4½ per cent) was paid to the North British, leaving an available balance for shareholders of £1,050, with £15 being carried to the reserve fund.

Here and There

In January 1867 heavy snow fell across East Fife and not only was the main line blocked but the first St Andrews branch train of the day only succeeded in reaching Leuchars shortly after 1 pm, after having to receive assistance on the climb to Milton Junction and main line trains were severely disrupted for several days. Such incidents were not unusual as the branch line ran through fairly exposed country and the local press reported each blockage, often in detail. A particularly dramatic account of the weather appeared on 8th January, 1875:

> The snowstorm, which took place on the evening of New Year's Day, and very severe in St Andrews and district, and miles of the road were blocked up with drift to the depth of six to eight feet. The train due here at 7.40 p.m. that day did not arrive here until about 11 o'clock in the forenoon of Saturday. Two engines were attached to the carriages, and when just a little over the bridge spanning the Eden the tender of the foremost engine in consequence of a deep snow wreath went off the line and all efforts to put it on again and proceed were unavailing. The passengers, or the greater part of them, remained in the carriages until four in the morning, when several started for St Andrews on foot. The remainder did not reach their destination until Saturday forenoon. Their quarters must have been very cold and disagreeable.

Minor mishaps included an incident in January 1868 when it was reported that a piston on a locomotive burst and all traffic was stopped for some hours – this account sems to be inaccurate as it would have been more likely at that time for a piston rod to fracture or part company with the piston and the cylinder would have been a more probable candidate to sustain a 'burst'. A report in the *East Fife Record* of 25th April, 1863 informed its readers that:

> On Monday forenoon an ass strayed on to the St Andrews branch … at Mussel Road crossing, and wandered along the line within a short distance of Guardbridge, when a train came up and knocked the poor donkey over, killing it on the spot. No damage was done to the train.

A more serious incident was reported in the *Journal* of 15th July, 1870:

On Saturday night, as the last train from St Andrews was nearing Edenside, the engine-driver perceived the rails some hundred yards or so before him to be covered by what he took to be birds. As the train, however, drew nearer the spot, he discovered that he was mistaken, and at once reversed his engine. The train, however, could not be stopped before it had dashed on to what proved to be a number of iron chains, spikes and other metal objects used on the railways. These covered the rails for some two or three hundred yards. Fortunately the 'cow-catchers' in front of the locomotive were instrumental in knocking off a number of the obstructive articles, so that the engine wheels only knocked them into the ground, and the train was stopped in time to prevent a catastrophe from the continued obstruction. Happily no damage was done, but had the train being going the other way, when going in which direction the engine is generally placed tender first, the locomotive must certainly have been thrown off the rails. Information of the extraordinary attempt to upset the train was at once given to the police, and Inspector Watson of St Andrews set to work to discover the offenders. It is understood that two boys, aged seven and nine years respectively, are the authors of the mischief which they seem to have perpetuated, in the idea that it was a frolic. They were apprehended, and brought to Cupar on Monday morning, but have in the meantime been liberated, on account of their extreme youth.

Another item which catches the flavour of its time appeared in the *Fifeshire Journal* of 9th March, 1871 under the heading of 'Narrow escape of the Fife Fox Hounds'.

On Friday, while the pack were out hunting and running on the scent on that portion of the line of rails between Seafield and Guardbridge, the train came dashing up and had it not been for the promptitude with which the engine-driver pulled up, the probability is that a large number of the pack would have been run over and killed.

The section of line which ran alongside the Eden near Guardbridge continued to give concern because of storm damage and eventually the company was forced to act after a particularly severe winter tempest at the beginning of 1877. As the *Fifeshire Journal* reported on 11th January of that year:

The railway between Leuchars and St Andrews has suffered more from this storm than it had done on any previous occasion. The strong gale from the east sent the water inland and the ballast had become much like mortar. Since Thursday night, a large squad of men collected from the branches of the section have been busy at work and the large portion of the line has been raised above the former level nearly two feet. The work was carried out on Sunday and Monday, the lifting of the rails with 'dumbies' being the chief feature of the repair. The ballast is obtained from the banks along the sides of the line, and Mr Turner, Inspector of the Permanent Way, is carrying out the work.

Perhaps the last accident on the independent St Andrews Railway occurred on 14th July, 1877 when two passengers, a Mr Slater and a Dr Archibald, were injured when a carriage on a train at Guardbridge had been 'drawn up beyond the platform and opposite a steep embankment near the station'. According to the *Journal:*

Slater first went out of the carriage and got down on the top of the embankment, but on assisting his friend, Dr Archibald, to alight with him, lost his balance, and together they rolled over the embankment and sustained injuries ... which they allege to be serious.

The sequel to this incident was that both Slater and Archibald sued the North British for £1,000 each in respect of their injuries but the action was subsequently settled before it came to court.

Other items from contemporary papers included the comings and goings of the railway staff which reflected the newly found labour mobility of Victorian Scotland - a typical item concerned, in the summer of 1868, the promotion of one Patmore, the station agent of St Andrews, to Manuel Junction on the Edinburgh to Glasgow main-line and his replacement by a Mr King, formerly the station agent at Fountainhall on the Waverley route from Edinburgh to Hawick. Safety of railway staff seems to have been somewhat illusory and the local newspapers were full of mishaps. A typical press report from 1869 recorded that:

> On Thursday evening, Alexander Leitch, railway porter [at St Andrews], while uncoupling a coal waggon from the passenger train was trapped in the rails, and his foot was run over and very seriously cut and injured. It is but a few weeks since he was able to resume his employment from a dislocation of the shoulder.

The end of 'ain auld sang'

The St Andrews Railway Company was similar to many small local railway companies throughout Britain in that it was formed by local interests to finance the construction of a railway branch line to connect their town, which had been by-passed by a trunk railway route, to the new main line system which was knitting together the economic fabric of an increasingly confident and prosperous nation. The venture proved to be successful and it contributed towards the growth of the town and its economy. The end to its independent existence came about as the result of the consolidation of the national railway system into a small number of large and powerful organizations such as the North British Railway (NBR) which, by virtue of its capital, assets and staff, was probably the largest joint stock company that Scotland had ever seen. The St Andrews Railway Company and its small, though very profitable line, became too small to survive as an independent entity at a time when in Britain the era of the locally-owned and locally-managed railway was coming to an end. The late 1870s saw a trade depression in the United Kingdom and, no doubt, the likelihood that this might affect the profitability of their own line helped to influence the Directors to seek to have their company absorbed by the only likely suitor, the North British. In any event the two companies were, by now, beginning to move closer together and in May 1875 they had come to an agreement relating to the running of through trains including a daily service to run to and from Burntisland and St Andrews during the summer months.

On 11th October, 1876 the following text was sent by the Board of the St Andrews Railway Company to all its shareholders and debenture holders:

> The shareholders are aware that the agreement with the North British Railway Company to work this line expires in July of next year. Your Directors had therefore to consider the terms of a new working agreement with the North British Railway or an amalgamation with that Company, such as has lately been gone into by the Leven & East

of Fife, and Peebles Railway companies. After certain negotiations, your Directors found that the terms asked by the North British Railway Company for working the line under a new lease were such that they could not agree to them.

At the same time, they were of the opinion that the line was too short to be worked independently with advantage. After several meetings, your Directors have at last come to an agreement with the North British Railway Directors, subject to the same being approved and confirmed by the shareholders at the Special Meeting called for 23 October – the principal item being that the shares of the St Andrews line get either a perpetual preferential dividend of 10.5% per annum, or be exchanged for £262 10s 4d of 4% new preference stock for each £100 of St Andrews stock with a lien in either case on the St Andrews Railway.

Further, that the North British Railway Company continue to give a service over the St Andrews Railway, at least equal to that now afforded …

The shareholders did give their consent and the absorption of the St Andrews Railway by the NBR took place under the North British Railway (Amalgamation) Act (40 & 41 Vict., cap. lxi). The preamble to the Act described it as 'An Act to amalgamate the St Andrews Railway Company, the Leven and East of Fife Railway Company, the Edinburgh, Loanhead and Roslin Railway and the Dunfermline and Queensferry Railway Company with the North British Railway …', the Act providing that the undertakings of those companies 'shall, subject to the contracts, obligation, debt and liabilities of these companies respectively be amalgamated with and form part of the undertaking of the Company … from the first day of August 1877'.

By the Act the North British was to acquire the entire issued share capital of the St Andrews Railway Company, comprising £21,000 in £10 shares, from the existing shareholders. In exchange for this, the St Andrews shareholders were to receive NBR lien shares of the same nominal amount, carrying a fixed preference dividend of 10½ per cent per annum and the new shares were to be called 'St Andrews lien stock'. The minutes of the final Board Meeting of the St Andrews Railway Company, held at St Andrews on Monday 17th December, 1877, stated that those present were Messrs Aikman, Jamieson, Meldrum and Purvis and went on:

> The Minutes of the General Meeting on 29th October, 1877 were read and signed. From these it appears that the balance, after paying all charges, was to be divided among the Directors … it was agreed by those present, as well as by Mr Orphat, who was absent, that the principle of distribution of the balance (which the Secretary states to be £176 12s. 0d.) should be to the respective periods of service at the board and the sum was therefore to be divided in the following shares:

		£	s.	d.
Mr Aikman	26 years	£70	12	10
Mr Orphat	10¼ years	27	17	0
Mr Purvis	9¾ years	26	9	9
Mr Meldrum	6¾ years	18	6	8
Admiral Dougall	6¾ years	16	19	8
Mr Jamieson	6 years	16	6	1
		176	12	0

The seal of the Company was ordered to be removed to be destroyed and brought back defaced to the Secretary.

Chapter Six

Creeping Back:
The St Andrews Branch 1877-1897

'In the hard familiar horse-box I am sitting once again;
Creeping back to St Andrews comes the slow North British Train ...'
R.F. Murray, *'Reflections of a Magistrand'*[*]

Crossing the Silvery Tay

There were few immediate changes to services over the St Andrews branch after its acquisition by the North British, largely because the new line from Leuchars to Dundee via St Fort and the Tay Bridge was still under construction but with the official opening of the new bridge to all traffic on the day before, and the start of the new timetable on 1st June, 1878, the St Andrews branch was transformed. A new station at Leuchars Junction was opened on that date, a couple of hundred yards north-east of the point at Milton where the St Andrews branch made a physical connection with the main line and immediately south of the point where the Tayport line made a junction with the new line connecting Leuchars to St Fort and the southern landfall of the Tay Bridge. The contractor for the new station was George Bruce of St Andrews, and Leuchars Junction, the name decided upon for the interchange point, had a single wide island platform with a west-facing bay platform for St Andrews trains and an east-facing bay platform for the Tayport line. Between the two bays was a fairly simple brick building with a canopy over the main line platforms; two new signal boxes, named Leuchars North and Leuchars South, guarded each junction.

The original Leuchars station, now marooned a half mile or so down the former main line to Tayport which had by now been relegated to the status of a branch line, was closed to passenger traffic on the day that Leuchars Junction was opened. However, the North British Railway obviously had second thoughts because the former station was reopened to passengers exactly six months later under the unimaginative name of Leuchars (Old); it had remained open to goods traffic in the interim as Leuchars Junction was only ever intended to handle passenger and parcels traffic.

On the opening of the Tay Bridge there was an immediate and sudden increase of traffic over the St Andrews branch but with the longer and busier trains which began to run over the line, further complaints were once again being made about the station there. In particular the inadequacy of its platform to deal with passengers was a source of comment and on 20th June, 1878 the *Fifeshire Journal* reported that 'last Saturday a train of excursionists from Dundee arrived with some 620 people and it was vexing to see the scrambling down of women and children'. The same newspaper went on to comment that

---

[*] A magistrand is a final (fourth) year undergraduate at St Andrews, first, second and third year students being known, respectively, as bejants (female: bejantines), semis and tertians.

the station was not suitable for anything other than 'the traffic of perambulators' and added that excursionists were also walking over the hallowed turf of the golf course and did not appear to understand the word 'fore' - it was, however, conceded that perhaps the notices prohibiting the crossing of the links were not being heeded because many of the families from Dundee could not, in fact, read.

The train service between St Andrews and Leuchars were increased to an all-time record of 12 daily services each way and a certain amount of summer commuting to and from Dundee was taking place. Other regular travellers included schoolchildren and students and it is entirely possible that the thrifty housewives of St Andrews followed their sisters in Newport and, in the words of William McGonagall,

> To Dundee will often resort,
> Which will bring to them profit and sport,
> By bringing cheap tea, bread and jam,
> And also some of Lipton's ham.

But the era of illiterate excursionists, commuters and cheap tea, came to an abrupt end, in McGonagall's words, 'On the last Sabbath Day of 1879, which will be remembered for a very long time'. On the evening of 29th December, the high girders of the bridge gave way and, along with the 5.20 pm from Burntisland to Dundee and its compliment of three crew and 75 passengers,* plunged into the swirling waters of the Tay taking with it Bouch's dreams. The ferry boats were pressed back into action and, once again, the Tayport branch became the main line to the north.

Sabbath Undefiled

From the very beginning of the branch line there was no Sunday train service over the St Andrews, Leven or East of Fife Railways and although there is some evidence that there was a certain amount of local opposition to the whole idea of Sunday train services, notably from the Strathtyrum estate trustees, it cannot be said that this particular part of Scotland was anything like a hotbed of sabbatarianism. The reasons for such an absence of Sunday trains were numerous† but included religious objections, the fear that 'vulgar trippers' would overwhelm decent folk and the purely economic arguments that Sunday trains would not pay - in later years further arguments against Sunday working were advanced by the nascent trade unions. When the North British took over, Sunday trains were run on the main line and on the Tayport to Dundee service but on the East Fife lines the Sabbath was not defiled by the sound of the whistle

---

* The passengers drowned included two St Andrews residents, George Ness a railway carriage cleaner and son-in-law of a local engine driver, and John Sharp, a joiner employed by Keiller & Sons of Dundee.
† For a general discussion on the subject of Sunday trains see Jack Simmons, *The Victorian Railway* (1991), Chapter 12.

or the clatter of passing trains. On 17th May, 1879 a letter to the *St Andrews Citizen*, made the following points:

> Sir, The concluding sentence in your last week's notice of the opening of the Newport and Tayport Railway, to the effect that a Sabbath railway service was about to be commenced via that route between St Andrews and Dundee, excited general surprise among your numerous readers and the public, no doubt divided feelings and different opinions. From my own part (and I believe I was joined in by not a few) I was inclined to say 'the news was too good to be true'. And so it turns out; for a perusal of the timetable, and a further knowledge of the real arrangements prove that the (what I consider to be) boon of a Sabbath railway service is to extend no further than Tayport, St Andrews being still denied the like privilege. More's the pity! Is it possible that in the transference of the St Andrews Railway to the North British it was made a 'sine qua non' that there should in no case be trains run on the former on Sundays? If so, this is surely legislation for the future with a vengeance.

The letter, which was signed 'No Humbug' produced no result. It is interesting to note that, in common with many minor lines in England and Wales and the great majority of such lines in Scotland, the St Andrews branch line was never to have a Sunday service, either under the North British or its statutory successors the LNER and BR, although those companies did operate a limited service between Thornton and Crail over the southern part of the Anstruther & St Andrews line. Perhaps if the St Andrews branch had survived to the end of the 20th century then the position might have been otherwise.

Rough Shunting at the Junction

At Leuchars Junction a number of minor accidents occurred in the NBR era due to what the company described as 'rough shunting of carriages'. These incidents usually involved locomotives backing on to branch trains waiting in the St Andrews bay platform, often with spectacular results. The practice of allowing passengers to await their connections by taking refuge in those carriages compounded the problem. Whether it was particular difficult for the locomotive crews to judge how far they should back their engines or merely the case that they were over-enthusiastic or careless was not clear but typical accidents included that which occurred on 12th April, 1880 which resulted in damages of £52 10s. being paid to a passenger, Mr Craig of New Steine, Brighton and 5s. 0d. being paid to a Mr A. Malcolm in respect of dressing Mr Craig's wounds. On another occasion the St Andrews branch train was shunted so vigorously into the bay at Leuchars that it demolished part of canopy valance and damaged the station toilets and, although no passengers waiting on the platform were injured, several had a near escape. The buffer stops in the bay were replaced and crews were given a stern warning to take more care in the future when carrying out such shunting.

Northwards from Anster

Although St Andrews had been joined to the national railway system since 1852, the landward connections to the East Neuk coastal burghs lying immediately to the south of the city remained poor. Two years after the opening of the St Andrews Railway, the first trains reached Leven, a port and manufacturing centre on the northern shores of the Forth. This six mile line was built and operated by the fiercely independent Leven Railway from a junction with the Edinburgh, Perth & Dundee Railway main line at Thornton, mid-way between Kirkcaldy and Markinch and followed the course of the Rivers Orr and Leven to its eponymous goal. Then, in 1857, the line was extended by a sister company, the independent East of Fife Railway, to run a further six miles or so along the coast past Lundin Links and Largo to a temporary terminus reasonably close to the landward village of Kilconquhar. The Leven and East of Fife companies now formally joined forces and, in the summer of 1863, managed to complete a further six miles of line to reach their true objective of Anstruther via the picturesque seaports and developing resorts of Elie, St Monans and Pittenweem. The new terminus was, perhaps, the only real potential source of traffic in the district for although it was of fairly little importance in its own right its harbour was already in the process of becoming the undisputed capital of the winter herring fisheries on the east coast and was to become famous for the huge amount of rail-borne traffic that it would generate.

Although with the opening of the Leven & East of Fife line Anstruther (often referred to locally as 'Anster') was now well served by rail, the irony arose that its nearest market town and regional centre, St Andrews, was some 44 miles and several hours away by way of the roundabout route via Thornton and Leuchars, whereas the distance by road was a mere eight miles by the direct road via Dunino and 16 miles by the coast road that ran through Crail and Kingsbarns. It was therefore little of a surprise that, within a few months of the completion of the Leven & East of Fife line, local agitation was suggesting that a line from Anstruther to Crail and beyond to the richly productive but sparsely populated farmland lying between there and St Andrews would not only be profitable but also highly desirable. Indeed a letter to the *Fifeshire Journal* commented that a survey of the route had already been carried out and that 'landed proprietors and farmers in the district are very favourable'. A previous correspondent had already opined that the area was 'a district unsurpassed in Fife for the fertility of its soil or the ability and enterprise of its agriculturists' and that of the proposed line its 'practicability and usefulness ... requires no demonstration'. But, practicable and useful though such a line might be, two attempts to get the scheme off the ground failed and it was not until 1877 that a provisional committee was formed and thereafter it took two years to raise the necessary capital and to make the Anstruther & St Andrews Railway company a reality.

New Station, New Traffic

The new line was to be some 16 miles in length and was to run from Anstruther Junction, adjacent to the Leven & East of Fife terminus, to St Andrews through a new passenger station at Anstruther and a westwards course to Crail. Here the line then turned north and passed through four rural and somewhat isolated stations at Kingsbarns, a mile west of the village of that name, Boarhills, situated slightly closer to the village it served, Stravithie, literally in the middle of nowhere, and Mount Melville, a mile and a half south of St Andrews on the main road to Largo. Apart from missing most of what centres of population actually existed - in the words of one irate shareholder 'they would have had a great deal more traffic if the stations had been made closer to the villages' - prospects for the line were said to be good and, from the very outset, it was intended that through goods and passenger traffic would be worked between the Anstruther & St Andrews Railway and the branch from Leuchars. In 1878 the North British indicated that they were willing to assist financially both in the building of a link between the Anstruther & St Andrews line and the original St Andrews Railway and also contribute to the provision of a new passenger station that would be situated nearer to the centre of the city than the existing one which, it was generally agreed, a had been woefully inadequate.

In March 1880 the promoters of the Anstruther & St Andrews and the Board of the North British entered into a working agreement whereby the NBR agreed to work the new line in return for a share of the gross receipts and, on 26th August of that year, the Anstruther & St Andrews Railway Act (43 & 44 Vict., cap. clxxx) was passed, although Parliamentary approval was only sought for the line to terminate at Argyle on the edge of the city. Construction work began rapidly, notwithstanding the bankruptcy of the principal contractor and at the end of 1882 a further agreement was reached to the effect that the North British would contribute £5,000 towards the cost of a new passenger station at St Andrews and the necessary linking line between the old and new stations in return for the use by that company of these facilities without payment of a charge or toll from the Anstruther & St Andrews company. The scheme was sanctioned by Parliament on 16th July, 1883 with the passing of a further Anstruther & St Andrews Railway Act (46 & 47 Vict. cap. c). At the beginning of May 1883 a goods service began to operate between Anstruther and Crail and on Saturday 1st September the line as far as Boarhills was opened to all traffic with St Andrews passengers being catered for by a special service of horsedrawn buses and existing carriers dealing with a small amount of through goods traffic.

Thereafter progress beyond Boarhills was slow, due to construction problems, the weather and further financial difficulties. By September 1886 the line was complete as far as the outskirts of St Andrews and plans were drawn up for the new passenger station which was to be situated in a shallow cutting half a mile south of the original terminus and close to the western end of Market Street, a mere stroll from the centre of the burgh. A single island platform was provided, and on this was to be sited waiting rooms, a parcels office, a refreshment room and other offices. A footbridge led up to the public road. The station was built

ST ANDREWS BRANCH.

Up Trains.

WEEK-DAYS.

Stations and Sidings.	Ms	Chs	1 Mix'd Pass. 1 2 3 Class	2 Pass. 1 2 3 Class	3 Pass. 1 2 3 Class	4 Goods	5 Pass. 1 2 3 Class	6 Pass. 1 2 3 Class	7 Goods	8 Mix'd Pass. 1 2 3 Class	9 Goods	10 Mix'd Pass. 1 2 3 Class	11 Pass. 1 2 3 Class	12 Goods	13 Pass. 1 2 3 Class	14 Mixed Pass. 1 2 3 Class	15 Pass. 1 2 3 Class
			a.m.	a.m.	a.m.	a.m.	a.m.	a.m.	p.m.	p.m.	p.m.	p.m.	p.m.	p.m.	p.m.	p.m.	p.m.
St Andrews dep.			6 25	7 39	8 10	8 15	10 5	11 30	12 35	1 15	...	3 25	4 30	...	6 20	7 15	9 25
*Seafield Siding ,,	2	0	......	......	......	......	......	......	12 40	......	......	......	......	......	......	......	......
*BrickWork Sid. ,,	3	29	...	...	......	......	......	......	12 45	......	......	......	......	5 10	......	......	......
Guardbridge ,,	3	43	6 35	7 39	8 20	8 30	10 15	11 40	12 50	1 25	2 25	3 34	4 40	5 10	6 30	7 25	9 35
Seggie Siding ,,	3	64	...	...	...	8 35	...	...	12 55	...	...	...	...	5 20	...	...	...
Leuchars Jc. arr.	4	57	6 43	7 44	8 27	8 45	10 22	11 45	12 58	1 30	2 35	3 39	4 45	5 25	6 35	7 30	9 45
Dundee arr.			...	...	9 38	...	‡	12 48	...	...	...	4 35	5 43	...	7 38	10 10	10 53
Perth ,,			...	8 45	......	...	12 10	......	...	4 0	......	5 50	7 0	...	......	10 0	......
Edinburgh ,,			...	9 37	12 35	......	12 45	......	...	3 48	......	...	7 14	...	......	......	...

No. 4.—Engine to do shunting at Leuchars as required.
No. 5.—On Tuesdays, connects with Market Train, due at Dundee at 12·5 p.m.
‡ No. 11.—Through Train from St Andrews to Tayport.

Down Trains.

WEEK-DAYS.

Stations and Sidings.	Distance from Leuchars Junction. Ms. Chs.	1 Goods a.m.	2 Pass. 1 2 3 Class a.m.	3 Pass. 1 2 3 Class a.m.	4 P'ss 1 2 3 Cl. a.m.	5 Mixed Pass. 1 2 3 Class a.m.	6 Goods a.m.	7 Pass. 1 2 3 Class a.m.	8 Mixed Pass. 1 2 3 Class p.m.	9 Goods p.m.	10 Mixed Pass. 1 2 3 Class p.m.	11 Goods p.m.	12 Pass. 1 2 3 Class p.m.	13 Pass. 1 2 3 Class p.m.	14	15 Pass. 1 2 3 Class p.m.	16 Pass. 1 2 3 Class p.m.
Edinburgh dep	...				6 30			9 30			1 30		4 0				7 20
Perth ,,	...			7 0	6 40			10 15			1 15			4 35			7 25
Dundee ,,	...		6 0			9 35			12 45		3 10		5 0			6 45	
Leuchars Jc. dep	0 73	6 45	7 0	7 50	9 10	10 33	10 40	11 55	1 43	2 5	4 3	4 45	5 55	6 45		7 40	9 55
Seggie Siding ,,	1 14	6 53	7 5	7 55	9 15	10 38	10 45					4 50					
Guardbridge ,,	1 28						10 50	12 0	1 48	2 15	4 8	4 55	6 0	6 50		7 45	10 0
*Brick Work Sid.,,	...						10 55										
Seafield Siding ,,	2 57						11 0										
St Andrews arr	4 57	7 5	7 15	8 2	9 25	10 50	11 10	12 10	2 0	Stp	4 20	Stop.	6 10	7 0		7 55	10 10

No. 6.—Engine to do shunting at St Andrews as required.

No. 12.—Through Train from Tayport to St Andrews.

The Trains on the St Andrews Branch will be available for Goods and Passenger Traffic, but the former will be wrought by any particular Train, provided time can be kept.

Seggie Siding.—Down Trains must not call at this Siding except when the Drivers are in possession of the Train Staff.

NBR working timetable, June 1883. Note the lengthy journey times to Dundee in the interval between the fall of the first Tay Bridge and the opening of the second.

to a limited budget and soon enough complaints were received that the narrow bridge and platforms were inadequate to cope with the considerable amount of luggage that the station subsequently handled. From the new station, the linking or junction line continued on an embankment wide enough for double track to the Petheram Bridge, which spanned the diverted public road to Guardbridge and replaced the nearby level crossing on the former main road which was then closed to all traffic; pedestrians were, however, then able to use a new wood and iron footbridge provided at the south end of the old station for that purpose. The line between Boarhills and the old St Andrews station was signalled by the Railway Signalling Company of Fazakerley, Liverpool and in the city two new signal boxes were provided, namely St Andrews (New), officially referred to as 'St Andrews Station' and St Andrews (Old), better known as St Andrews Links. The former was an unusual wooden structure with nine working levers and no spares and was situated at the west side of the new passenger station and adjacent to (and reached by) the footbridge while the latter, a more conventional brick and wood structure with 13 working and seven spare levers was a little beyond the north end of the old passenger station, opposite the engine shed. The line between the two was worked as a block section and south from the new passenger station the block section extended from there to Mount Melville. The old passenger station was now used solely as a goods depot and the platform within the original trainshed was used as loading bank. The layout and buildings of St Andrews (Old) were, however, unaltered and the latter were allowed to slowly deteriorate until their state was unfavourably commented on particularly as they were so visible from the Old Course and the most tourist-orientated parts of the city.

Railway Renaissance

The Anstruther & St Andrews Railway (A&StAR), together with the new passenger station and link line to the original branch from Leuchars, was opened to all traffic on 1st July, 1887. Although the basic pattern of services between Leuchars and St Andrews was little altered, certain trains were now extended over the new line to Thornton, via Crail and Anstruther and although few passengers chose to travel via such a circuitous route from St Andrews to the south, there was nevertheless a healthy stream of passengers travelling from Leven and the East Neuk burghs to St Andrews. These, no doubt, greatly appreciated not having to use the antiquated horse buses still operating in the area or the long rail journey with its lengthy wait for so-called connections at the windswept junction platforms at Thornton and Leuchars. What was, however, remarkable was that the new station had been provided timeously for even though the contribution of A&StAR traffic from the south was negligible, there was a huge influx of additional traffic from the north over the original St Andrews Railway branch line from Leuchars. The reasons for this were various but what was noticeable was that the city was becoming an increasingly important destination both for leisure traffic and scholars and, with the opening of the second Tay Bridge on 20th April, 1887 and the consequent provision of through trains from Dundee, commuters although that term was not then in use and the designation of 'contract ticket' traffic was a more contemporaneous one.

The city was reviving, helped in no small way by the railway, and with the increasing amount of middle-class seaside and golfing traffic and day trippers from Dundee and elsewhere, was becoming a well established seaside and golf resort. New purpose-built hotels were built and two new golf courses, the New and Jubilee, were opened respectively in 1894 and 1899. The ancient university, which in 1827 had been described by Robert Chambers in *The Picture of Scotland* as being the least prosperous in Scotland and the number of students seldom exceeding 140, began to undergo a metamorphosis and, following a threat in 1883 to transfer the undertaking to a new site in Dundee, a reorganization of St Andrews University took place in 1887 and, the student population began to rise rapidly with a large majority of them coming to study by train from all over Scotland and even, in some cases, from as far away as England. Another source of railway revenue was St Leonards School, a large mainly-boarding private school opened in 1877 as part of a nationwide drive to provide better education for girls. A junior school was added in 1894 and St Leonards, which still flourishes today as a coeducational establishment, provided many passengers and much luggage throughout the existence of the branch line. And, if all this were not enough, the population of the burgh was on the increase from just under 5,000 at the opening of the St Andrews Railway to 6,400 in 1881, 6,850 in 1891 and 7,600 by the time of the first census of the 20th century.

Eden Re-bridged

With the increasing loads and weight of both passenger and goods trains on the St Andrews branch, and the increasing popularity of St Andrews as a destination following upon the opening of the Tay Bridge and its successor and the new line from Anstruther, concerns were expressed as to the continuing suitability of the bridges over the River Eden and Motray Burn. These bridges were, essentially, the same wooden structures carried on deep wooden piles that had been designed by Bouch for the line some 30 years before and, despite the continual patching-up and partial rebuilding, it had become evident that they now had reached the end of their lives. It appears that these concerns were being voiced not only by the engineers of the NBR but also by members of the public and, as the *Fifeshire Journal* commented that in relation to the Eden crossing 'some passengers were often afraid to cross it, and many were the head shakings and murmurs of timid passengers'. Accordingly on 13th June, 1889 the NBR Works Committee approved contracts being placed with Goodwin, Jardine and Company of Motherwell for the supply and placing of new wrought-iron girder bridges over the Motray Burn in the sum of £2,493 9s. 0d. and that over the Eden, a larger-five span structure, in the sum of £5,388 4s. 1d., with the sinking of the caissons and the carrying out of the masonry work to be done by James Young & Sons of Edinburgh. The bridges were to be completed by 1st November, 1889 under payment of a penalty and the work appears to have been carried out expeditiously, the *Journal* of 4th July commenting on the Eden bridge project that:

ST ANDREWS AND RAILWAY ACCOMMODATION.

AT A MEETING OF ST ANDREWS TOWN COUNCIL LAST NIGHT COUNCILLOR LINSKILL REMARKED—" THE STATION IS PRACTICALLY BUNKERED."

A 'squib' directed at the failure to provide proper accommodation at St Andrews, 1894. The original, with annotations showing the station master, provost and councillor is in the NBR correspondence file, apparently having been sent to the company by the station master himself! *Authors' Collection*

A newspaper cartoon of 1896 showing passengers awaiting their connection to the branch train. The station depicted is the original one at Leuchars, burnt down by suffragettes in 1913. *Authors' Collection*

THE RAILWAY RACE TO ST ANDREWS.

WAITING AT LEUCHARS JUNCTION.

The structure is being erected close to the side of the other, and it is thought probable that by engaging a numerous staff of workmen from Saturday evening to Monday morning every week, during which time there is no railway traffic, that the bridge will be placed in its proper position on three successive Sundays, without hindering traffic.

Both of the new bridges carried trains for 80 years with little trouble and their remains can still be seen to this day.

Disaster at the Links

On the evening of Saturday 11th July, 1896 the 5.56 pm passenger train from Thornton Junction to Dundee was, characteristically, running some 45 minutes late when it arrived at St Andrews station. At about the same time the 8.05 pm branch passenger train from Leuchars Junction, which normally waited for the Thornton train to clear the branch line before departing, was timeously dispatched. In accordance with the custom that had grown up in order to avoid excessive delays, the 8.05 was due to be shunted into a siding at the Links goods station to allow the Thornton train to pass it. Hauled by Drummond 4-4-0T No. 111 (the former *Clackmannan*) and consisting of a guard's van and two third-class carriages, the 8.05 was duly signalled to run into the siding normally used for that purpose. Driver Andrew Campbell, however, failed to reduce his speed to an appropriate level and the train failed to stop in time, colliding with the buffer-stops and damaging a coal wagon, two fish vans and a third class carriage stabled there as well as causing damage to the carriages of the train and to the locomotive, which was derailed.* Fifteen passengers were injured, some seriously. Driver Campbell was charged at Cupar Sheriff Court with a culpable breach of duty and, although found not guilty by the jury, the North British fined him £4 but, because of his excellent character, allowed him to continue in the company's employ although he was relegated to the duties of driving the Ladybank shunting engine. The fireman, who it was said 'was due to go abroad shortly', received a caution. The passengers' claims were duly settled at £300 in total, exclusive of doctors' fees and other expenses.

When the North British carried out its investigations, the company discovered that the Westinghouse brake on the locomotive had failed some four hours before the accident and that the driver had neglected to observe the rule applicable to such circumstances. More to the point the practice of shunting passenger trains at the Links station to enable another to pass was condemned, as was the practice of propelling empty stock between the two stations. Accordingly it was recommended that both signal boxes should be extended and altered to make them suitable for the introduction of train tablet apparatus at a cost of £45 13s. and that a proper carriage siding be provided at the New station. The former was done, but it appears the latter suggestion was not acted upon.

* The stock damaged included 'passenger guards van No. 124 (telescoped with engine, 2 floorboards broken), third class carriage No. 846 (side glass broken), do. No. 343 (side glass cracked), locomotive wagon containing coal, No. 4499, separated from its four wheels tilted against front of engine, contents emptied and otherwise damaged, fish wagon (empty) No. 48454 with guard rod bent, do. No. 48586, buffer locked with carriage and end beam and board broken; engine derailed and badly damaged'.

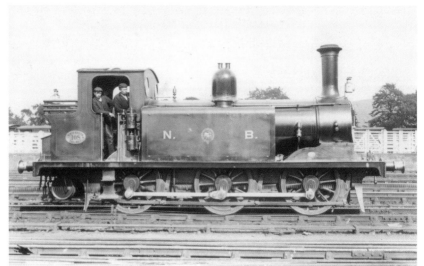

NBR Drummond 'Terrier' No. 108, originally bearing the name *St Andrews*, built for the branch in 1878 and used on it until transferred to Perth in 1890. The locomotive, which lost its name early on, was finally withdrawn in 1925.   *Pete Westwater Collection*

Fin-de-Siecle

By the last decade of the century the St Andrews branch had been radically altered from its primitive earlier existence. Longer trains hauled by more powerful locomotives, improved gas-lit carriages and a plethora of through services patronised by a flood of summer passengers attracted by golf, the delights of the seaside, and 'culture'. Equally importantly, by the fact that it was no longer necessary to embark on the stomach-churning ferries after the opening of the Forth Bridge in 1890, all of those factors combined to ensure that the line had lost its earlier eccentricities and was by now very much a standard NBR product with only a few remaining vestiges of its pioneer spirit. Working was now very much by the book whilst installation of new signalling and shorter block sections eradicated much of the previously haphazard nature of operation. In 1894 the only intermediate station, Guardbridge, received some much needed modernisation with the addition of a new station building on the sole platform supplementing the original St Andrews Railway booking office which was situated at right angles to the line. In addition a third siding was added to the goods yard at Guardsbridge and on 19th March of that year a signal box, replacing the original wooden gate box, was opened next to the level crossing there. With these alterations at Guardbridge completed, passengers now were relatively satisfied with the new and adequate accommodation at all three stations on the branch, with the possible exception of Leuchars Junction where complaints and sarcastic comments about the perceived shortcomings continued to be heard from time to time.

Chapter Seven

Into the New Century:
The North British Railway 1897-1922

'A quick service of trains to St Andrews would do more than anything to make the Ancient City more prosperous than it had ever been.'

Harry Anstruther

The Edwardian Summer

At the turn of the 20th century the North British Railway had consolidated its position to become the largest of all of the Scottish railway companies and, in the words of railway historian Hamilton Ellis, 'it may not have been an exemplary enterprise but it was, undoubtedly, great'. In Fife the railway had secured a virtual monopoly and its main line, crossing the Forth by a great cantilever bridge and the Tay by the less spectacular replacement for Bouch's bridge, was paralleled to the east by the sweep of the coastal loop line which brought through trains from the south to St Andrews via the East Neuk and from the north via Leuchars. To some the company appeared to have reached the zenith of its powers and prosperity but appearances were often deceptive and, notwithstanding the fact that the motor vehicle was still very much in its infancy and the coal trade was continuing to expand, the company's resources were already well stretched and much needed improvements were put on hold to await more rewarding times.

In August 1897 the shareholders of the beleaguered Anstruther & St Andrews company sold out to the North British in a deal which rescued them but must have been of dubious benefit to the larger company. This move was, perhaps, an inevitable one and just as the shareholders of the St Andrews Railway, wishing their line to enjoy the benefits of fresh capital and much-needed modernisation, had sold out 18 years before. Part of the impetus had come from the need to comply with the new Board of Trade regulations designed to ensure passenger safety in a more stringent age, part came from the desire to improve the train to take an expected influx of heavier and faster trains running on an improved service at higher speeds and all of this suggested that money, a commodity that was in short supply on the Anstruther & St Andrews Railway, was required. The improvements came rapidly with the opening of a passing loop at Stravithie, enhancements to the stations at Crail and Anstruther and a general overhaul of the by now rather antiquated facilities on the Leven & East of Fife section further east. Particularly during the summer holiday season, which in Fife really only encompassed the months of July and August, severe congestion was experienced on the coastal loop line and in particular the sections between Thornton and Leven and St Andrews and Leuchars and, in the summer of 1898, proposals were put forward by the NBR Board for the reconstruction of those two sections as double track lines with rebuilt stations and bridges designed to take heavier traffic. In view of the costs involved the proposals were shelved and although the section to Leven was eventually doubled in 1910, Leuchars to St Andrews was destined to remain as a single track line despite the considerable capital spent on the enforced rebuilding of both St Andrews and Leuchars Junction stations.

St Andrews destroyed

The first significant change to affect the St Andrews branch in the new century occured when on 6th July, 1901 the *Fife News* reported under the headline of 'Extraordinary Series of Fires at St Andrews' that:

> The fire fiend has been specially active since the arrival of the new fire engine in St Andrews Within a fortnight, no fewer than three fires have occurred at the railway station. Shortly after seven o'clock on Saturday night a great commotion was caused in South Street, when the clattering fire bell rang out the tocsin of alarm to summon the fire brigade. When it was known that the old station was ablaze, remarks such as 'It will be a pity if the whole place is not burned to the ground' were made on all sides. A large crowd assembled to witness the steam fire engine turn out, this being the first occasion on which it has been used to extinguish a fire.

It appeared that this fire had broken out at about 7 pm on the night of Saturday 29th June when smoke was seen to be pouring out of the office at the north end of the wooden goods shed which had formerly served as the passenger station prior to the opening of the new station in 1887. The alarm was raised immediately and a telephone message was sent from the signal box to McGee, the station agent who then sent a further message via the police station to the fire brigade. In the interim the railway employees still at work in the yard attempted to put the flames out with pails of water:

> The brigade turned out with commendable smartness and in about twenty minutes they had a jet playing upon the conflagration. By the time the brigade arrived, however, the fire had obtained a firm hold of the wooden shed and office and little could be done to save them. At the time of the outbreak a goods train was in the yard and by it most of the goods had been taken up and thus saved from being destroyed. Only a few sundry articles remained and these were removed by the men to a place of safety.

The fire was eventually brought under control three hours after it had first been noticed but the shed and office were said to be a complete wreck along with the books and records kept in it and 20 shillings in copper coins totally destroyed. The damage was estimated at £300 and considerable disruption was caused to traffic on the line. The *Fife News* somewhat caustically remarked that:

> The old station buildings, which are in a very dilapidated condition have long been an eyesore and now that part of them has been destroyed, it is to be hoped that the company in its reconstruction operation will carry out extensive improvements here.

Worse, however, was to follow. On the night of Wednesday 3rd July another fire broke out, this time at the 'new' passenger station which, in consequence, was almost totally destroyed.

About midnight, Miss Woodcock - whose house is situated close to the station - and several gentlemen who happened to be abroad at the time, had their attention drawn to a bright glow in the vicinity of the station, and they were not long in being made aware of the fact that the station was ablaze. The very heavy haar, which last night enveloped everything, concealed the existence of the burning until it had made considerable headway. The conflagration in its early stages could not therefore be observed from the stationmaster's house at the old station, but as soon as the seat of the fire was known, the fire brigade was summoned with all possible haste. The police were telephoned to from Mr W.R. Kermath's shop and they very quickly called out the brigade. Considering the late hour, the brigade deserve much credit for turning out so smartly. They fortunately got the advantage of the new ten-inch main at the hydrant opposite Hope Park church and in a very short time they had their engine in full swing with two jets playing upon the doomed buildings. The engine worked splendidly but the flames had got so thorough a hold that it was only possible to save the stairway leading to the station, the bookstall, the signal cabin and the gentleman's lavatory. The entire damage done is roughly estimated at £2,000.

An interesting coda to the story was provided by the fact that a St Andrews lady who was married the following day 'had her marriage outfit lying in the parcels office and, of course, lost everything'. History does not relate what she wore at the ceremony on that Thursday!

The cause of the two fires was never ascertained although there was a strong feeling locally that a wilful fire-raiser had been at work.

Phoenix Rising

The fire at the new station had effectively destroyed the whole of the passenger accommodation there and once the remains had been cleared away the North British was left with the problem of providing temporary facilities for the forthcoming summer season as well as considering what do to in the long term. On 16th July, 1901 William Jackson, the NBR General Manager, travelled in a special train to St Andrews to meet a deputation of the Town Council, who urged him to consider greatly enhanced facilities when the station was rebuilt. The North British considered the matter carefully but concluded that a simple rebuild of the station on the existing site, reusing the existing island platform would cost some £3,800 and would be covered by their fire insurance policy, while a radical re-planning of the station on the lines suggested would amount to some £16,382 due to the heavy engineering and other expensive works which would need to be carried out. As usual the Board dragged their heels and on 18th December, 1901 the Board of Trade in London received the following letter from the St Andrews Town Council pointing out that since the station was destroyed:

The Railway Company have done little or nothing to provide accommodation for the passengers. A great deal of unnecessary delay has been caused and the company are in the meantime making no adequate provision for the passenger traffic with the result that the passengers arriving at or leaving St Andrews in the cold wintry weather are obliged to stand on the platform without shelter.

The station, which was erected in 1887, has always been quite inadequate for the requirements of the place. It is situated in a hollow by means of a very inconvenient and almost dangerous stair leading from the higher level of the road outside. As St Andrews is a residential place with several large schools, very considerable quantities of luggage are received and despatched at the station throughout the year and during the summer season enormous quantities of luggage fall to be handled. The platform has found to be much too narrow for the necessities of the traffic and complaints about it have been made. It may also be mentioned that the space available for cabs &c at the station is much too small and that the roadway giving access to the sidings at the North side of the station has an inconveniently steep gradient.

The Council went on to point out that since the meeting in July, at which the North British said that they would give due consideration to the Council's views, 'there has been no communication from them' and the first they knew of the plans were when they were announced to the public without any chance to comment thereon:

It is understood that the Railway Company do not propose to increase the platform accommodation and that the buildings will be erected practically on the old site. But even though the buildings were put up as to leave a much greater space at the point where the staircase meets the platform, the main cause of complaint - the extreme narrowness of the platform combined with the bad access - would still remain unanswered.

The North British replied to the Board of Trade that, immediately after the fire, they had taken steps to erect 'temporary shelters' and had gone on to provide copies of the plans for proposed rebuilding. Even though the St Andrews Town Council commented that the plans were 'grossly inadequate' the North British stuck to their guns and accepted Kinnear, Moodie & Company's tender for the rebuilding at a total cost of £3,496; the only concession to improving the facilities being a goods hoist to take luggage to and from the platform at a cost of £360. Originally the hoist was to be hydraulically powered but, on the grounds of economy, a 'gas engine' was substituted apparently on the grounds that the annual water charge would be too high. In May 1903 the buildings were completed but the complaints continued, principally in relation to congestion on the platforms and the inability of the sole footbridge to cope with pedestrian traffic. On 20th June, 1905 the company's district traffic superintendent in Dundee wrote to the head office that:

The question of an additional exit from the St Andrews station has been mentioned by two St Andrews gentlemen lately and I have myself been a witness of the congested state of the platforms and of the confusion resulting from two streams of passengers meeting on the stair, especially on Saturdays. This would be largely avoided were an overhead bridge put up at the other end and I shall be glad to know if this can now be got on with.

The General Manager rejected the proposal, stating that the £180 cost could not be justified since 'the present time is not an opportune time for carrying out the work' but the congestion could not be ignored and on 25th June, 1906 it was recorded that the new bridge had been completed. For several years views were again expressed that the station facilities were inadequate. There was even a proposal to build a new station at the Old station site but in December 1911 the superintendent of the line wrote to the General Manager that 'So far as the extension of the passenger station is concerned, keeping in view that St Andrews is not an industrial centre, I am of the opinion that the necessity for extension in this direction is very far off'. This view was, indeed, correct and the rebuilt station survived in much the same form until the cessation of services in 1969.

Ever Better

In the first decade of the new century the North British could justifiably claim that they had made a success of the holiday trade in East Fife. Further enhancements to the line's capacity had been made to Cameron Bridge, Leven, St Monance and Elie and although St Andrews was still served by a single-line from Leuchars, it was an extremely busy one with the company proclaiming that St Andrews station handled the greatest annual number of passengers of any place between Edinburgh and Dundee - indeed 140,000 passengers were booked to St Andrews in the financial year of 1905, a figure far greater than Cupar or Inverkeithing and, if one took into account the considerable number of day trippers and excursionists, comparable in numbers only to the great mercantile town of Kirkcaldy. And, in the age when the railway was still the preferred method of transport for the rich, much of this traffic travelled in first class carriages. In the contemporaneous *Pageant of the Forth*, Stewart Dick emphasised this by describing St Andrews as a place where

> the cream of the fashionable world pours into every summer, yet it still manages to maintain its dignity and its aloofness. It has its fashionable villas, its great hotels; everything is arranged for visitors on the best scale, yet it never degenerates into a northern Brighton. Golf at St Andrews is not a frivolous pastime, it is a serious business.

A short-lived, and presumably commercially unsuccessful, innovation appeared in the summer of 1913 when a through composite carriage from St Andrews was attached at Leuchars to an Aberdeen to Kings Cross service. The experiment was not repeated in 1914. What was, however, still somewhat surprising was the absence of any regular Sunday service to St Andrews.

A Long Way Round to Perth

On 25th January, 1909 the independent Newburgh & North of Fife Railway* was opened and with this St Andrews acquired a new daily train service to and from Perth. Prior to this time passengers desiring to travel between the two towns required to travel via Ladybank or Dundee, but the new service enabled not only an elimination of the draughty waits at junction stations but also the chance to travel through the quiet and hilly farmlands south of the Tay. The 34-mile journey, completed at an average speed of less than 30 mph, began on the original NBR line from Perth to Newburgh, then over the 13 miles through Lindores, Luthrie, Kilmany and St Fort. There were three trains a day from Perth to Dundee but the 11.50 am from Perth was halted at St Fort West where the front three coaches travelled onwards over the Tay Bridge while the rear coach, an elderly six-wheeled composite, was taken on from St Fort West by the St Andrews goods engine to that town, arriving there at 1.10; the return service left St Andrews at 1.55 and arrived back at Perth at 3.10. Apart from a temporary wartime cessation of the service in July 1916, the result of staff shortages, the direct train to Perth continued to run until 1926, when it became a casualty of the General Strike and was never resurrected for, by then, a direct

---

* The N&NFR remained independent from the NBR until 1923, when both were absorbed into the LNER.

Left: NBR ticket from St Andrews to Perth via the 'old' route through Ladybank, *c.*1900.

Right: A ha'penny ticket between the two Leuchars stations. Surely the cheapest fare between any two stations on the North British system.

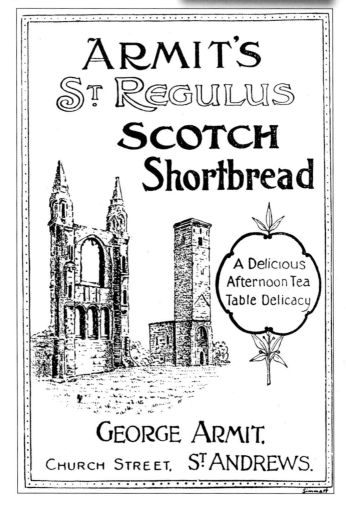

motor bus service was in operation between the towns. Other direct train services from St Andrews before the First War included three daily services to Tayport, two to Cupar, five to Anstruther and Thornton and a regular service of local trains to Leuchars.

Passengers Protest

In the early years of the century the local newspapers contained a series of complaints about the East Fife passenger service or, rather, the way in which it was being run and comments were made that 'a motor car service along the Fife coast, say from Kirkcaldy to St Andrews ... would be a great success and convenience'. Then the St Andrews District Committee of the Fife County Council weighed in with suggestions for improved services and suggested that the branch between Leuchars and St Andrews should be doubled. In December of 1905, the Committee made a further series of suggestions to the North British, the principal points of which were that there should be separate sidings and lines at Leuchars to enable the St Andrews and coast trains to run independently into the station without fouling the main line, the doubling of the St Andrews branch, the provision of a 'properly covered' platform at Leuchars, the running of through carriages from Edinburgh to St Andrews, improving the timing and punctuality of the services, the provision of printed tickets at all stations to prevent delays in booking and sundry other matters. At the council's meeting to discuss the matter Sir William Erskine remarked, amidst laughter, that they would be near the millennium before all of this was done - this was a rather optimistic view as, in reality, most of the matters complained of were never dealt with.

In the autumn of 1908 there was an unprecedented series of complaints from members of the public in response to alterations made to the passenger timetable on the East Fife lines. Some interesting light was thrown on the travelling habits of local people as a result. The alterations had been forced upon the company by a severe financial crisis and some 100 weekday trains were to be withdrawn including several East Fife services, all with effect from 1st November. The first complaint came from the St Andrews Town Council who protested against the withdrawal of the first train of the day, the 6 am service from St Andrews to Leuchars. This had been run mainly as a mail train to connect with services to Dundee and Edinburgh, giving same day deliveries to all Scottish towns as well as a number of major English towns but carried few passengers – indeed the North British confirmed that the service was very poorly patronised carrying only two or three passengers *per week*, invariably bound for Guardbridge or Leuchars only. This complaint was dismissed summarily since it had been the decision of the postal authorities no longer to support the train and the practical effect of its withdrawal was minimal with the only real casualty being the mail destined for England.

Another grievance about retiming was received from a man who complained that he could no longer reside in St Andrews because of the poor connections to there from his work in Dundee in the evening peak hours. This view was backed up by the St Andrews Town Council who remarked that a considerable number of Dundee merchants would probably move to St Andrews if a train arriving in St Andrews at 8 am were put on. The Fife County Council District Committee protested about a lack of notice of the changes, causing them to reschedule their meetings.

Apart from the timetable changes, there were the usual grumbles about bad connections, inconsistent fare structures and, from St Andrews, a complaint that the branch trains were provided only with what were described as 'poor' carriages. A draft letter was prepared in reply stating that 'the carriages on the St Andrews branch will compare favourably with those on other branch lines, but of course they are not like those on the through main-line trains'. William Fulton Jackson, NBR General Manager, must have felt that this reply was rather anodyne for he added in hand to this draft that pious but incomprehensible sentiment that 'should an opportunity arise which would admit of our moving the stock on the St Andrews branch, advantage will be taken of the same'.

Suffragettes Strike

During the early hours of Monday 30th June, 1913 the station buildings at Leuchars were burnt to the ground. It was widely suspected that this deliberate act was carried out by renegade women in support of the cause of women's suffrage. There had been public meetings locally in favour of the respectable, if controversial, Women's Social and Political Union but a more militant group or groups had been touring the country causing damage by wilful fire-raising of buildings thought to have some particular significance, such as the parish church in Whitekirk, East Lothian which was regularly attended by the former Prime Minister, A.J. Balfour. Other activities included attacks on railway installations,* bombs in postboxes and other incidents which were designed to disrupt communications and to ensure that the question of votes for women were kept on the political agenda. St Andrews, presumably because of its university connections, was a particular target and a university building was set on fire. Then it was the turn of Leuchars Junction and, as the *Fife News & Coast Chronicle* of 5th July, 1913 reported:

> Leuchars Junction railway station was completely wrecked by fire during the early hours of Monday, only stone and brick and ironwork being left standing. A number of tin flasks which apparently contained some inflammable liquid were found at the spot where the fire originated, proving that incendiaries had been at work As the flasks were mostly of the same pattern as those found after the burning outrage by suffragists at the Gatty Marine Laboratory, St Andrews, the other week, this latest time is being laid at the door of the militants ...
>
> The station agent, Mr James Unwin, resides at Leuchars old station, nearly a mile off. As no trains stop at the junction on Sundays (although Sunday 'locals' call at Leuchars Old Station) the station is always closed up on Saturday night, not to be re-opened till Monday morning. Last Saturday night the staff departed as usual after the last train for St Andrews had left. On Sunday night, Police Constable Crighton, Leuchars, had a look over the station at twenty minutes to twelve and everything was then all right.

---

* Amongst the other railway casualties of the suffragette campaign were the station buildings at Saunderton (Great Western & Great Central Joint), Croxley (London & North Western) and Kenton (North Eastern), while arson attempts were made on the stations at Bangor (Bangor & County Down) and Aylesbury (Great Western & Metropolitan Joint) and an attempt was made to destroy the Whalley viaduct (Lancashire & Yorkshire).

About two hundred yards north of the junction is a signal cabin and signalman, Geo Evans, who was on duty, saw something that startled him as he was looking in the direction of the station at 1.25 am. Smoke was rising skywards from the centre of the station buildings, and there was a lurid glow of fire. With all haste Evans ran to the station and found the booking hall burning fiercely. It was plainly evident that the flames had a firm hold of the place and that the fire was beyond the stage when the efforts of one man could subdue it. Evans therefore ran back along the line to the village and aroused Mr Unwin and some other railway officials residing there. Within a few minutes of the alarm being given, all the resident railway workers were running for the station, the lurid glow from which was becoming larger every minute. A message to Guardbridge aroused the Paperworks fire brigade and in a considerably short time the fire engine was on the way to the station. By two o'clock the hose was playing upon the burning building but already the station was doomed and the water had little effect.

Some reports additionally claimed that three women were seen speeding away from the scene of the crime in a motor car and that some suffragette literature had been left at the station. Whatever the motive for the attack, the perpetrators were never identified or caught.

Before the rebuilding of Leuchars took place, however, an old proposal was again revived, namely the idea of building a new westerly spur from the St Andrews branch to the main line so that through trains could be run from Cupar to the Fife coastal line and thus both the necessity to change trains at Leuchars Junction and of incurring the cost of rebuilding and staffing the station there could be avoided. The *Fife News* commented that:

> The scheme proposes to lay less than half a mile of rails branching off the main-line at the South signal cabin before Leuchars is reached, curving to Guardbridge station and trains for St Andrews would leave Cupar and go direct to St Andrews. Leuchars Old Station would be the station for Leuchars, and there would be special trains from Dundee to and from St Andrews and the coast. Both passengers from north and south will benefit by the tedious wait at the junction at Leuchars being made unnecessary. At the time of the Highland Show Cupar station was greatly improved with new waiting rooms, stairs and lengthened and higher platforms. The heavy traffic during the Show week was handled better than it is in many centres showing that Cupar station has many possibilities.

One of the guiding lights behind this scheme was H.T. Anstruther, brother of Sir Ralph and a Director of the North British, and there was considerable local support for it, both from the Cupar area and from the East Neuk:

> St Andrews Town Council ... have long complained of the delay between the South and St Andrews and have pointed out that passengers going by the same train from the South reach Aberdeen almost as soon as they get to St Andrews. Seeing the Town Council have lately revised the Links Golfing Regulations at great expense, St Andrews looks to an increased number of visitors, not only during the summer but at Easter and other golfing seasons. A quick service of trains to St Andrews would do more than anything else to make the Ancient City more prosperous than it has ever been.

Rumours abounded that the rebuilding of Leuchars Junction was 'on hold' until the scheme was costed but these rumours appear to have had little foundation in fact and within weeks the reconstruction of the station was in hand.

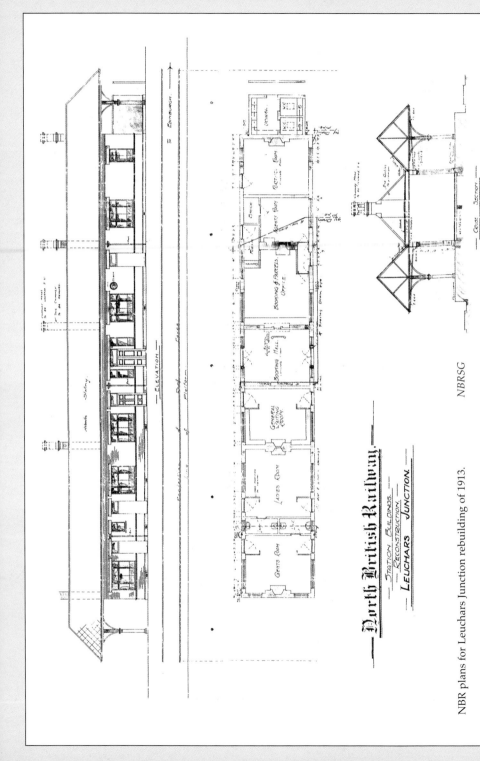

NBR plans for Leuchars Junction rebuilding of 1913.   *NBRSG*

Leuchars Junction station buildings from the east, November 2006 - this neat NBR structure which replaced the station burnt down by the sufferagettes has survived in use to the present day.   *A.M. Hajducki*

Defence of the Realm

On 3rd August, 1914 war was declared between Germany and Britain and, as an immediate consequence, the North Brtish came under government control. An attempt was made to discourage unnecessary travel, although the only casualties on the St Andrews branch were the seasonal through coach to London and, from March 1916, the first train of the day from Dundee to Crail. Perhaps more significantly the nationwide raising of fares by 50 per cent to combat rising inflation and dwindling resources led to a downturn in local passenger bookings with St Andrews recording a fall between 1916 and 1917 of some 30 per cent, Guardbridge of some 40 per cent and with Leuchars Old and Junction recording a similar fall of 40 per cent; noticeably, however, St Andrews recorded only a minimal fall in revenue while Guardbridge and Leuchars Junction had a slight increase. Goods traffic, on the other hand, remained fairly static despite the government's attempts to beat the U-boat blockade by growing more food at home, additional traffic from this source being off-set no doubt by the absence of visitors and the effect of the absence of so many local young men.

The major local development was undoubtedly that of the construction, from 1916 onwards, of the Royal Naval Air Services Leuchars airfield* where, a hard surface runway was constructed on flat land to the south east of the village, which was already in use as a rudimentary airfield, and was served by the existing rail connection to the Tayport line by a short branch which left it roughly halfway between the Junction and Old stations. The building materials came via the main line and were booked through Leuchars (Old) and the ponderously-named H.M. Aerodrome Siding. The amount of merchandise and minerals handled at Leuchars (Old) in 1918 increased dramatically from an annual average of some 7 to 8,000 tons to some 44,000 tons, 26,000 of which

---

* The origins of the airfield and its subsequent railway history are dealt with in Chapter Fifteen.

NBR locomotives Nos. 321 and 1421 shedded at St Andrews, *c.*1919; locomotive shed in the background.   *H. Stirling Everard/W. Hennigan Collection*

NBR Holmes 'P' class (LNER 'G7') No. 587 waits at the up platform at Leuchars Junction *c.*1920 with a St Andrews branch passenger train - note the large lumps of coal on the bunker, a sign that this photograph dates from before the days of machine-cut coal!

Leslie Tomsett/W. Hennigan Collection

Holmes 'C' class 0-6-0 and 'P' class 0-4-4T locomotives Nos. 776 and 587 on a down train of mixed stock leaving St Andrews for Leuchars, *c.*1920. *NBRSG Collection*

NBR No. 251 passing the Links station, *c.*1920. Note the old footbridge and, to the right, the station master's garden. *W. Hennigan Collection*

NBR No. 1338 simmers in the Tayport bay at Leuchars Junction while awaiting its next turn of work, *c*.1920.   *W. Hennigan Collection*

NBR No. 1320 heads a Leuchars local out of St Andrews, 1922.
                                          H. Stirling Everard/W. Hennigan Collection

were conveyed in the period from July to December. Passenger traffic was greatly augmented at Leuchars Junction where the following passenger numbers were booked at the station:

Six months ending		
	31st December, 1917	10,724
	30th June, 1918	74,040
	31st December, 1918	254,303
	30th June, 1919	48,526

Thereafter the figures for passengers at the station are between 50 and 150 per cent higher than the pre-war averages and one can only assume that this extra traffic was directly attributable to the presence of the RAF.

While the airfield was being built a special workmen's train was operated between St Andrews and Leuchars Junction for the benefit of civilian employees employed on the construction works. This service, which is shown as operating in the October 1918 working timetable, left St Andrews at 6.25 am and reached Leuchars at 6.35 am with a return working leaving at 6.08 pm and arriving back at St Andrews at 6.18 showing that in wartime a 12-hour shift was not regarded as being in any way exceptional.

The End of the North British

When the war ended and the government handed back control of the railways to their owners, all was not well. On the one hand, passenger figures by 1920 were, in the case of St Andrews and Guardbridge up to pre-war figures and still rising, whereas Leuchars Junction had shown a permanent substantial increase due to the airfield and in all cases revenue was up. Goods figures, fuelled by the short post-war boom, were also encouraging but despite the apparent rise in the sums being remitted by local stations to the NBR head office galloping inflation and greatly increased fuel, materials and wages costs had meant that the real effect of monies received was a negative one. Industrial action resulted in strikes of railwaymen in 1919 and coal miners in 1921, both of which impacted on the St Andrews branch. Economies followed on 3rd October, 1921 when Leuchars (Old) station was closed to passengers. This was hardly surprising as the annual number of passenger bookings there had declined from over 13,000 at the turn of the century down to about 7,000 in the last full year and although the station was situated in the centre of the village, the meagre train service between Tayport and Leuchars Junction did not encourage trade. The fact that Leuchars Junction, with a much better service and through services to Aberdeen, Edinburgh and London, was only half a mile away clearly brought about the demise of the original EP&D passenger station.

When the Railways Act 1921 was eventually passed it was clear that an east coast Grouping was to include both the North British and Great North of Scotland Companies and William Whitelaw, the ebullient Chairman of the North British, was to become Chairman of the new London & North Eastern Railway.

Dundee, Tayport, and St Andrews.

Week-days only.

To Perth.

(Upper table — St Andrews to Dundee)

		a.m.	a.m.	a.m.	a.m.	a.m.	a.m.	a.m.	a.m.	a.m.	C	a.m.	A	a.m.	p.m.	p.m.	p.m.	p.m.	p.m.	p.m.	p.m.	p.m.	p.m.	p.m.	p.m.	p.m.	p.m.	p.m.	p.m.	p.m.	p.m.	p.m.	p.m.	p.m.
St Andrews	lev.	7 13			8		9 33		10 3	10 3	11 9	11 35	12 9	12 42	1 39	2 10	2 47		3 25			4 15	4 24		5 33	6 25		6 54		7 34	8 19	8 30		9 30
Guard Bridge		7 25			8		9 42		10 42				12 51	12 51			2 57						4 31		5 42			7 4		7 43	8 28	8 39		9 39
Leuchars Jo.	arr.			8 14			9 54		10 45		11 45		12 9	12 54											5 45			7 6		7 46	8 31	8 42		9 42
	lev.			9 7			9 50		10 45				12 11		1 512	1 6							4 29		5 54			7 10		8 358	357	8 40		
Tayport		6 227	20	8 26		9 20	10 1		11 20	11 20	12 21		1 131	1 13	2 39		3 133			4 465	235		6 236	43	7 7		7 55		8 489		0	9 22		10 19
East Newport		6 297	27	8 33		9 30	10 9		11 27		12 28		1 201	20	2 46		3 203	20		4 535	445		6 396	50	8 0		8 0		8 549		3	9 29		10 26
West Newport		6 327	30	8 36		9 33	10 12		11 30		12 31		1 231	23	2 49		3 233	24		4 565	05		6 426	53	8 5		8 5		9 0			9 32		10 29
Wormit		6 357	34	8 41		9 37	10 16		11 34		12 35		1 271	27	2 53		3 273	4		4 595	05	436	6 466	57	8 9		8 9	7 13	9 7			9 36		10 33
St Fort							9 56															5 0												
Esplanade	arr.	6 427	40	8 47	9 14		10 22					12 19	1 331	33	3 0		3 344	10		85	85	8	5 27	3	8 15		8 15		9 135		42	9 42		10 40
Dundee (T.B.)	arr.	6 447	42	8 49	9 45		10 24				11 41		1 351	35	3 2		3 364	12		85	58	8	5 47	5	8 17		8 17		8 509		15	9 44		1040

B — C

(Lower table — Dundee to St Andrews)

Leaves Perth 11·30 a.m.

		a.m.	a.m.	a.m.	a.m.	a.m.	a.m.	a.m.	a.m.	a.m.	a.m.	a.m.	p.m.	p.m.	p.m.	p.m.	p.m.	p.m.	p.m.	p.m.	p.m.	p.m.	p.m.	p.m.	p.m.
Dundee (T.B.)	lev.	6 50	7 30	7 40	7 56	8 47	9 13		1030	11 51	1230	1 6	12 49	1 52	2 15	3 21	4 17	4 55	5 54	6 14	7 20	8 18	8 40	9 50	10 46
Esplanade		6 57	7 397	47	8 88	50			1033	11 54	1234		1 31	5 52	2 18	3 244	20	4 59	576	17	7 23	8 43		9 53	
St Fort									1039	12 0	1241		12 561	92	24	3 304	26	5	6 3	23	7 29	38	8 49		9 59	1053
Wormit		7 2	7 447	54	8 569	1	9 20		1044	12 5	1246		1 421	4	6 296	29	3 354	31	5 166	32	7 34	8 54		10 8	1058
West Newport		7 6	7 487	58	9 09	5	9 25		1048	12 9	1250	1 51	1	222	102	33	3 394	35	5 206	36	7 38	8 58		10 8	11 2
East Newport		7 9	7 538	3	9 39	10			1053	12 14	1256	1 101	27	2 152	51	3 444	40	5 256	40	7 43	9 -3		1013	11 7
Tayport	arr.	7 11			8 16	9 6				1 6								6 28		7 44			
Leuchars Jo.	arr.	7 36		8 16			9 45		1110	1147	1228	1 11	2 593	26	4 495	15	5 157	36	9 68	53	9 65	10 89
	lev.	7 40		8 28			10 2		1114		1232		2 593		4 535	22	9 37	5 9	9 65	9 65	
Guard Bridge				8 32			10 6						3 3		5 15				10 8		9 69	10 35
St Andrews	arr.	7 48		8 40		9 16	1014		1122	1157	1240	1 23	3 113	38	5 30		6 196	47	8 179	3	107	1043

A — Through Train—Edinburgh to Dundee.
B — Through Train—Dundee to Edinburgh.
C — Through Train from Glasgow to Arbroath.
¶ For additional trains between Leuchars and Dundee, see Edinburgh and Dundee Section.

The first LNER summer timetable, July 1923.

Chapter Eight

Under English Rule:
The London & North Eastern Railway 1923-1947

'The continuance of this state of things can only result in traders taking to motor transport for the conveyance of their goods.'
LNER Report, 1927

Home Truths

When, on 1st January, 1923, the North British passed into the hands of the London & North Eastern Railway whose headquarters were in London and whose empire stretched from there to Lossiemouth and from Wrexham to Great Yarmouth. The local arrangements for train control and traffic management of the St Andrews branch were kept on initially, although the new initials L. & N. E. R. (abbreviated in 1924 to LNER) began to appear on locomotives and stock and on timetables, posters and other publicity. What was perhaps worrying, though, was that local management, no doubt lulled by the temporary increase in passenger figures, had failed to take into account the emergence of a serious new rival, the motor bus. Largely unregulated and with a ready pool of trained drivers and surplus vehicles left over from the recent war, several local entrepreneurs were tempted to start up their own local services which either ran parallel to, or in some cases took a more direct route, to the St Andrews and Tayport lines and their connections. Among the early pioneers were Clow's Motors who began, in 1922, a service between St Andrews and Newport via Guardbridge and Leuchars to connect up with the ferry service over the Tay and the General Motor Carrying Company of Kirkcaldy who augmented this route with their own buses so that each company connected with alternate ferries giving a comprehensive overall service. A further operator on this route was Johnstone's of Tayport who operated a similar service from 1930 onwards.

With an absence of any direct road connection between St Andrews and Dundee, through traffic between those places was relatively unaffected by these ventures, and long-distance traffic to Glasgow, Edinburgh and London was still unrivalled due to an absence of long-distance coach services but local traffic between St Andrews, Guardbridge and Leuchars, and also between Leuchars, Tayport and Newport was greatly affected, particularly as the buses ran direct through Leuchars village (formerly served by the more convenient Leuchars (Old) station). In 1921 Grant's of Cupar started up a service from St Andrews to Cupar via Dairsie and Guardbridge and this in time became a daily service which enabled passengers to avoid the inconvenient change of trains and wait at Leuchars Junction - if only the NBR had heeded the proposals put forward for a direct link to Cupar via a new spur at Leuchars, perhaps this traffic would not have been lost to the railway! In March 1927 Fuller's of Newburgh started up a direct service from St Andrews to Perth via Newburgh in replacement of the direct Perth to St Andrews train withdrawn in the previous year. At the same time the motor lorry was beginning to have a small, but ever increasing, effect on local goods traffic and these losses were to mount in the following years. The effects of motor vehicle competition were further felt after the General Strike which commenced on Tuesday 4th May, 1926 when virtually all local LNER staff failed to report for work and the entire service between Leuchars and St Andrews was temporarily withdrawn. However, some of the men began to drift back to work in the middle of that same week and by the middle of the following week both passenger and goods services on the branch were virtually back to normal, although much goodwill and traffic had been lost to the railway. The public had discovered, many for the first time, that they now had a realistic alternative to their local train.

First Class Folly

By the 1920s passengers seem to have become more vociferous in their protests to the LNER, possibly because at the dawn of the motor bus age they might have sensed that the railway would be more sympathetic to their plight in view of the availability of an alternative. A typical complaint was published in the Dundee *Evening Telegraph* during the summer of 1925:

> On a recent Saturday afternoon, while travelling from Dundee to St Andrews (writes a Fife correspondent) I had the rare experience of being pushed into a first-class carriage because the thirds were full. This luxurious travelling, however, was destined to be short-lived and my last state was destined to be worse than the first. Reaching Leuchars, where the tickets are checked, I was informed that the accommodation was now available in the third class and was asked to change. The unwilling transfer was made, and after passengers from an incoming train were absorbed, the carriages were absolutely crowded out again. At Guardbridge another influx took place and the ticket collector unblushingly accepted sixteen tickets and one-half out of the compartment. The whole of the third class was run much the same condition and not a single first-class seat was occupied. Why such conditions should be allowed to continue is beyond explanation. It is nothing short of egregious folly to run the first-class carriages empty. The companies themselves have proved it. Statistical departments can show no profits other than those garnered from the third-class and from excursion trains.

Official enquiries were made and although it was admitted that the train, the 2.15 pm from Dundee on Saturday 15th August 1925 'was admittedly heavy particularly between Leuchars Junction and St Andrews, there was nothing to call for criticism such as is contained in the newspaper paragraph'. Once again the indifference of railway management to the ordinary passenger is shown - a recurrent theme at the time - and the folly of operating first-class carriages when, apart from the business traffic, there was little demand was clearly demonstrated. The reality was that leisure travel by those who could afford to pay the significantly higher first-class fares had already been largely lost to the private car in the same way that the third-class traffic would subsequently be lost to the motor bus.

Quicker by Rail

Although the North British had issued a limited number of pictorial posters of holiday places served by their system, it was the LNER who excelled in producing excellent and colourful examples of this form of art, the style being described as simplified realism rather than the more stylised art deco style of the Continental railways. Scottish golf resorts featured in the programme and examples were produced for North Berwick, Cruden Bay and, of course, St Andrews, all with the LNER slogan 'It's Quicker by Rail'. In 1925 the advertising manager of the company, W.M. Teasdale, commissioned from Henry George Gawthorn a view of ladies putting on the Old Course with the beach behind them and the Royal and Ancient club house in the background and this was issued as a poster with white on black lettering reading 'St Andrews, Home of the Royal and Ancient Game'. Possibly one of the most famous of all pre-war railway posters, Gawthorn's design proved popular with the public and became such an iconic image that it was reproduced on a Japanese poster to advertise the 1984 Open and a copy of the original was, in 2001, sold at Christie's for £21,150 - a then record sum for a British railway poster. A separate version of the original was issued in the US and Canada and bore the company name as 'The London & North Eastern Railway of Great Britain'. In 1929 the LNER adopted the clean and pleasing Gill Sans typeface and this was used on a number of subsequent posters of St Andrews when Teasdale's successor, Cecil Dandridge, commissioned several well-known commercial artists of the day to paint and design posters in the standard double royal (40 x 25 inches) and quad royal (40 x 50 inches) sizes. Arthur C. Michael was responsible for a picture of a golfer swinging his club on the Old Course and Fred J. Taylor was paid £50 for a striking view of St Andrews castle perched on the clifftops; both became quad posters and met with public approval, so much so that when exhibitions of posters were mounted across the country, examples could be purchased for 5s. 0d. or 2s. 6d. depending on size. Another poster, with artwork by A.R. Thomson, was issued in 1931 and featured contrasting sketches of early 19th century golfers and their modern equivalents above the slogan 'Then and Now - 600 Golf Courses. LNER including St Andrews!'

Whether any of these posters had the desired effect of boosting the tourist traffic to St Andrews is unclear, but they, in conjunction with slogans such as 'LNER - the Drier Side of Britain', and the later 'Meet the Sun on the East Coast' would certainly have raised the profile of the LNER as 'the holiday line'. The posters were the only publicity specially directed towards St Andrews, although the town did feature in more general handbooks such as the LNER Holiday Handbook and other publications aimed at golfers, ramblers and holidaymakers.

South Street, St Andrews, *c.*1935. This Valentine's postcard view shows two waiting buses outside Madras College - the leading vehicle is on a Perth service after the demise of the direct railway service between those cities. *Authors' Collection*

A wonderful example of the LNER poster painter's art from the 1930s, much reproduced locally in the post-railway era. *Britsh Rail*

ST. ANDREWS THE HOME OF THE ROYAL AND ANCIENT GAME

ILLUSTRATED GUIDE FREE FROM TOWN CLERK OR ANY L·N·E·R OFFICE OR AGENCY

Inconvenience and Delay

Although Leuchars (Old) had been closed to passengers since 1921 it was still a very busy goods depot, both for the surrounding area and the RAF camp but also as a transfer point where wagons were shunted and exchanged to and from the St Andrews branch. But a combination of the inconvenient layout of the station and traffic congestion at certain times of the year meant that lengthy shunting had to take place over the level crossing in the centre of the village. Complaints were received by the LNER that not only were local traders using the station being held up and inconvenienced but general motor traffic on the busy main road was also being greatly delayed. By 1927 these complaints were so vociferous that the company had to act. An official LNER report stated that:

In winter months the siding facilities at the Goods Station are taxed to the utmost and consequently have to be shunted over the level crossing at least three times a day. This cannot be avoided because wagons drawn from or into the loading bank have to cross the level crossing as does use of the delivery siding which can only be reached via the loading bank siding. Each shunt of the loading bank can occupy an engine for about an hour and a good proportion of this requires use of the level crossing. The level crossing is an exceptionally busy one and the view for approaching vehicles from either direction of the actual state of the crossing is very restricted and when shunting movements are prolonged it always entails a serious hold-up to vehicles. Loading and discharge of goods is also held up. This causes serious inconvenience to farmers and others who have horses or motor lorries at the station loading or discharging traffic. The continuance of this state of things can only result in traders taking to motor transport for conveyance of their goods.

On 5th July of that year the company announced a proposal to make alterations to the sidings serving the loading bank in order to alleviate the problem at an estimated cost of £362 and this was duly authorized and carried out. Ironically the tonnages of merchandise, minerals and coal and the number of livestock handled at Leuchars (Old) went into a sharp decline after 1927 and goods receipts at that station fell by one-third between 1927 and 1934. To many local motorists, however, the hold-ups at local level crossings, particularly those at Leuchars (Old) and Guardbridge were still felt to be a great source of inconvenience and delay and many could not wait for the day when East Fife would be free of such antiquated nuisances.

The Railway Fights Back

Although the North British had operated a limited number of bus services before World War I, the bus services which were now in operation in the St Andrews area were all privately-run and unconnected to the railway. The LNER had no direct involvement with the buses and could do little to stop the largely unrestricted and damaging competition from them. In 1928 the Railway (Road Transport) Act gave the company powers to buy out the opposition but it was clear that this move would be opposed by the existing bus operators themselves. Accordingly the LNER bought a controlling interest in the bus company of Walter Alexander & Sons via the Scottish Motor Traction Company of Edinburgh (SMT) and by the mid-1930s the latter company had acquired virtually all the bus operators in East Fife; from

THE
NEW PICTURE HOUSE

ST. ANDREWS

Telephone 509

FIFE'S FINEST

Cinema advertisement.

From the St Andrews Official Guide, 1939 edition

A 1938 rival to the railway.

From the St Andrews Official Guide, 1939 edition

that time the buses operated under the fleetname and in the distinctive blue (later red) and cream livery of Alexanders, latterly as part of the nationalised Scottish Bus Group until their eventual privatisation long after St Andrews had lost its train services. For many years there was a limited degree of co-operation between Alexanders and the LNER, such as the inter-availability of tickets (particularly useful on Sundays when the St Andrews branch was closed to all traffic) but ultimately there was little attempt to feed bus services into the railway and the acquisition of the bus companies did little to help the railway in what eventually turned out to be a losing battle.

However, as the country's financial situation began to improve from the early 1930s, the immediate financial pressures on the LNER were gradually lifted but the traffic lost to road transport never returned. Passenger figures for St Andrews showed an inexorable decline from a peak of 176,000 bookings in 1925 to figures of below 140,000 by 1932 whereas revenue figures showed an even more alarming descent from a peak of nearly £32,000 of receipts in 1925 to £20,500 in 1932, an indication, perhaps, that those remaining passengers after the disastrous contemporaneous trade slump preferred to travel at reduced third class fares and take advantage of all the special offers that the LNER made available. Local passenger traffic over the branch had, to all intents and purposes, been lost to the buses but long-distance traffic, feeding into the national network at Leuchars, held up.

Goods traffic was a different matter and as the decade progressed much of the profitable traffic was lost to motor lorries with heavy traffic, sundries and livestock remaining largely rail-hauled, notwithstanding the fact that it was only marginally profitable to the railways witnessed by the fact that goods receipts at Guardbridge and St Andrews had fallen sharply, by the early 1930s. New sources of revenue included an early attempt by the railways to develop the container market, the provision of express and 'door-to-door' services and other innovations but none of these succeeded in stopping the slow leaching-away of goods traffic and although the four great British railway companies campaigned for a 'Special Deal' in their fight against the largely unregulated road traffic industry, they made little headway.

A Dundee to Edinburgh express, hauled by an LNER 'D11' class 4-4-0 passes through Leuchars Junction while NBR 'C16' class No. 9512 waits with a train in the Tayport branch bay platform, August 1936.   *J.G. Anderson*

An unusual visitor at Leuchars - a Great Central 'O4/1' class 2-8-0 travels southbound from Dundee towards the Junction with a train of wooden-bodied coal wagons, *c.*1938.
Dr W. Rhind Brown Collection

Fortunes of War

When World War II broke out in September 1939, the Railway Executive Committee, set up by the Government to manage Britain's railways, announced an immediate reduction in railway passenger train services but these were restored within a few days and the timetable was little altered thereafter. What was immediately apparent, though, was that the departure of holidaymakers coincided with an increase in military traffic as territorials were mobilised and, eventually, conscription took effect. New faces and new nationalities were seen - in 1940 Polish army engineers, stationed in St Andrews and at Tayport, began to build and garrison the coastal defences designed to prevent a feared German invasion from Norway and trains were used both to bring them to the area and to carry the materials for the massive concrete anti-tank blocks which they constructed. The Fife armoured train, also used for coastal defence and for a time almost exclusively crewed by Poles, made several journeys along the line and spent much time in the area.* The Poles were followed by Czechs, Canadians and Americans, the latter troops often being fascinated to visit the 'home of golf'. Indigenous tourists continued to visit the area, albeit in lesser numbers and were often hampered by the war-time restrictions on travel - in

* The armoured train operations over the Fife Coast line is dealt with more fully in *The Leven & East of Fife Railway.*

June 1942 the *St Andrews Citizen* stated that the city had still much to offer the visitor and that it was, even during those dark days, 'truly an ideal resort for holidaymakers, young and old'.

In common with many burghs on the east coast of Scotland, St Andrews received its fair share of children evacuated from the inner city areas of Glasgow and Edinburgh and, in September 1939, 200 or so of these young evacuees arrived by rail with further contingents arriving sporadically throughout the war. In common with Scottish practice, and in contradistinction to England, many of these evacuees were accompanied by their mothers, and the majority of them stayed only a short time. For, in reality, St Andrews was less safe than Edinburgh due to its proximity to RAF Leuchars and not only did German planes regularly pass overhead but a number of raids in the autumn of 1940 and summer of 1942 caused much damage and several casualties. Somewhat pathetically, the victims, in one particularly bad raid, included a family from Dundee killed when their holiday lodgings in Nelson Street were destroyed by a bomb. Guardbridge was another target and although the railway escaped damage, a chimney at the paper mill was damaged and many windows, including those at the Seggie crossing keeper's cottage, were blown out; in the same attack a lady waiting for a bus was killed and three children going to school were injured by bullets sprayed upon them by the Luftwaffe. A not infrequent local hazard during this time were the crippled RAF planes which crashed while attempting to land at Leuchars, and although no major damage was done to the railway in these incidents local railwaymen assisted the members of the Guardbridge paper mill's fire brigade in clearing up the wreckage.

Per Ardua ad Astra

One wartime feature that did generate a great deal of additional traffic was RAF Leuchars, an established air base close to Leuchars Junction and served by a siding off the old Edinburgh, Perth & Dundee line between that station and Leuchars (Old). This airfield was favourably situated for the defence of the eastern coastline of Britain and, after an early start in World War I, the facilities had grown considerably, causing the once quiet Tentsmuir to take on a new appearance. In the 1920s John Geddie, in *The Fringes of Fife*, commented that:

> The presence of the latest and strangest of human inventions is declared in the brand new buildings of the Aerodrome, set against the woods that surround the ancient house of Earlshall. Overhead there hovers and buzzes something that looks not so much like a monstrous bird of the air as a stupendous dragon fly, but swifter and more powerful than any Roc of eastern fable.

Over the years the airfield had expanded to take over two farms and a large tract of Tentsmuir while immediately prior to 1939 RAF Leuchars was extended yet further. In its role as a bomber and fighter station, as well as a training establishment, the airfield played a vital role in World War II but RAF Leuchars generated comparatively little traffic on the branch line apart from service

Barely a month after VE day, NBR 4-4-2T 'Yorkie' No. 9141 (built by the Yorkshire Engine Co.), approaches St Andrews with the 6.45 pm from Leuchars, 11th June, 1945.   *J.L. Stevenson*

NBR 4-4-2T No. 9141 running bunker first on the 7.15 pm St Andrews to Leuchars service on 11th June, 1945; the train has just passed the St Andrews Links starting signal and is approaching the Golfers' bridge.   *J.L. Stevenson*

personnel travelling off-duty to St Andrews to sample its cinemas, cafes and dancehalls although Dundee, with an altogether livelier nightlife and a Sunday train service, was probably a greater magnet. At Leuchars (Old) building materials, stores, aircraft parts and fuel and a wide variety of other connected merchandise was regularly handled in large quantities throughout the war, both at the goods yard and in the dedicated siding leading into and connected with the RAF internal railway and during this period Leuchars Junction handled a heavy additional passenger traffic resulting from the greatly increased use and importance of the airfield.

Post World War II Blues

With the advent of peace, the holiday traffic returned in force but the LNER was left in a poor state. Locomotives and stock and local stations had received little maintenance during the war and were now dirty and run-down but, despite a shortage of cash and materials, the company was still determined to make an effort.

In 1946 the LNER began issuing holiday guides again and St Andrews featured prominently as a destination for holidaymakers by rail. But the tide was turning and, with the gradual lifting of fuel rationing and other restrictions and the diversion of buses from their wartime routes, competition was once more in the air.

The following year services were extensively disrupted by bad weather with heavy snow falls and a prolonged cold spell coinciding with a severe coal shortage, and extensive summer flooding. If that were not enough, record numbers of holidaymakers sought to discover the delights of St Andrews by rail at the same time that the beleaguered LNER was also fighting a rearguard action to prevent the Socialist government from nationalising Britain's transport system including its railways; a campaign that, it has to be said, received little support from unions and passengers alike who in that idealistic era had little time for what many Fifers (but possibly not some of the more genteel St Andreans) regarded as the death throes of an outdated capitalist regime. The State prevailed and, as from midnight on 31st December, 1947, the LNER ceased to exist as a transport operator with the Railway Executive of the British Transport Commission taking control of its assets.

Ex-NBR Holmes class 'C' (LNER 'J36') 0-6-0 No. 5330 in LNER green livery at the north end of St Andrews station, Thursday 17th April, 1947. *J.L. Stevenson*

'One-armed golfers at St Andrews' - the caption says it all but note the ex-NBR 'M' class 4-4-2T No. 9043 passing in the background. *W. Hennigan Collection*

Chapter Nine

The Lion on the Wheel:
British Railways 1948-1969

'For a town of its size and geographical location,
St Andrews is very well served by the railway'

St Andrews Town Council, 1967

The Emperor's New Clothes

The British Railways (BR) era began innocuously enough with the change of ownership being marked by the arrival of the totem symbol on publicity and, later, on station signs in the attractive Scottish Region Caledonian-blue colours. Locomotives and stock gradually altered their liveries; tanks and tenders acquired the crest of an emaciated lion balancing on a wheel while carriages appeared in maroon or the main line livery of 'blood and custard'. The level of pre-war services were gradually restored, including the 'Fife Coast Express' which had been suspended in 1939 but was reinstated on 23rd May, 1949 although now running only between St Andrews and Glasgow Queen Street via Crail. In 1950 articulated streamlined stock from the former 'Silver Jubilee'* of the LNER was allocated to the service (although no restaurant facilities were provided) and the 'Express' continued to run throughout the decade. However as the decade progressed it was becoming increasingly clear that, despite the buoyant summer holidays trains, the use of local trains by the general public was clearly on the wane.

The entry for St Andrews in the *Third Statistical Account of Fife,*† published in 1952, after a brief history of the railway, concluded that:

…even when … this line (i.e. the line from Leuchars) was joined up with the one from Anstruther, it remained a branch and, moreover, left untouched an extensive area to the west of the town. Now, ample bus services radiate from St Andrews to many towns, even as far away as Glasgow. Perhaps more important, they link the town with virtually every neighbouring locality.

An interesting throwback to the early days of the St Andrews Railway, when similar sentiments were being expressed, occurs later in the same account when the annual Lammas Fair is being described:

---

* A short-lived LNER crack express train run between London and Newcastle and suspended on the outbreak of war. A fuller account of the 'Fife Coast Express' will appear in *The Leven & East of Fife Railway*.

† The *Statistical Account of Scotland* was first published in 1796-8 and was designed to reflect everyday life in each parish, including industries, transport and housing and 'the quantum of happiness enjoyed by its inhabitants and the means of its future improvement'. The second account was published in the 1830s and gives a good account of Scotland in the immediate pre-railway age while the third, published after World War II (the Fife volume appearing in 1951), tells of how Scotland's railways were faring in the motor age; it is selectively quoted in this chapter.

Locomotive shed, signal box and platelayers huts at St Andrews Links, 15th May, 1949.

J.L. Stevenson

St Andrews shed - a good view for modellers, *c.*1950.   *W. Hennigan Collection*

St Andrews, 2nd May, 1949. The south end showing the signal box and down platform on the left, and the up platform on the right. *J.L. Stevenson*

A panoramic view of the north end of St Andrews showing the dock platform, water tower, oil lamp store, train in the up platform, elevated passenger walkway, lift headgear housing, walkway to signal box, down starting and distant signals on a lattice posts and NBR-pattern trackwork, c.1950. *NBRSG Collection*

Centenary special - a small ceremony to mark the 100th anniversary of the opening of St Andrews Railway: Tuesday 1st July, 1952.   *W. Hennigan Collection*

'J37' class 0-6-0 No. 64634 backs the branch set out of St Andrews station before running round the carriages and forming the next departure, 1955.   *Nigel Dyckhoff*

The gaiety of the Lammas Fair is a welcome and accepted feature of the life of St Andrews, but a more recent manifestation of revelry is viewed with less enthusiasm, and has been the subject of many protests. This is the conduct of some of the summer-time day trippers, who come, in buses, sometimes from as far as the Clyde valley, to spend a Sunday in the town. In the region of 100 buses have been counted, and streets, beaches and putting-greens are thronged ... Unfortunately drunks, rowdies and litter-louts are all too frequently apparent, and ... useful as is the revenue from these incursions, local opinion holds that it is very dearly gained.

At least the railway could not be blamed for this unwelcome incursion for, even after World War II, there were still no Sunday trains to St Andrews!

The entry for Leuchars, after commenting on how the village became the centre of a wide agricultural district following on the opening of the original station on the Tayport line in 1848, notes that:

Travelling facilities are adequately provided, not only for the village but for all parts of the parish, except for the outlying districts of Tentsmuir. An hourly service connects Newport Ferry, Tayport, Leuchars, Guardbridge and St Andrews while the landward parts are within easy reach of the bus route from Newport to Cupar via Balmullo and Dairsie. The railway service, although very good, is not used to the same extent probably because of the higher fares and the half-mile that separates it from the village. It is mainly used for long journeys, and by those local people whose daily work takes them from Dundee to Cupar. There is a local garage which provides a taxi service.

Declining Goods

On the goods front, things were in an even more serious decline. The local rural economy was facing serious difficulties caused by the disappearance of indigenous small-scale industries and from the railway's point of view, however, the downturn was even more pronounced. The motor lorry had been an ever present threat to short and medium length journeys since the end of World War I and had taken away much of the local traffic between St Andrews and other parts of Fife. The absence of road bridges over the Forth and Tay helped to preserve some of the longer distance traffic and although firms such as Danskins of Strathkinness were already making inroads into longer distance traffic the hiving off of British Road Services from the British Transport Commission exacerbated the competition that the railway was facing.

In June 1955 a national strike was called by ASLEF, the railway footplatemen's union, and considerable disruption to local goods services resulted. One unfortunate consequence of this strike was that some of the largest users of the railway in East Fife deserted to other forms of transport, the biggest loss being the esparto grass traffic of the Guard Bridge Paper Company Ltd where the heavy loads formerly conveyed by rail were, after the strike, carried by a fleet of six new lorries owned by the company.

The ability to convey goods from door-to-door and to avoid the damage and pilfering that often occurred in the transhipment between lorry and railway were contributory factors to the steady decline in goods traffic at Leuchars (Old), Guardbridge and St Andrews. But the truth was that by the 1950s the carriage of

St Andrews looking north from the dock platform, *c.*1955. Note the trackwork detail including the check rails.

Nigel Dyckhoff

less than full wagon-loads of general merchandise which the railway was bound to convey in pursuance of its common carrier obligations had become largely unprofitable and the cumbersome and labour intensive methods of handling such goods in the antiquated local goods yards ensured that this traffic was an increasing burden on the already fragile economics of the St Andrews branch. In an attempt to cut costs and to make the carriage of goods by rail in the area more attractive British Railways attempted, towards the end of the decade, to concentrate traffic at St Andrews and to deliver and collect over a wide hinterland traffic that might have used the smaller local yards and sidings, using a dedicated fleet of vans and Scammell 'Scarab' vehicles. Whether these measures did little more than delay the inevitable must, however, remain a moot point.

Tayport No More

Until 1954 passenger services in the east of Fife remained remarkably intact but in September of that year Dairsie station, on the main line between Cupar and Leuchars, was closed. Then, barely a year later, it was announced that, with effect from 9th January, 1956, the section of the original Edinburgh, Perth & Dundee Railway main line between Leuchars (Old) and Tayport was to be closed to all traffic, although this news would have come as little surprise to anyone. With the opening of the first Tay Bridge the train service on this section had been drastically reduced with the diversion of most trains to the new line to Dundee via St Fort and the bridge and the newly-opened continuation of the old line between Tayport and the bridge via Newport seeing a healthy amount of local and commuter traffic to Dundee. When the first Tay Bridge fell services on the original line were revived but the revival was a temporary one and, with the opening of the second Tay Bridge, the Leuchars to Tayport section again lost most of its trains. By World War I there were few trains using the line and eventually in 1921 Leuchars (Old) station was closed to passengers and thereafter the former main line was reduced to a single track branch. By the late 1940s all that remained were the three passenger services per day that operated from Dundee to Leuchars via Tayport, two of them being extended to St Andrews. Given the timing of the services, they were of little use to anyone other than the intrepid railway enthusiast, the parallel bus service being quicker and more convenient.

Saturday 7th January, 1956 saw the last trains over the line, with the Leuchars northern bay seeing its last Tayport train leave at 1 pm and the last train of all, the 5.10 pm Edinburgh Waverley to Dundee Tay Bridge via Crail and Tayport, arrived at Leuchars Junction behind 'D30' class No. 62430 *Jingling Geordie* to find a small welcoming party. At 8.51 the train departed for Tayport and, on arrival there nine minutes later, it was greeted by a crowd complete with a lone piper who played the lament 'Lochaber No More'. This, according to the report in the *Dundee Courier* was the nearest refrain to 'Leuchars No More'. And so it was, for the line between Leuchars (Old) and Tayport (Morton's Siding) was completely abandoned and passed into history with little comment from the public and only a scarce mention in the railway press. Leuchars (Old) station remained open for goods traffic in the meantime, the short section of line from there to Leuchars North Junction being reduced to single track on 8th June, 1959.

Leuchars (Old) station looking towards the Junction and showing the former level crossing, truncated lines and general air of dereliction, c.1958.   *J. McEwan*

LMS Ivatt '2MT' class 2-6-0 No. 46464 at Leuchars (Old), 1957. This engine was employed as the Leuchars Pilot and frequently worked the St Andrews branch freight traffic.   *George Bett*

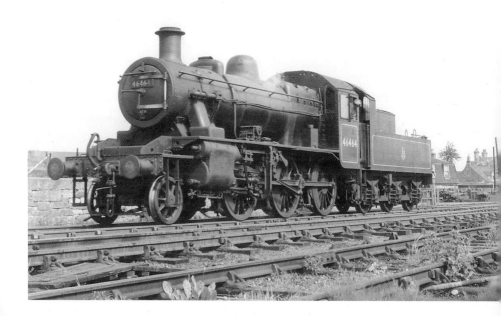

Trackside view of Leuchars Junction, 22nd August, 1958; note the presence of the ashes next to the St Andrews branch bay platform and Gresley spare coach in the siding.   *A.G. Ellis*

NBR 'J36' class No. 65333 on the 1.26 pm branch working to St Andrews at Leuchars Junction, 25th April, 1959; the locomotive was withdrawn from service five months later.   *J.L. Stevenson*

'D49' class 4-4-0 No. 62708 *Argyllshire* on a southbound passenger train leaving Leuchars Junction 'wrong line'; the train will regain the correct line at the crossover at Milton Junction. Note the maroon-painted teak coach and red and cream BR Mark I coaches and the 'B1' with a branch train in the St Andrews dock. *W.A.C. Smith*

Thompson 'B1' class 4-6-0 No. 61132 with a Dundee to St Andrews via St Fort train composed of LNER-pattern stock enters the up main line platform at Leuchars Junction while an Aberdeen-bound train made up of BR Mark I coaches heads in the other direction; 3rd November, 1958.
Hamish Stevenson

'J36' class 0-6-0 No. 65330 arrives at Guardbridge station with a train bound for St Andrews with the fireman holding out the token for the signalman to exchange, 22nd August, 1958. *A.G. Ellis*

A classic photograph of Guardbridge station on 9th August, 1958 with Thompson 'B1' No. 61133 arriving with the 2.10 pm Dundee Tay Bridge to Edinburgh Waverley via St Andrews service.
W.A.C. Smith

BR Standard class '4MT' No. 76109 at Guardbridge with the 2.15 pm Dundee Tay Bridge to Edinburgh Waverley, 3rd October, 1959. *Roy Hamilton*

'B1' class 4-6-0 No. 61147 with the 2.10 pm to Edinburgh via Crail and a train of Gresley coaches in 'blood and custard' livery, passes under the replacement footbridge at St Andrews Links, 12th January, 1957. *J.L. Stevenson*

Sunshine at the south end of St Andrews with 'D30' class 4-4-0 No. 62418 *The Pirate* on the 2.17pm Dundee to Thornton train, 8th September, 1955.   *H.C. Casserley*

LNER 'J39' class 0-6-0 No. 64792 about to depart from St Andrews for Dundee with an afternoon passenger train, 1957.   *Jim Page*

ST. ANDREWS

GUIDE FREE FROM TOWN CLERK, ST. ANDREWS, FIFE

Train services and fares from  stations, offices and agencies

BR Scottish Region poster for St Andrews, 1957. The artist was the well-known Dundee artist, James McIntosh Patrick. *British Rail*

The Diesels Arrive

In an effort to avert further closures and combat declining patronage and rising costs, British Railways began to introduce diesel-multiple units (dmus) on a number of Scottish routes towards the end of the 1950s and on 15th June, 1959 twin units replaced steam-hauled trains on certain local services including those running between Dundee, Leuchars and St Andrews.* At the same time efforts were made to publicise St Andrews and, in an echo of pre-war days, two pictorial posters of the town were issued. Less striking than the 1930s examples, one depicted artwork by Frank H. Mason and featured the dunes with the sands of the west bay being enjoyed by holidaymakers while the second had a view of the Old Course with the town in the background with artwork by the renowned Dundee artist James McIntosh Patrick. Both posters bore the rather more sober legend 'St Andrews – Guide Free From Town Clerk, St Andrews, Fife' above the British Railways totem and the McIntosh Patrick poster, like some of its LNER predecessors, is still widely available as a reproduction. In May 1960 a further spate of dieselisation led to a complete recasting of the Scottish East coast timetable and the appearance of multiple unit working on Edinburgh to Dundee local services and on services between Glasgow and Edinburgh and the East Fife coastal route although some of these services had, in fact, been diesel-worked in the previous summer. The steam locomotive was not, however, completely banished because a handful of services did not succumb to the diesel multiple unit and these included a daily working between Dundee and St Andrews worked by the Leuchars pilot engine and some additional seasonal and special trains. Goods services continued to be steam-worked and diesel locomotive workings over the St Andrews branch between Leven and Leuchars were few. As a consequence of the arrival of the multiple-units, the motive power sub-depots at St Andrews Links and Anstruther (Old) were both closed and thereafter the remaining steam locomotives still in use were shedded at either Dundee or Thornton. Another casualty was the 'Fife Coast Express' which ran for the last time on 5th September, 1959.

The diesel units on local services were popular with the travelling public because of their speed, perceived modernity and comparative cleanliness and, not least, because of the fine views that could be had through the cab windows of such delights as the crossing of the Tay Bridge and the run along the banks of the Eden with the ever increasing prospect of the beach, Old Course and city. What they could not do, however, was stop the continuing long-term haemorrhage of passenger traffic but they did provide a temporary boost with, according to BR sources, an increase in passenger traffic on the St Andrews to Dundee service of between 10 and 15 per cent. However, even though the running costs of the multiple units were much reduced from the steam trains they replaced, the basic faults of the line remained, namely the fact that the stations were inconveniently situated for passengers, that there was still often a need to change trains at Leuchars and that the trains did not run to a regular 'clockface' timetable, there was no Sunday service and that, for local journeys in Fife, the bus was usually cheaper and, sometimes, faster.

* Other services that became dmu-worked on the same day included Aberdeen to Peterhead and Fraserburgh and the St Combs branch and local trains between Perth and Blair Atholl.

Metro-Cammell twin-car dmu crossing the River Eden at Guardbridge with the 5.04 pm from St Andrews to Leuchars, 3rd October, 1959. The unit is in its earliest green livery without yellow 'whiskers' and has just been sent to Dundee to work this service.   *Douglas Hume*

A Metro-Cammell dmu coasts towards St Andrews with a panorama of town, beach and golf course in the background, August 1960.   *Authors' Collection*

Farewell to the Anstruther & St Andrews

As far back as 1937 it had been realised that the Anstruther & St Andrews line, particularly the section between Crail and St Andrews, was of marginal viability and in that year the LNER had investigated the operation of the East Fife coast line as two separate branches namely a Leuchars to St Andrews section and the Thornton to Crail section with the complete closure of the line that linked the two. The intermediate stations between Crail and St Andrews had all been closed to passengers in 1930 and what services on that section of line remained after World War II were often lightly-used, particularly in the winter months. By 1960 the whole of the line east of Leven had little goods traffic and was only busy with passengers on public holidays and on summer weekends when additional trains, including Sunday trains, were operated. The line was still fully staffed and signalled and little attempts had been made to reduce costs but the holiday traffic could no longer subsidise the whole line and the end was probably inevitable. In March 1963 the British Railways Board, under the Chairmanship of Dr Richard Beeching, published their far-reaching report into the re-shaping of the national railway network and, notwithstanding the rumours circulating locally prior to this, there was public dismay that the whole of the line between Leven, Anstruther, Crail and St Andrews was listed for complete closure. Local opinion was mobilised but despite their best efforts the passenger and goods service from St Andrews to Crail was withdrawn on 4th September, 1965, and the last passenger train between Crail and Leven operated the following day with the goods service over that section being withdrawn on 18th July, 1966. The line south of the new station in the town had been completely abandoned and, once again, St Andrews had been relegated to the terminus of the original branch line from Leuchars.

Guardbridge Gone

Passenger traffic figures at Guardbridge station had been in a downward spiral since the end of World War II, largely due to the relentless bus competition and the fact that new building in the village had tended to be at some distance from the station but close enough to a bus stop to jeopardise what passenger traffic the railway might have retained. In 1944 all the St Andrews branch trains called at Guardbridge station; by 1954 many were omitting the stop. In 1964 of the 24 trains running daily between Leuchars and St Andrews only nine called at Guardbridge; there was a total absence of any train between 8.25 am and 2.11 pm while in the other direction only seven trains from the St Andrews direction called at the station. The evening service was so sparse as to be practically worthless. No attempts were made to have more trains call there or to save costs such as making Guardbridge an unstaffed halt. Few protests were made when it was suggested that the station be closed, as foreshadowed in the Beeching report. In February 1965 the Minister of Transport informed the local Member of Parliament that he was giving his consent to the closure to passengers of Guardbridge station and the closure notices were duly posted. The last passenger

Leuchars Junction looking north, *c.*1962 with the St Andrews branch dmu in the bay; the overgrown sidings, water tank, air base, RAF houses and parish church can all be seen. Note the absence of the present main road.   *J. McEwan Collection*

Guardbridge in the 1960s showing a close-up of the level crossing gates and the original St Andrews Railway station building with the later NBR waiting room visible in the background.
Authors' Collection

train to call there was the 11.0 pm Saturdays Only Leuchars to St Andrews service which called at Guardbridge at 11.4 pm on the evening of Saturday 4th September, 1965, the station having outlived the St Andrews to Crail line by a mere 5½ hours. Parcels traffic to and from Guardbridge was thereafter collected and delivered by road from Cupar - an ominous development so far as the much nearer St Andrews stations were concerned.

Goods Depart; A Hotel Arrives

In St Andrews things continued on much as they had before, indeed in October 1964 an application was made by the British Railways Board to St Andrews Town Council for power to reconstruct and modernise the station in the town and to provide a new bookstall; planning permission was granted. The council, in the same month, protested to the Board against their proposals to withdraw the Leuchars Junction stop from the London sleeper trains as an economy measure but do not appear to have mounted any protest against the proposed closure of the line to Crail and Anstruther. On 2nd August, 1965, a month before the line to Crail was in fact closed, outline planning permission was granted to British Transport Hotels, the BR subsidiary that ran the former railway hotels, to build a new hotel on the site of the still-open goods station at St Andrews (Links); the Town Council noted, in giving their consent, that arrangements were in hand for the closure of the Links station. This closure followed when, with effect from 20th June, 1966 the goods stations at Guardbridge and St Andrews (Links) were closed to all traffic, general goods now being received and dispatched by British Railways lorries from Cupar. The remaining wagon load traffic for the Guardbridge paper mill was served by trip workings from Leuchars. Now that the branch no longer had a goods service, St Andrews business people began to complain, somewhat belatedly, about delayed deliveries and the poor service which they felt they were now receiving; the sundries traffic continued to be carried in the guard's van sections of the diesel multiple units.

The Links station site was rapidly cleared and construction began on the new hotel, the first railway hotel to be built in 30 years. Designed by Curtis & Davis of New York in a style which resembled 'a chest of drawers with all the drawers sticking out', the hotel was felt by many in the town to have reached an architectural nadir for St Andrews; ironically the building ended up costing some 20 per cent over the initial estimate. The 'topping-out' ceremony took place on 16th December, 1967 and 'after long deliberation' British Transport Hotels imaginatively named the new hotel 'The Old Course Hotel' after the famous nearby links. The hotel opened on 25th June, 1968* and, for a brief period, the forlorn dmus trundled past the new building. Initially a commercial failure,† the hotel was later grandiloquently renamed 'The Old Course Golf and

---

* Contemporary with the Hotel, the former St Andrews Railway station master's house at the Links was converted into a public house and was named 'The Jigger Inn'.

† In its third year of operation the hotel lost £60,000, in the face of a forecast profit of £123,000. The initial overnight rates for a room with facilities was £6 5s. 0d. for a single and £7 0s. 0d. for a double with suites available at £15 10s. 0d. per night; breakfast in all cases was an extra at 14s. 6d. per person. A contemporary guest house establishment in St Andrews was charging between 15s. 0d. and 21s. 0d. for a double room with breakfast.

Thompson 'B1' class 4-6-0 No. 61340 on a branch empty coal working from St Andrews heads north through Leuchars Junction on 20th June, 1964; coal at this time was still being delivered to St Andrews Links, Guard Bridge and Seggie sidings.   *J.L. Stevenson*

'B1' class No. 61402 on Leuchars pilot duties shunting at St Andrews Links on 14th March, 1963.
Mike MacDonald

Country Club' and survives to this day. Enlarged in 1982 and now in private hands, it cannot in all honesty be described as one of St Andrew's architectural gems - indeed it has been said that 'the name's implied elegance is belied by the blockwork and render reality'.* Whether the hotel was ever destined to cater for rail passengers was a matter of some controversy but it seems likely that those likely to patronise the 'Old Course' would have been expected to travel by road from Leuchars rather than have to endure the rattling dmu on the branch which would pass by and terminate half a mile distant. Indeed the initial publicity for the Hotel made no reference to any rail connection at St Andrews and the brochures issued in July 1968 state that 'A hotel bus will meet passengers at Leuchars Junction'.

Latter Days

Leuchars (Old), however, remained open to goods for a few months more, finally succumbing on 6th November, 1967, having outlived all other local goods stations by more than a year. Following this closure the formation of the line between the RAF siding and Leuchars (Old) station was abandoned and the site quickly reverted to nature.

The St Andrews branch continued to function and on a summer Saturday as the well-filled diesel multiple-units arrived and departed, business still appeared to be good. However changes were afoot. The timetable alterations consequent upon the closure of the Crail line meant that there were bound to be changes to the Leuchars - St Andrews service. A report prepared by a sub-committee of the Town Council on the line was forwarded to British Rail (the new trading name for the BRB) makes interesting reading:

> For a town of its size and geographical location, St Andrews is very well served by the railway. An average of about 700 passengers per day use the train to come into St Andrews and the same number make outward journeys. Yet there is virtually an hourly service to Dundee from early morning until late evening and the service to Edinburgh is almost as good. With one or two exceptions, no train leaves or arrives in St Andrews carrying more than a good bus-load of passengers. Some carry only a car-load. Traffic, as might be expected, is concentrated into two peak periods, with the result that 20 per cent of the trains carry over 30 per cent of the passengers. Furthermore the opening of the Tay Road Bridge in 1966 is bound adversely to affect railway passenger traffic ...

The report went on to comment specifically on the trains to Leuchars and Dundee which were to be withdrawn or re-timed:

> Those taken off, 9.34 am, 12.13 pm (which was a Fife Coast train starting at Glasgow), 1.30 pm and 7.42 pm carried among them an average total of only 65 people a day, 10, 30, 20 and 5 respectively. Since there are other trains departing from St Andrews within half-an-hour of these times, we cannot claim that the removal of these trains has caused widespread hardship or inconvenience. Certainly some individuals have been inconvenienced and have had to alter their personal arrangements. The old 9.19 am trains has been re-timed at 9.25 am and no longer goes straight through to Dundee.

* Gifford, *The Buildings of Scotland: Fife*, 1988 - the sale of the British Transport Hotels was only the first step in the disastrous breaking up of British Rail, an event for which neither of the main political parties now seem willing to take responsibility for or to do anything about.

A panoramic view of Guardbridge from the west and looking towards St Andrews; this 1965 view was taken in the brief period between the closure of the station to passengers and the closure of the small goods yard to all traffic.   *Jim Page Collection*

Ivatt class '2MT' 2-6-0 No. 46464 on Leuchars pilot duties shunts a train past Leuchars (North) signal box towards Leuchars (Old) on 11th March, 1966, shortly before closure of this part of the former Tayport line.   *Mike MacDonald*

Passengers for Dundee must wait at Leuchars for a minimum of 30 minutes and arrive in Dundee at 10.19 am at the earliest. On the average, the 9.19 used to carry about 40 people a day from St Andrews. It seems fair to claim that this particular change is highly inconvenient to a significant number of people. The inconvenience could be obviated by continuing the 9.25 am through to Dundee. We understand that this revision is under consideration by British Rail and that a request from this Town Council might help them to decide favourably.

The 9.25 was, indeed, retimed to 9.20 and ran through to Dundee with effect from 3rd January, 1966 but the Council's other requests fell on stony ground. They had observed that while certain trains carried few passengers the loss or retiming of them caused considerable inconvenience - an example being the 9.15 pm from Dundee which was brought forward to 9.02 since the admittedly fewer than 20 night-school pupils who regularly travelled on this service would now either have to miss the end of their classes or wait for the last train of the day, the 10.50 pm.

On 25th April, 1966, as part of a reorganization of 'human resources' by BR in Scotland, the post of station master at St Andrews was abolished, his duties instead being carried out by Alan Chamberlain, the BR Area Manager in Dundee. On 29th August, 1966 the Town Council authorized their Parks Committee to assist British Rail in the improvement of St Andrews station gardens after the Council had passed a resolution drawing their attention to the poor condition of the flower pots and beds at the station. In addition they enquired as to why the station was to have no services on the forthcoming 26th December and 2nd January, a consequence of the creeping shut-down of the railways during festive periods. The impending shut-down was, however, to prove to be a rather more alarming one.

It was the opening of the Tay Road Bridge that, directly, led to the end of all services on the St Andrews branch. Until then bus passengers intending to travel to the North had to go via the Newport to Dundee ferry service,* a journey which involved changing modes of transport and frequent delays caused by congestion or the vagaries of the weather. Considering that a good proportion of the passenger traffic from St Andrews was bound for Dundee, the St Andrews branch had had an assured future so long as the ferries continued to operate. A road bridge over the Tay had been long-mooted but difficult to justify on economic grounds, but political considerations dictated otherwise and a concrete road crossing over the Tay finally became a reality in August 1966, albeit one which was, on any financial criteria, hard to justify. During the construction of the Tay Road Bridge the ferry services were disrupted and, as a consequence, there was a not insignificant increase in the number of cross-Tay railway passengers but this additional traffic was only temporary and, as had been expected, the opening of the road bridge had a disastrous effect on the revenue of the St Andrews branch, as well as foreshadowing the end of services over the remaining portion of the Tayport branch as far as Newport-on-Tay. According to figures released by BR after two passenger censuses had been taken, in September 1966, i.e. immediately after the bridge was opened, the number of rail passengers joining and alighting at St Andrews on a weekday was 608 and 560 respectively, with Saturday figures of 519 and 576. By the

---

* The Broughty Ferry to Tayport ferry service did not outlive World War II.

following March, when new travel patterns via the bridge had come into effect, the figures had dropped to 361 and 351 on weekdays and 390 and 405 on Saturdays. This demonstrated a weekday reduction of some 40 per cent and a Saturday fall of 28 per cent, suggesting, not surprisingly, that it was the Dundee commuter traffic that was the most affected and that season-ticket holders were deserting the railway for their cars or for the greatly improved bus services between the two towns. But the figures also demonstrated another even more alarming trend - each weekday train on the branch was only carrying an average of 18 passengers and Saturday trains were carrying 20 which, given that the loadings were not equal on all services, confirmed that most trains were not only failing to meet their costs from fares collected but were almost certainly running at a heavy loss. With the new bridge and better bus services, there was little hope of any new significant passenger flows over the branch line; the fall in numbers was likely to continue.

It therefore was perhaps inevitable when, on 20th March, 1967, the British Railways Board published an advance notice under section 54 of the Transport Act 1962 of their intention to discontinue railway passenger services on the Leuchars to St Andrews line and to close St Andrews station to all traffic. This did not come as a complete shot out of the blue, as many had predicted that the closure of the line to Crail was only the precursor of St Andrews also losing its service, but the Council nevertheless resolved that Sir John Gilmour be asked to put a question to the Minister of Transport regarding the reasons for this proposal with a view to preparing objections. Subsequently the Council, together with a number of associations and corporate bodies, made representations to the Ministry that no action should be taken pending receipt of a report by the Tayside Planning Group. They urged all those affected to lodge objections with the Transport Users' Consultative Committee for Scotland on the grounds that hardship would be caused by the closure of the line and also to submit hardship claims to the Clerk of the Fife County Council. But, to many, it seemed as though the British Railways Board had already made up their mind.

Over But Not Quite Out

One good source of revenue in the past had been the excursion train which had brought hundreds (and, on occasions, thousands) of trippers of all sorts to St Andrews with a consequent boost to local cafes, restaurants, shops and other attractions. It was inevitable that much of this traffic would be lost to the motor coach but even in the 1960s there were still a handful of additional and excursion trains which visited the city to say nothing of the regular television trains for schoolchildren, enthusiasts specials and even specials organized by university students. An example of the latter was the train arranged by John Purvis which, in October 1960, conveyed 150 students dressed in period costume around the East Neuk and formed the first (and last) service to call at Stravithie in 30 years; catering was provided by female undergraduates and the proceeds went to an educational charity.

Special trains continued to travel over the line throughout the 1960s, although latterly these tended to be diesel-hauled, and such services included BR staff excursion trains, specials run for outside organizations such as the Johnny Walker distillery and a train run for the 1964 Golf Open which included the Scottish Region's General Manager's saloon. A particularly poignant trip was that run on 12th October, 1966 when a large party of St Andrews students was taken by a special train to Dundee to witness the last St Andrews graduation ceremony at Queen's College, Dundee as the new academic year was to see the birth of Dundee University as an independent academic body. This occasion was an historic one in more ways than one for it was to form the last ever steam-hauled passenger train on the branch.* In the following year the revenue from such traffic was effectively lost for ever when, on 3rd September, 1967 the signalling on the branch was abolished and henceforth the line was worked as 'one engine in steam' with the box at St Andrews Station abolished and Guardbridge reduced to function only as a gate box. A few days later, on September 10th, the final excursion train was run, a diesel-hauled special from Glasgow run on behalf of aluminium company Alcan which achieved another 'first and last' by being run on a Sunday - a most unusual occurrence, but presumably made possible by the fact that signalmen were no longer required to be paid for an extra shift since the surviving box at Leuchars South remained open all weekend. Within months the former down platform at St Andrews was put out of use and the track serving it lifted, all remaining trains now being required to use the up platform, the sole surviving face of the island. With the consequent abolition of the run-round loop, no loco-hauled excursion could ever use the branch again and with a tight and inflexible timetable in place it was doubtful if a multiple-unit special could be squeezed in either. Worse still, the reduction in staff and the growing dereliction at St Andrews made it look as though the line was destined for early closure.

Defeat in the Victory Hall

On Thursday 2nd November, 1967 the official public hearing on the proposed closure of the St Andrews branch took place at the Victory Memorial Hall in St Andrews, convened by the Transport Users' Consultative Committee (TUCC) and chaired by Mr E.W. Craig of Glasgow. He began the meeting by stating that:

My Committee have noted that reference had been made to the possible industrial development of the area. In that connection the Minister would seek advice from the Scottish Secretary as to the possible consequences of any contemplated industrial development in the area. It was only right also that the Minister should be made aware of any individual cases of hardship that would arise from the closure in this direction. It was from that aspect, and that only, that the inquiry would be conducted.

Evidence was given by Sir John Gilmour, MP for East Fife, who said that no decision should be taken while the Government were considering the new

---

* The last steam engines of all to visit St Andrews were a pair of 'B1s' in April 1967 - for an account of this see Chapter Fifteen.

St Andrews shed on 22nd January, 1967 showing the interior after removal of the rails and shortly before demolition.   *Hamish Stevenson*

Metro-Cammell dmu crossing the Petheram bridge at St Andrews on the 13.50 to Dundee, 8th April, 1968.   *Nicholas Walker*

Transport Bill* and that both the University and the tourist trade would be harmed by the withdrawal of a train service which, in the long run, would be a seriously retrograde step. On behalf of the County Council it was stressed that elderly and infirm people would be affected adversely and that the interchange between bus and train at Leuchars was inadequate - a point mentioned by several subsequent speakers. The Provost of St Andrews then presented a petition with some 2,174 signatures against the proposed closure and said that this was a private petition which had been got up at very short notice but which, nevertheless, reflected the strength of local feeling. On the question of the replacement buses it was said that:

> The service offered as an alternative to the present rail service was so totally inadequate that it would be cynical to describe it as an alternative at all ... By rail to Leuchars took ten minutes and it required twice that time by bus. After that passengers would have to clamber over the bridge to the platform in all kinds of weather. The time taken to travel to Dundee would become very much more. It required 25 minutes just now and would take 48 minutes by bus ... The bus would mean hardship to older people and to mothers with children. There was also the fact that rail travellers could take 150 lb. of luggage,† but only 60 lb. by bus. That represented hardship to students and to girls travelling to school.

Other representations were made by the St Andrews Merchants' Association and, on behalf of St Andrews University, by its Secretary A.N. Mitchell who stated that:

> The closure would inflict great hardships on its students, who had to travel six times per year to and from their homes. There were about 2,400 students involved and the existing rail service was often strained at the times when they travelled. Indeed the closure would represent not only a big hardship, but a considerable problem as the bus service proposed was completely inadequate as a substitute. It was arranged to meet certain trains only and not all of them, although all were in use by returning students over a period of four or five days in October ... In the restricted service there was not such a bus after 6.30, and such arrangements could not cater for some 2,000 students ... They also maintained that a small service of trains could still be run that would meet the case of commercial hardship and still be a financially viable proposition.

Representations were then made by Major G.R. Ormiston, who represented St Leonard's School. He commented, after saying that the school contained some 420 boarders and between 70 and 80 teachers, that:

> The girls all came from various parts of Britain and travelled by rail. There were 12 days per year when they were using the railway, and also some of them at half-term holidays. Withdrawal would mean that they would have young children hanging about shivering at Leuchars Station or Cupar waiting for trains. Similarly they would arrive in large batches at these places and the school would require to find its own transport to bring them to St Andrews.

---

* Sir John was referring to what was to become Section 56 of the Transport Act 1968, a radical measure which authorized a direct government subsidy (Public Service Obligation Grants) for loss-making services which it considered desirable to retain on social grounds.
† This was a reference to the standard luggage allowance for first class passengers; second class passengers were allowed 100 lb. - a considerable advance over what one could expect to take by ordinary bus.

Twin-car Gloucester RC&W dmu on the 14.53 St Andrews to Leuchars approaching the Petheram bridge with the new University buildings prominent in the background, 8th April, 1968. *Nicholas Walker*

The 10.58 Leuchars Junction to St Andrews passing the Old Course Hotel, St Andrews Day, 1968 -note how the former goods shed is now fenced off. *Hamish Stevenson*

The St Andrews Labour Party, represented by the Revd Helen Woods, drew attention to the hardship that would be suffered by the poorer, older and weaker people of the area by the proposed change and emphasised that the Minister of Transport, Barbara Castle, 'herself had stated that the railway existed to serve the community, and her Party saw other forms of transport being helped by taxpayer's money both at home and abroad'. Other individuals gave examples of personal hardship that they would suffer and these included a regular St Andrews to Broughty Ferry commuter, a Dundee commuter and other regular users.

The British Rail case was presented by A.B. Arundale, divisional manager, East Coast Division, Edinburgh, who said that:

> The St Andrews line was yet another example of a steady decline in use over the years, while the completion of the Tay Road Bridge [opened in the previous year] had introduced a drastic new element into the situation. In the six years from 1960 passenger use had declined from 90,000 to a figure of 66,000 in 1966. In the same period there has been a slight increase in season tickets issued from 1,700 to about 1,900. At Leuchars there has been a decrease in 9.1 per cent in passenger journeys, with an abrupt decline with the opening of the road bridge in St Andrews journeys of 38.1 per cent. At Dundee in the same period tickets and season tickets issued show a slight increase, confirming that the real field of economic rail travel was on an inter-city basis rather than on local lines. A comprehensive survey showed that season ticket holders were over double figures, namely 11 and 12, on two of the trains in daily service, and on all other trains they were in single figures only. In regard to the use of trains on special occasions, a recent student return coincided with a big golf tournament, and the use of the service was only marginally greater than in an ordinary week.
>
> In regard to the complaint by Sir John Gilmour and others about elderly and infirm people and the Leuchars bridge, arrangements would be made to allow the sleeper crossing to be used. The running of smaller and fewer trains would effect some minor economies, but would not make the line profitable ... With regard to the 2,174 signatures on the petition, if each made one journey per year this would reflect itself in the number of annual journeys, but would not make the line profitable.

Confirmation was given by Mr Arundale that British Rail had no intention of closing Leuchars station 'on the sort of business being done at present ... but we are very much at the mercy of the people using the train', while Mr W. Sim, General Manager of W. Alexander & Sons (Fife) Ltd gave an assurance that his company would be able to provide a bus service on the lines that had been referred to'. By the end of the same month a recommendation was being made by the TUCC to the Minister of Transport that they could see no grounds upon which the St Andrews branch should not be closed to passenger traffic.

A Slender Chance

On 2nd December the *St Andrews Citizen* stated, in an editorial, that the impending charge would be

> ... no surprise to the local people who followed closely the tenor of the recent inquiry. That does not lessen the shock of disappointment and dismay generally felt at the considerable blow dealt this week to the local economy. Not everyone in, or coming to

St Andrews branch train on a dreich December day in 1968 - the tree stump, wind-swept bent and the lonely telegraph poles all contribute to the bleakness of the scene.   *Hamish Stevenson*

The 11.15 St Andrews to Leuchars passes the Links goods shed on the left and the new Old Course Hotel on the right with the former station master's house on the far right. This picture, taken on St Andrews Day, 1968, shows the hotel and railway in the brief period when they co-existed.   *Hamish Stevenson*

In the dying days of the branch a Metro-Cammell dmu waits at the sole remaining platform in St Andrews, 7th December, 1968. *M.B. Smith*

Twin car Metro-Cammell dmu leaves the St Andrews bay platform at Leuchars Junction in the last month of the branch service, 7th December, 1968. *M.B. Smith*

A dmu bound for Leuchars passes the closed Guardbridge station in December 1968; note the lifted sidings. The former signal box remains in use as a gate box.   *Douglas Yuill*

Metro-Cammell dmu on 11.15 am St Andrews to Leuchars leaving the former station on a frosty December morning with the steeple of Hope Park church visible in the background.
Hamish Stevenson

St Andrews, owns or can command a car. Many holiday visitors to the town have had to rely on the train service. Substitution of a bus service will mean greater inconvenience for them and could well be the deciding factor in fixing further holiday venues. For car-less residents, and they are the majority including also students and St Leonards' girls, the closure of the passenger line takes them back more than a century ago when Leuchars was the nearest railway point. Today's bus is certainly slighter faster than a stage coach, but this is the space age, we are told ...

Notwithstanding the recommendation, the Minister's decision was anxiously awaited and on 5th August, 1968 a letter from the Minister of Transport confirmed that she had given her consent to the closure of the line 'subject to certain conditions requiring alternative bus services' and that she did not propose to make a grant under the Public Service Obligation. The St Andrews Town Council, while recognising that this was both an economic and political decision, suggested that one of their number, Councillor S. McDowall, prepare a report on the subject and this he duly submitted in the following terms:

At a meeting of the Town Council on Monday 2nd September, 1968 at which the closure proposal was discussed, Councillor Ritchie and I made suggestions about possible ways in which the line might be kept open. I promised to submit written suggestions.

First, it seems to me, taking a short view, the closure of the line makes economic sense on any normal basis of accounting. The volume of traffic simply does not justify its remaining in operation. It is true that on a few days in the year the line is comparatively busy but for most of the time it carries only a handful of passengers. On the other hand, if we take a longer view, there is a strong likelihood that with an increase in population, many of whom would work on the other side of the Tay, and with parking space for private cars becoming increasingly scarce and expensive, the demand for railway travel, especially for daily commuting, will revive. The long term interests of St Andrews might well suffer if the rail link is broken. In the meantime we hardly expect British Rail or the British taxpayer to underwrite the loss on this line merely to save the occasional convenience of few travellers. If we really want the line kept open, knowing that the losses will inevitably be heavy, we must offer something more than protests.

Baillie Ritchie has suggested that the line could be run much more cheaply than it is at present. One-man railcar operation, the closure of the station building at St Andrews with tickets being issued at Leuchars and the adoption of an automatic level crossing at Guardbridge would clearly produce substantial operating economies. I fear, however, that there are formidable technical difficulties, including safety regulations and manning rules, which would require to be overcome. Furthermore, a proportion of the present loss on the line must be attributed to its share of central overheads. I do not know how large this amount is, but it would presumably be unaffected by operating economies. At all events, I do not think that we could presume to make general suggestions about operating economies to British Rail unless we had carried out a detailed study of the possibilities.

A short term solution could be to offer to make good to British Rail part or the whole of the operating loss on the line. The Council will note that Dundee Corporation has just agreed to pay Autair a subsidy to keep the Dundee to London air link open. Frankly I believe that this is the only slender hope of keeping the line open. This is something which the Council would have to ascertain. If this suggestion meets with approval then the following immediate action could be taken:

enquiry of British Rail if such a proposal is acceptable to them *in principle*;

enquiry of the Fife County Council if they would consider making a contribution to the annual subsidy

Withdrawal of Passenger Train Services between Leuchars Junction and St. Andrews, on and from Monday, 6th January, 1969

ALTERNATIVE SERVICES BY RAIL AND ROAD

The Scottish Region of British Railways have announced that the passenger services between

LEUCHARS JUNCTION and ST. ANDREWS

will be withdrawn on and from MONDAY, 6th JANUARY, 1969, and that the following passenger station will be closed:—

ST. ANDREWS

This pamphlet contains the following information:—

1. Summary of principal passenger train services departing and arriving at Dundee, Leuchars Junction and Cupar.
   (For full details of train services in operation until 4th May, 1969, see Public Time-table and Supplements.)

2. Additional bus services between St. Andrews and Leuchars Junction Station, with train connections.

3. Bus services between St. Andrews and Dundee.

4. Additional bus services between St. Andrews and Dundee.

5. Summary of bus services between St. Andrews and Cupar.

6. Other alternative bus services.

7. Sketch maps of Cupar and Dundee.

8. Arrangements for Parcels Traffic.

9. Car Parking facilities.

Further information regarding passenger and parcels services may be obtained from the Area Manager, Dundee (Tel. No. 0382-21041).

The front cover of the leaflet distributed to passengers in late 1968. *Authors' Collection*

If the answers from British Rail were favourable, we could enter into discussions with them to discover what the annual cost would be. Only then would it be possible to decide *rationally* if we really wanted to keep this line open.

On 7th October, 1968 British Rail confirmed to the Town Council that the proposed closure date of 6th January, 1969 would be maintained unless a firm undertaking was received from the Council that they were prepared to meet the full costs of keeping the service running. There was an offer from the General Manager of British Rail, Scotland, to meet the Council and the Scottish Railway Development Association suggested that the Council meet them to discuss possible methods of operating the line more cheaply. As if to scupper any possibility of Council support, British Rail told them on 4th November that the estimated cost of maintaining the service had now increased to some £20,000 per year.* Undaunted, on 18th November, the Council resolved to write to the Minister requesting that a reconsideration of whether or not a subsidy to cover these losses should be made. By this time, however, all hope had for all practical purposes all hope had been lost and on 7th December, 1968, following observations by the BRB that there had been an absence of any undertaking by the St Andrews Town Council, the official closure notices were posted.

Close of Play

The *St Andrews Citizen* made a final plea, saying that:

> With the closing of the branch railway line ... just a few days off, extreme perturbation is being expressed on all sides by the town people. The Town Council are already alarmed at the fact that out of the 21 main line trains which stop at Leuchars daily, only about 6 are being met by buses from St Andrews. Passengers from other trains will have to depend on the bus service that passes through Leuchars village, half a mile from the station ... The Merchants Association, Hotelkeepers and the Students Representative Council have all expressed their deep concerns. Even the request by the students to defer the closing by one day to enable students to get back for the new term have been refused.

The newspaper concluded that in relation to the impending closure 'the general opinion is that it will be a disaster for St Andrews'.

The last trains to and from St Andrews ran on Saturday 4th January, 1969, the official closure date being Monday 6th January. Somewhat overshadowed by the closure on the same date of the entire 98 mile Waverley Route through the Borders, the St Andrews branch nevertheless was given a good send-off by local residents and University students. The final train, the 11.07 pm Leuchars to St Andrews driven by a local man Jock Speed, arrived to a varied musical repertoire including 'Last Train to St Andrews', an adaptation of the contemporary ballad 'Last Train to San Fernando'. The passengers on the train included a party from the University Conservative Association who were,

---

* At the TUCC hearing BR representatives had stated that the line was losing some £24,000 annually, but it was unclear if this included a capital element or whether any potential losses of main line traffic occasioned by the branch closure had been included.

The last train from St Andrews to Leuchars, the 22.32 on 4th January, 1969.
Authors' Collection

apparently, the last first-class passengers on the line.* A contemporary report in the *Dundee Courier* recorded that:

> There were lively scenes to mark the last journey from Leuchars to St Andrews at 11.07 pm, but no enthusiasm. The train carried a large number of passengers, many of then University students and townspeople who had travelled on the last train out of St Andrews at 10.32 pm in order to make the sentimental journey back on the 11.07. Many of the travellers asked to be allowed to keep their tickets as souvenirs of the occasion. The last journey on Saturday took almost half an hour because unknown travellers managed to do £25 worth of communication cord pulling for nothing. Five times during the five mile journey, the diesel came to a halt and each time the guard walked through the compartments to see innocent-looking passengers who 'knew nothing'. On the St Andrews platform a group of students sang calypsos about the closing of the station. As the empty train drew out of St Andrews on its way to the depot in Dundee, passengers joined in singing 'Auld Lang Syne' and sent up three cheers for the St Andrews railway staff.

The empty diesel set, driven by driver Allan Watson of Brechin, departed a few minutes later and St Andrews was thereby severed from the national railway network. On the same day the remaining goods traffic to the Guardbridge paper mill was also withdrawn and the whole of the branch line, together with the signal box at Leuchars South, was closed to all traffic. On the road between St Andrews and Leuchars a mere handful of additional bus services were put on.

* They included Douglas Mason, future architect of the poll tax and Allan Stewart, later to become a well-known if controversial Scottish MP; at a dinner of the Conservative Association held in a local hotel later that month the Vice-President stated that he 'looked forward to the return of a Conservative government in 1971' and made a plea for the return of the St Andrews branch line. The Tories did return in 1970, the branch line remained closed and the parliamentary seat was subsequently lost to the Liberals!

Chapter Ten

St Andrews Derailed:
From Closure to the Present Day

*'A rail ticket marked London to St Andrews would
surely tempt many foreign travellers.'*
Sir Menzies Campbell, MP

St Andrews No More

As soon as the Minister of Transport had given her consent to the closure of the St Andrews to Leuchars branch, the St Andrews Town Council intimated to the British Railways Board, in August 1968, that they would be interested in acquiring both the passenger station and some of the trackbed between there and the Links station - the latter location, of course, having disappeared into the grounds of the Old Course Hotel. A suggestion, made to the *St Andrews Citizen* a week after the closure, that the Leuchars to St Andrews branch be saved and operated as a preserved railway came to naught, the writer acknowledging that 'such a venture has not as yet been tried in Scotland'.* Tracklifting began at the Leuchars end of the branch in 1969, the contractors apparently being unaware that the line from Crail to St Andrews was no longer in existence since local rumour has it that some of the track at the Leuchars end had already been lifted and had to be hastily re-laid so that the demolition train could reach St Andrews to commence work from that end. St Andrews (New) station buildings found a new but temporary use as the clubhouse of the Ichthus Youth Club, a council-backed venture, but this reincarnation was short-lived and in July 1972 the once well-kept buildings were completely demolished and the whole site built up to the level of the island platform so that the area could then be used as an extension of the large North Haugh car park to the north - an ignominious end, as it was rightly said, to nearly 120 years of local enterprise! The junction line over the embankment towards the Petheram bridge became a landscaped footpath and the bridge deck was removed for scrap not long afterwards. The stone abutments, with their carved nameplates, remain but whether the many hundreds of motorists who pass by every day notice them or appreciate their significance is a matter of doubt. Another curious survivor of the railway age in the city is in the two street names 'Station Road' and, half a mile away, 'Old Station Road', still so-named long after both stations have disappeared. The former St Andrews Railway station master's house at the Links station somehow escaped demolition and now survives as the Jigger Inn, dominated by the now inappropriately 'Surrey suburban-styled' Old Course Hotel behind it, whose car park extends over the path of the line. The trackbed of the railway across the links and along by the banks of the Eden can still be traced and railway fencing and gates still survive in places.

* The same fate befell the proposal to save the Dollar and Haddington branch lines but eventually the Scottish Railway Preservation Society succeeded with the Bo'ness & Kinneil line and a breakaway group went on to save the Strathspey line from Aviemore to Boat of Garten; at the time of writing this latter line has been extended to Broomhill and work is underway on completing the re-opening of the line to Grantown-on-Spey.

At Guardbridge the Guard Bridge Hotel (two words, as in the title of the papermill!) still stands next to the piers of the Eden viaduct; the hotel, which often formed the backdrop to photographs of trains crossing the river, contains a number of relics including the original NBR drinking fountain from the village station on the front wall and, inside, the wooden signal box nameboard and a number of pictures of the line in action. Of Guardbridge station and its level crossing nothing remains and there is now little evidence of the Seggie siding and the connection to the still flourishing papermill now operated by Curtis Fine Papers. From the village a footpath runs past the papermill reservoir to the banks of the Motray where the remains of the railway viaduct are there for all to see. The route of the branch line can be easily distinguished from the window of a main-line train passing the now vanished Milton Junction.

At Leuchars for St Andrews station (its current name) the St Andrews bay has been filled in and a new footbridge built* but Leuchars North signal box remains and the line is still mechanically signalled. The first few yards of the Tayport line lead to the now disconnected RAF siding which is heavily overgrown with weeds. The level crossing here has vanished but on the airfield side a short stretch of track on the internal railway has been left *in situ* as a memorial. Of Leuchars (Old) station there are no remains although the adjacent Old Hotel survives as a reference point while to the north of the vanished level crossing here the trackbed is still visible and now forms a footpath.

The Bus Departs

As with the case of so many other similar closed branch lines in Britain, the replacement bus services failed to live up to their promise, especially after the last remaining part of the coastal line, from Leven to Thornton Junction, closed nine months after the St Andrews branch. The main bus service, Alexander's existing Route 355, which ran approximately hourly between Dundee and Leven via St Andrews and the coast, started its journey at the Seagate bus station in Dundee rather than from Tay Bridge railway station and, at its southern end, terminated at Leven bus station where passengers had to change to travel onwards to Kirkcaldy where main line railway connections could be made. Between St Andrews and Leuchars some additional buses were put on to serve the station there, but after a short period these buses were withdrawn due to poor patronage arising out of the poor connections caused by late running trains and problems with keeping to the bus schedules. Many now relied on their own cars to drive to Leuchars Junction and local taxi and private hire companies enjoyed a bonanza caused by the absence of buses. Eventually in 1988 the re-named Leuchars station acquired a new suffix, 'Leuchars for St Andrews'. There were many who thought that, from a public transport point of view, this was nothing more than a joke as it was clear that the Scottish Bus Group had little real interest in providing any truly connecting service between the city and its railhead - a disgraceful example of two nationalised concerns who had little regard for the real interests of the travelling public! The privatisation and break-up of the Scottish Bus Group did little to improve this situation and the timekeeping, comfort, ambience and

---

* See Chapter Fifteen.

appearance of the buses used on the routes that paralleled the railway, together with the fact that no dedicated connections are maintained at 'Leuchars Interchange' (the grandly-named bus shelter outside the station),* give potential passengers little reason to abandon their cars, unless, of course, like students and many others, they do not possess one. Perplexed tourists at Waverley, when told that they must complete their journey to St Andrews by bus or taxi from Leuchars, are still heard to remark 'Gee, you mean there's no train to there?'

Starlink

In 1989 a pressure group named Starlink, or the St Andrews Rail Link, was formed with a stated aim of 'reconnecting the town to the rail system in the interests of convenience for travellers, the alleviation of traffic congestion and reduction of car-generated pollution'.† Amongst the supporters of the scheme are local councillors, tourist organizations, the Railway Development Society, members of the European and Scottish Parliaments and the North East Fife MP and former Liberal Democrat Leader, Sir Menzies Campbell, in whose words:

> . . . as a recognised tourist attraction, the town deserves the best possible transport links. On environmental grounds greater emphasis should be placed on rail travel. A rail ticket marked London to St Andrews would surely tempt many foreign travellers.

The success of the Starlink campaign, which has now been active for some 17 years, has been mixed. In December 1994 it was announced that North East Fife District Council, the 1975 successor to the St Andrews Town Council, had called for a report which would seek to explore the feasibility of a new branch line from St Andrews to Cupar, which would have constituted something of a revival of the 1913 proposals following upon the destruction of Leuchars Junction. The matter had arisen in connection with a scheme to electrify the main line between Edinburgh and Aberdeen and the Council were anxious to explore the possibilities of either Cupar or Leuchars as the new junction. Although it was recognised that a link such as the one proposed would be an expensive one likely to cost 'at least £1 million', the idea of such a new line 'was too narrow when sustainable development was being sought'. The proposal was, accordingly, not followed through. A subsequent study by the Fife and South Tayside Rail Study concluded that there was no case for the reinstatement of the St Andrews branch line but in 2002 the Scottish Executive, in its modification to the Fife Council Structure Plan (Fife Council having succeeded its local predecessor in 1996), safeguarded the former route of the branch line;# the Starlink group continue to campaign for the reinstatement of the Leuchars to St Andrews line.

* The official reason usually given is that a dedicated bus to meet every train would be impracticable, given the supposed inability of trains to run to their timetable. Perhaps a more flexible demand-responsive minibus service would be the answer.
† For the Starlink website see www.louisxiv.demon.uk/starlink
# Proposal PT2, 'Land for the following routes and facilities will be safeguarded from prejudicial development and identified in the local plan, in accordance with the Local Transport Strategy: The Leven and St Andrews lines including new stations, subject to review through Local Transport Strategy', was accepted by the Scottish Executive in August 2002, the Scottish Parliament being demonstrably much more railway-minded and environmentally aware than Westminster.

Poster advertising the 2005 Open and 'Golflink' service.   *A.M. Hajducki*

What is, however, abundantly clear is that there is a very definite need for a proper and dedicated link that would serve all trains, start at the station and terminate in the middle of St Andrews. An obvious first step would be for First Scotrail, Cross-Country (the Arriva group's replacement for Virgin Cross Country) and National Express East Coast (the replacement for GNER), the three privately-owned train operating companies who now run services on the Edinburgh to Dundee line, to provide an integrated bus service which, if successful, could later be transmuted into a railway service.* There are many local commuters who now use the Leuchars car park, mainly due to the disproportionate increase in passenger fares between Leuchars and Dundee causing many who would have commuted from the latter station to use the free parking facilities at Leuchars, and at least some of these could possibly be persuaded to abandon their cars in favour of a reinstated railway line.

At potential peak periods, such as the beginning and end of the academic terms at the university and the now co-educational St Leonards school, traffic at Leuchars can be heavy and when the Open Golf Championships are held at St Andrews traffic for the few days that the event is on could well justify special trains shuttling up and down a new St Andrews branch line. A valuable illustration of this potential is provided by the special rail-and-bus service operated during the Opens at St Andrews under the golfing umbrella title of 'Golflink'. In 1999 a total of 40,995 out of the 157,000 persons attending the Open at Carnoustie, the course at which is still directly served by rail, travelled by train - a percentage of 26.1 per cent of such visitors which could even be improved upon if the railway arrangements had been better organized and more flexible. In 2000 the Open was, once again, held at St Andrews and 29,500, or 15 per cent, of those attending, travelled by rail and the Golflink buses. According to Jane Ann Liston, a local councillor and the energetic convenor of Starlink 'it is clear that the train journey terminating five miles short of the course, requiring a change to a bus, has been a major discouragement to golf fans travelling by train' while a Scotrail spokesman added that 'Carnoustie had the station practically on the first tee which was a big advantage for a lot of people'. This may well be the case but on dreich winter days when visitors are few and the commuters choose to remain in their cars, the demand for a railway is less than obvious and even the most optimistic supporters of a scheme to resurrect the branch line must have some doubts if the whistle will ever be heard again next to the banks of the Eden. However the motto of St Andrews being *'dum spiro spero'* or 'where there is life, there is hope' may, in the end, prove the authors wrong!

Raking Over the Ashes

We are now more than a generation on from that January evening when the last train occupied the remaining platform at St Andrews station and it is worth looking, for a last time, at the railways that served that town, using the benefit of hindsight and history. The St Andrews Railway was a solidly-founded local enterprise that paid its way and helped to make the town the tourist, university

---

* Particularly as the parent bodies of these companies are themselves bus or coach operators!

The forlorn piers of the Eden viaduct at Guardbridge, November 2006.   *A.M. Hajducki*

The NBR water fountain from Guardbridge station in its present home of the Guard Bridge Hotel.   *A.M. Hajducki*

The gaunt remains of the Motray viaduct, December 2006.   *A.M.Hajducki*

A winter afternoon view of Leuchars Junction from the north, showing the new footbridge, November 2006.   *A.M. Hajducki*

Leuchars from the up platform looking towards Leuchars Old with the North signal box in the background, December 2006.   *A.M. Hajducki*

and golfing centre that it is today by first of all halting its decline and then by enabling visitors, pupils and students, enthusiasts of the world-famous golf course and locals alike to travel to and fro in what was once a cheap and efficient manner. Likewise its goods station serviced farmers, shops, hotels and the many residential establishments in the town. The turning point came after World War II when cheaper and more flexible forms of transport came on the scene and the veneer of bustle and prosperity began to wear thin on the now-nationalised branch line. The final blow came with the advent of the opening of the Forth and Tay road bridges which opened up Fife and closed many of its remaining railways. In an age when the green agenda was all but unknown, the line succumbed to what was seen by many as the cost-cutting mismanagement of a Labour Government, albeit only after a last-ditch campaign by local people and their representatives. Since then the population of St Andrews has increased from around 9,5000 to about 15,000 and student numbers at the university have trebled, traffic congestion has become a real problem and local people now travel much further to work than they did. So whether this is truly the end of the St Andrews branch story is, as yet, unknown and perhaps a subsequent edition of this book will recount a tale of optimism and rebirth - only the blind seer of time can tell.

The site of St Andrews station, August 2005 - the retaining wall and railings give a clue to the position from which this photograph was taken although part of the cutting has been filled in.   *Dr W. Rhind Brown*

Chapter Eleven

Scholars and Spectators:
Passenger Traffic on the St Andrews Railway

'Now the railway has brought us within a reasonable reach
of the rest of the world'

Fifeshire Journal, 1852

Passenger traffic on the St Andrews branch was extremely varied and interesting in nature and included local farmers and tradesmen, schoolchildren and university scholars, Dundee commuters, holidaymakers and day-trippers, golfers and service personnel, evacuees and a myriad of other Fifers and Non-Fifers alike. This chapter attempts first of all to deal with passenger traffic at each station travelling southwards from Leuchars, and then with sections dealing with regular services and special trains.

Leuchars

In the early years the Old station at Leuchars was used mainly by passengers transferring to the St Andrews branch trains and there was little originating traffic there, save a few locals who travelled on business to Dundee via Tayport. With the opening of the second Tay Bridge in 1887 the Old station lost most of its trains and passengers, limping on until closure in 1921 - a closure that even pre-dated the competition from the nascent motor bus notwithstanding the more convenient position of the station in regard to the old village. Following upon the expansion of the airfield, the village also grew and although Leuchars Junction was, principally, an exchange station for the St Andrews branch and, to a much lesser extent, the Tayport line, it was from the time of World War I onwards, also a centre for originating traffic, albeit most of this traffic being destined for main line stations to the south. By 1950 this local traffic was fairly substantial and RAF personnel, their families and those who worked for them used Leuchars Junction a great deal with the local buses making comparatively small inroads into this valuable source of revenue. By 1950 there were about 900 servicemen of all ranks stationed at the RAF camp and, according to the *Third Statistical Account*, 'the officers' houses, consisting of 5 permanent and 4 temporary villas, are situated in the village, while 69 houses in the camp itself are used as married quarters'. With the closure of the St Andrews branch in 1969 Leuchars became the railhead for a wide area of north-east Fife and has remained so until the present day. There are a substantial amount of daily commuters to Edinburgh and a healthy long-distance traffic both to the South and the North with a fair degree of tourist, golf and academic traffic coming from main line destinations, attracted by the arguably misleading 'Leuchars for St Andrews' branding in the timetable. The station is now served by an hourly First Scotrail service from Edinburgh to Aberdeen, by a handful of London to

Aberdeen trains and by cross-country services from Dundee to Birmingham and the South-West; additional traffic is generated by the annual September air display at RAF Leuchars. The future of Leuchars station seems to be secure, despite the very real worries back in the 1960s that the station would not survive long without its branch line.

Guardbridge

The only intermediate passenger station on the branch, Guardbridge had something of a chequered career. In the early years the station had few passengers, serving only a handful of houses, the Seggie estate and the moribund distillery but with the opening of the paper mill passenger numbers began to build up to a sufficient number to justify the NBR upgrading the facilities here by providing a new platform waiting room and offices in 1894. By the 20th century the station was a busy one, outstripping places like Crail, but its demise was a spectacular one brought about by the advent of the motor bus on the parallel main road providing a direct service to the centre of both St Andrews and Leuchars village and after World War II less than half the scheduled services on the branch line called at the station - the fact that it was an easy walk from Leuchars Junction to the village did not help to engender much local traffic. There was little in the way of commuter traffic - the workers at the paper mill, the only real source of employment, would travel by foot from their homes in places like Strathkinness, Dairsie and Balmullo and, as a result of the policy of the mill's owners, in latter years they tended to live in the company's own houses in and around the mill. Passenger traffic eventually dwindled to such levels that the station was recommended for closure in the Beeching Report and the last trains called there in September 1965, some 3½ years before the demise of the branch line on which it was situated.

St Andrews

St Andrews station was, in its heyday, not only the busiest station on the line but indeed one of the busiest stations on the North British system outside of the major conurbations. The number of tickets sold there annually outstripped the combined total of all of the other stations between Leuchars and Crail. The nature of the traffic was extremely varied and included school and university pupils, holidaymakers and daytrippers, commuters and business travellers in contrast to the types of passengers who used, say, Anstruther or Kingsbarns stations. As the *Third Statistical Account of Fife* commented, as late as 1952,

This geographically eastern corner of Fife has come to represent something like the social 'West End' of the county - a place in which the well-to-do have their abodes and to which many outsiders flock for education, for commercial purposes and for entertainment.

The vast majority of all travellers came from the Leuchars direction with traffic from the Crail direction being comparatively light. Throughout its existence St Andrews station never had a Sunday service and although this might have made a difference to traffic there at least in the 20th century, the exact effect of the absence of Sunday trains on the viability of the branch line will, perhaps, never be known. The station was always busiest in the summer with the highest traffic flows in July and August, starting with the Edinburgh Trades and Glasgow Fair holidays - traditionally the first two and last two weeks in July respectively. The increase in passengers extended throughout the school holidays (both English and Scottish for then, as now, they did not wholly coincide) and lasting well into September with other seasonal peaks at Easter, Whitsun and the Autumn bank holiday. There were several distinctive categories of leisure traveller including those who came to spend their summer holiday in hotels and guest houses convenient for the sandy beaches and other childrens' attractions that the town had to offer, those who came to see the historic remains and cultural attractions of St Andrews and those who used the town as a base to tour the surrounding countryside and coastline either by bus or by using one of the local 'Rail Rover' tickets first issued in the 1930s. During World War II there was an upturn in the number of servicemen visiting St Andrews and airmen, Polish and Czech soldiers and British Army personnel all used the railway; in addition evacuees from Glasgow, Clydebank, Dundee and Edinburgh all travelled to their temporary homes in St Andrews by train.

Other annual highlights at the passenger station included the additional traffic caused by the annual Lammas Fair in August when hundreds of extra travellers from stations throughout Fife (including all of those between Leven and Leuchars) attended by using ordinary service trains and, in the earlier years, special trains). The relatively local nature of this traffic, however, was peculiarly susceptible to motor-bus competition and the special fares and additional strengthening of trains by adding extra carriages did not survive the World War II. Other regular seasonal attractions included motor cycle speed championships held in July, swimming galas held in July and August, the Eden golf tournament held in August and the Scottish Hard Court Tennis Tournament held in August. Once again much of this traffic was lost to local buses but the railway did tend to retain the longer-distance visitors to these events.

Commuters were a steady and dependable year-round traffic source at St Andrews and although their numbers never rose above the 40-50 mark they boosted revenues by their daily journeys to and from Dundee; with the opening of the Tay Road Bridge, inevitably much of this traffic was lost.

Golf

Golf was a year-round attraction at St Andrews (or at least from about March to November, when the weather would turn so inhospitable that only the most intrepid visitors would venture forth to see the delights of the links) and many were drawn to St Andrews from America and Europe to savour the atmosphere

From the NBR *Official Handbook*, 1912.

ST. ANDREWS

A LOVELY AND HISTORIC UNIVERSITY TOWN
AND THE SUNNIEST SPOT IN SCOTLAND

FOUR GOLF COURSES
Including the far-famed Championship Old Course.
All courses open to visitors. Moderate green fees.

NINE PUBLIC TENNIS COURTS
on which the Scottish Hard Courts Championships
are played annually in August.

Splendid Public Putting Greens

Boating, Bathing (large open-air Swimming Pond) ; Riding ; River,
Loch and Sea Fishing ; Bowling ; Cinemas, Theatre, Dancing; Safe
beaches and glorious sands.

EXCELLENT ACCOMMODATION IN HOTELS, BOARDING HOUSES AND
APARTMENTS.

For List of Hotels apply to the Town Clerk, St. Andrews, Fife

Advertisement from *BR Holiday Haunts, Scotland*, 1961 edition.

John Braid solves a tricky problem that will enable him to go on and win the 1905 St Andrews Open. *Authors' Collection*

No. 46463 in the Tayport bay at Leuchars Junction heating up three coaches to form an additional Leuchars-St Andrews shuttle for the Open Championship, July 1964. *M.B.Smith*

of the 'Home of Golf'. This trade was particularly encouraged by the railway since it often involved first class travel to and from London or Edinburgh and was often regarded, from a revenue point of view, as the icing on the cake.* When the railway arrived there was only one course, the Old Course, but three new courses were subsequently opened, namely the New in 1894, the Jubilee in 1899 and the Eden in 1913. From 1897 the Royal and Ancient was recognised as the rule-giving authority in all countries except the United States and Mexico where the US Golf Association controls the game. The highlight in the St Andrews golf calendar was, and still is, the few days at the height of the summer season when the British Open championships were held on the Old Course and these were held at regular intervals throughout the period when the railway served St Andrews.† The first Open to which passengers travelled by rail was in 1873 but it was not until the end of the century that the crowds began to form. Those familiar with the Open would be surprised by the fact that it was only with the advent of full television coverage in 1957 that the number of spectators really took off. During the days on which the Open was held branch line trains were strengthened by the addition of two or three coaches, as were connecting Edinburgh to Aberdeen services. It was usual to have a special morning train run from Edinburgh to St Andrews via Leuchars which returned at 5.30 in the evening along with another special from Dundee to St Andrews run at the same times, while the branch line service was augmented as necessary. Spare carriages were kept at the Links goods station. As a result of the Suez crisis and subsequent fuel rationing St Andrews was selected as the venue of the 1957 Open because of its easy accessibility by rail although, by a strange irony, petrol-rationing had ended by the time the Open was held. Two further Opens were rail-served but the private car and bus had attracted most of the traffic and it was only later that traffic congestion led to the introduction of the 'Golflink' dedicated bus service from Leuchars with special fares including connecting trains and these continue to the present day.

One oddity of the Opens in the railway era was that railway services had to be suspended at crucial moments in play and shots were played through the goods yard and across the track - a local rule being that 'the grass within the railway fence, the grass bounding the roads at the Corner of the Dyke and at the seventeenth hole, shall not be considered hazards'. In the 1905 Open the celebrated James Braid, a Fifer from Earlsferry, while playing the 16th hole in the final round while attempting to get the ball out of the bunker beyond the Principal's Nose:

> …got it on to the railway and … found it lying in a horrible place, tucked up against one of the iron chairs in which the rails rest. I took my niblick and tried to hook it out but did not succeed, the ball moving only a few yards, and being in much the same position against the rail. With my fourth I got it back on the course.

Despite this setback, Braid went on to win the Championship handsomely!

---

* This traffic was, in LNER days, enhanced by the issue of some attractive pictorial posters, see Chapter Eight.
† These years were 1873, 1876, 1879, 1882, 1885, 1888, 1891, 1895 and 1900 (two-day events), 1905, 1910, 1921, 1927, 1933, 1939, 1946, 1955, 1957, 1960 and 1964 (three-day events). In 1873 the winner received £11; in 1964 the sum was £1,500 while 20 years later this had risen to £55,000.

NOTICE

EDEN COURSE
GOLFERS ARE REQUESTED
NOT TO PLAY OFF FROM
THE FAIRWAY OR FROM THE
TEEING GROUND WHEN THE

TRAINS ARE PASSING

A warning to the incautious - November 1964.   *J.L. Stevenson*

Students and schoolchildren

St Andrews University was another source of income, particularly after the revival of that ancient institution in the 1870s and its subsequent reorganization; new buildings, halls of residence and the Gatty Marine Laboratory were all added and in 1892 women were, for the first time, allowed to matriculate. A large number of undergraduates, postgraduates and lecturers began to use St Andrews station, particularly at the start and end of every term along with their luggage and 'cycles by the score'. The branch line became imbued in university lore, so much so that it featured in literary works by undergraduates which appeared regularly in student publications. It would, indeed, hardly be an exaggeration to say that it was the railway that saved St Andrews University from a complete demise. Other traffic generated by students included regular trips to and from the University College of Dundee which, in 1954, became the Queen's College, Dundee in the University of St Andrews. Every year until 1967, when that institution attained full independence as the University of Dundee, its students travelled to St Andrews by a chartered train to attend graduation ceremonies. A small number of St Andrews graduates lived at home or in lodgings elsewhere in the East Neuk and travelled by train from Anstruther, Crail and Kingsbarns by rail but the reluctance of the North British to grant them reduced fares and the general paucity of the train service helped to kill off this potential source of revenue. On occasions the Railway and Transport Society of Queen's College, Dundee organized trips by chartered train to destinations of interest including, on 1st May, 1965, a journey around the Fife coast line.

Another important and regular source of revenue at St Andrews was provided by the staff and pupils of St Leonards School for Girls, an independent school catering for girls founded in 1877 as part of a widespread national movement to provide good education for middle-class girls; a junior school was added in 1894. In time St Leonard's gained a formidable reputation as one of Britain's premier girls' schools and attracted pupils from all over the country so that it eventually had a number of day pupils and some 420 or so boarders, with a staff of between 70 and 80 teachers. The boarders travelled to and from St Andrews by rail at the beginning and end of every school term and their arrival and departure, heralded by a heavy traffic in trunks and other baggage which was sent from the school as luggage in advance, was a regular feature of the local railway scene right up until the closure of the line. In 1913 a typical Special Traffic Notice stated that on 2nd April one of the St Andrews to Leuchars services 'conveys through vehicles for Kings Cross with pupils from St Leonard's School' to mark the end of term. Four weeks later, on 30th April, there is mention of a special express train from Edinburgh to St Andrews which 'conveys St Leonard's School Party arriving by ordinary trains from the South - 50 from Kings Cross, 35 from Manchester and 35 from Liverpool'. The Christmas 1931 travel arrangements for the school's pupils are reproduced in *Appendix Three* to this book and give a valuable insight into how the railway dealt with the complex administration of this traffic, something that would be inconceivable to the present-day companies. Former St Andrews station master, J.M. Bennett, recalled that, in the 1950s:

HATS OFF TO ST. LEONARDS SCHOOL!

In 1887 the chaps agreed that our Agnata's Cambridge performance packed more punch than any of theirs. She stood alone in the first division of the first class in Classics! A classic achievement indeed, and just the first of many subsequent triumphs for St. Leonards girls.

HONOUR TO AGNATA FRANCES RAMSAY !
(CAMBRIDGE, JUNE, 1887.)

IT'S ALWAYS LADIES FIRST AT ST. LEONARDS SCHOOL, ST. ANDREWS, FIFE. Telephone: 0334 72126.

When the Girls' school broke up at the end of each term there were widespread bookings and mountains of 'Luggage in Advance'. The morning of despatch saw two lorries with assisting porters running round the various 'houses' collecting the packages and taking them to the Goods station for loading to their respective vans. Everything was arranged in advance and very few snags cropped up. A lump sum in respect of gratuity was included in settlements and a fair proportion distributed to all concerned in the relative work.

The school protested at the closure of St Andrews station but even today many of its pupils make their homeward journeys by train from Leuchars, albeit using other transport to get there! Other schools whose pupils used the train included Lathallan School and New Park preparatory school and these also attracted similar traffic to St Leonards while some day pupils from Madras College used the train to travel to and from their homes in Crail and Leuchars.

Ordinary Trains

The basic pattern of ordinary passenger train services over the St Andrews Railway remained fairly constant from the time of the opening of the line until the latter part of the 19th century and consisted of short four- and six-wheeled wooden coaches in which all four classes of passengers were carried. All early trains operated from Leuchars (Old) to St Andrews only but after the opening of Leuchars Junction and the Tay Bridge line trains were extended to run from Cupar, Dundee and Tayport, and, with the opening of the North Fife line in 1909, a daily return service to Perth was also operated. Most services, however, on the St Andrews branch continued to operate only as Leuchars to St Andrews shuttles. By 1892 trains conveyed first and third class passengers only and were the subject of continual complaints by local passengers who thought that East Fife was the graveyard of ancient and unsatisfactory stock deemed too poor and decrepit to be used elsewhere; although it would have to be admitted that the North British was not generally noted for treating its passengers well. The opening of the Forth Bridge in 1890 brought through Glasgow and Edinburgh to Anstruther services, a handful of which were eventually extended to Crail and even to St Andrews (and, in one case, to Dundee) but the North British preferred its passengers for St Andrews to travel via Leuchars rather than by the coast line, although tickets were valid by either route.

The 20th century saw the widespread introduction of bogie carriages, eventually lit by electricity, but their state was often still the subject of controversy particularly in winter when train compartments were said to be cold and miserable. Foot warmers, in effect tin hot water bottles, were provided in first class compartments between Leuchars and St Andrews but these were largely ineffectual and none were provided between Anstruther and St Andrews; later advent of steam-heating of carriages must have been welcomed by the hardy Fifers and their winter visitors. Gradually newer stock appeared on other services but it was not until after World War II that ex-North British stock was augmented by corridor stock of Gresley, Thompson and, latterly, BR

* The Highland Show was originally peripatetic, only settling in its permanent home at Ingliston, near Edinburgh, in 1965

NBR class 'M' 4-4-0 No. 735 on a passenger train approaching Leuchars Junction from Leuchars (Old), September 1925. *Thomas Middlemass/W. Hennigan Collection*

NBR class 'M' 0-4-4T No. 355 on a St Andrews train in the bay platform at Dundee Tay Bridge station, *c*.1920. *NBRSG Collection*

NBR Holmes class 'P' 0-4-4T No. 589 on a Perth to St Andrews direct service passing (*on left*) St Andrews Links box and (*right*) the engine shed, 1921. *W. Hennigan Collection*

NBR class 'P' 0-4-4T No. 589 at Perth shed - this was the regular locomotive used on the Perth to St Andrews direct service via the North Fife line, August 1924.

Robert McCulloch/W. Hennigan Collection

NBR class 'M' 4-4-0 No. 735 on Edinburgh to Dundee via Crail train approaching St Andrews Links parallel to the old alignment of the A91 to Guardbridge, 1922. Note the patriotic BP roadside advertisement.   *S. Ellingworth/W. Hennigan Collection*

NBR Reid class 'K' 'Intermediate' 4-4-0 No. 885 awaiting departure at Leuchars Junction on an Edinburgh via Crail train, *c.*1920; note the headboard and smokebox wing-plates.
                    H. Stirling Everard/W. Hennigan Collection

Mark I origin, the latter being subject to special speed restrictions because of the length of the carriages and the extreme curvature of the line at Guardbridge station. The number of Leuchars to St Andrews trains had doubled by World War II and through trains ran from Dundee, mostly via St Fort but with a handful via Tayport and a few continued southwards to Edinburgh via Crail. One exotic train that operated over the branch for many years was the Fife Coast Express, a prestigious service that dated from 1912 and which provided a summer through service from Glasgow and Edinburgh to the Fife coastal resorts. In 1920 the train from Glasgow was extended from Crail over the Anstruther & St Andrews line to St Andrews, complete with a morning service of breakfast and an afternoon service of tea. A further extension, largely for operating purposes and without the restaurant car, occurred in 1923 when the train ran beyond St Andrews to Dundee. The service was suspended during the War and upon its resumption in 1949 it once again terminated at St Andrews; the Fife Coast Express ran for the last time in 1959.

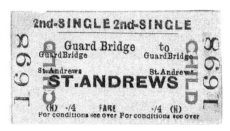

A Thompson 'B1' class 4-6-0 from St Margarets (with homemade headboard) on a special excursion for Leith Walk Schools of Edinburgh in the up platform at St Andrews on 29th March, 1960.   *Alex Coupar*

The advent of dieselisation brought a radical overhaul to parts of the timetable and for a time some St Andrews services operated through Dundee to Arbroath and Broughty Ferry for operational reasons and all regular St Andrews branch services shuttles from Dundee and Leuchars were run by dmus although a Dundee to Edinburgh via Crail service continued to be steam-hauled. For a period Glasgow services at the weekends ran from the former Caledonian Railway's Buchanan Street station rather than the North British Queen Street and this led to ex-LMS carriages appearing on these trains. When the Anstruther & St Andrews line was closed the diesel shuttles continued but no longer called at Guardbridge and although small alterations were made this timetable continued until the St Andrews branch was closed in 1969; the driving cars of the diesel multiple units had small first-class saloons but this class of traffic was little used in later years. Apart from a brief period in 1913 there were no through carriages to destinations south of Edinburgh or Glasgow via the coast line or south of Leuchars Junction by trains running via Guardbridge.

Extraordinary Trains

Special trains were run on frequent occasions and were a feature of the St Andrews Railway from its opening day - a selection of items contained in the North British 'Supplementary Advice of Special Trains' traffic notices in a typical three-month period in 1913 included, on 12th June a 'Master Bakers Guaranteed Excursion' from St Andrews to Dunfermline (Upper) and back from Dunfermline (Lower) was run at a fare of 2s. 6d. Nine days later an Alloa to St Andrews and back special for Carsebridge Distillery Employees Guaranteed Outing for 2s. 9d. was run. Other similar documents show a great

Ex-GNR Ivatt 'D1' 4-4-0 No. 3051 and ex-NBR Reid 'D34' 4-4-0 No. 9287 *Glen Gyle* on an up train approaching St Andrews from Leuchars, 1925. *NBRSG Collection*

'B1' No. 61278 on a charter train to Dundee waits at the down platform at St Andrews while a twin car Metro-Cammell dmu arrives on a Leuchars service in January 1965.
Mike MacDonald

variety of services and these include specials run on behalf of the employees of various companies right up until the closure of the line and the regular through trains run on behalf of local schools to Edinburgh and beyond, some of which were routed via Dunfermline Lower. Organizations which had special trains run on their behalf included youth associations such as the Scouts, Girl Guides, Sunday schools and the Boys Brigade; Freemasons and similar societies, bowling and other sporting clubs as well as ad hoc parties. The North British and its successors also ran special services from such diverse places as Glasgow, Hamilton, Ayr, Leven and Linlithgow often with reduced fares and these tended to operate on half-closing days, on public holidays (which, as now, varied from town to town) and during summer evenings. In the early years special trains from St Andrews were operated to such destinations as Aberdeen, Arbroath, Perth, Stirling, Ayr, Edinburgh, Glasgow (especially for the 1938 Empire Exhibition) and, occasionally, to English destinations such as Blackpool and even as far as London for national events. Schools trains, often using the facilities of the Scottish Region Television train, were run. Railway enthusiast's specials operated over the branch line on several occasions from 1960 onwards and these were, inevitably, well photographed.

Type '2' locomotive No. D5122 at Guardbridge on the 'Alcan' special, 10th September, 1967 - the only recorded occasion on which a passenger service was operated over the branch on a Sunday and (*below*) the same train at St Andrews.   *J.L. Stevenson (Both)*

NBR class 'K' 4-4-0 No. 886 on Leuchars Pilot working at St Andrews Links, *c.1922.*
H. Stirling Everard/W. Hennigan Collection

NBR Nos. 598 and 1421 double-head a northbound goods out of St Andrews Links in 1922.
H. Stirling Everard/W. Hennigan Collection

Chapter Twelve

Coal and Clay:
Freight Traffic on the St Andrews Railway

'St Andrews must be virtually unique for a town of 10,000 inhabitants, in having no industrial establishments that employ more than a handful of workers'
Third Statistical Account, Fife

The goods traffic on the St Andrews branch was of a varied nature and included coal (for both household and industrial uses), building materials, sand and gravel, fish and shellfish and a plethora of sundry goods such as parcels, golf clubs, stock for local shops, beer, wine and spirits and almost every other variety of miscellaneous traffic that comes to mind. The biggest single consignee and consignor of goods for many years was the Guardbridge Paper Mill and this traffic is dealt with separately in the following chapter. In this chapter agricultural, fish and coal traffic is dealt with first of all, followed by a station-by-station account of each station or siding running southwards from Leuchars, with the exception of Seggie, and concluding with a survey of the changing pattern of goods services between Leuchars and Crail over the years.

Fish, Chips and Sugar Beet

Although there were in the early days of the railway a number of fishing vessels whose home harbours were at Guardbridge and St Andrews, they generated little in the way of railborne fish traffic. The reason for such small numbers of boats had much to do with the inhospitable nature of the coastline here with rough seas and the sand bar at the mouth of the Eden presenting hazards to even the most experienced of seamen. In view of the importance of outgoing fish traffic on the southern part of the Fife Coast line, it is perhaps ironic that the only fish handled in any quantities at St Andrews goods yard was a relatively small amount of inward traffic from the ports of Montrose and Arbroath. When it came to shellfish, some of the annual harvest gathered in the estuary of the Eden off Tentsmuir did travel by rail from Guardbridge, but the vast majority of this once-substantial trade was taken by sea to markets in the North of Scotland.

Agricultural traffic was two-way and included livestock and, more importantly, arable goods and general agricultural requisites. The principal crops handled were potatoes and sugar beet. The potato traffic was conveyed in unventilated vans and was mainly bound for East Anglia whereas the beet traffic, conveyed in open wagons, were destined for the sugar beet factory in Cupar; both sources of traffic survived until the closure of the branch for general goods traffic.

Traders wagon owned by St Andrews coal merchants, Benzie, and built by Hurst Nelson & Co.
HMRS Collection

An example of a 10 ton sprung-buffered wagon built by R.Y. Pickering of Wishaw for A. Benzie & Son. The plate reads 'Return to Blairadam Colliery', a West Fife pit owned by the Blairadam Colliery Co. *HMRS Collection*

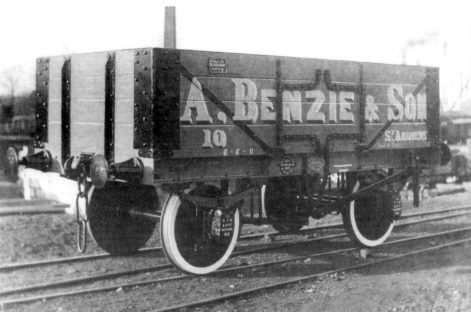

Coal and yet more Coal

All of the goods stations and sidings on the line handled coal in greater or lesser quantities depending largely on whether or not the station served a sizeable community or not and whether there were any industrial concerns locally. The quietest stations in this respect were, unsurprisingly, the four stations between Crail and St Andrews and much of the coal handled was for domestic or agricultural use. Coal fires, cooking ranges and hot water systems (where found) all relied on this fuel and coal was brought from the Tyne and West of Scotland pits in the early days until it was supplemented and then largely supplanted by rail-borne coal from the Fife Coal Company, the Wemyss estates and other collieries closer at hand. The town of St Andrews was a major user of coal with the local schools, university, hotels and boarding houses all having a great need for coal and on a annual basis some 2,000 to 3,000 full wagons of coal were unloaded at the goods station there. Most coal was handled by local coal merchants, those in St Andrews who had stances at the Links station included Brown & Sons, Benzie & Son, Brand and Rutherford and Grubb and the yard was, accordingly, an important point of distribution of coal by road to the surrounding area.

Some of these merchants had their own private owner wagons* and those known to the authors to have had such wagons included, in St Andrews, A. Benzie & Son and Brown & Sons. Benzie had a total of five private owner wagons, all of which were operated out of St Andrews Links goods yard. The wagons bore the numbers 6 to 10, suggesting that they may have been replacements for an earlier fleet. Four of the wagons were built by Hurst Nelson of Motherwell and were of 8 ton capacity with solid buffers; their NBR register plate numbers were 4680, 4681, 4682 and 6124 and these were fleet numbers 6 to 9 and were placed on the line on 24th March, 1900. The remaining wagon was a 10 ton example built by R.Y. Pickering of Wishaw with sprung buffers and was register plate number 8922 - this was fleet number 10 and was built, according to the Pickering records, on 14th June, 1897.The livery used for all of these wagons was dark blue for the body with white lettering shaded black. Other St Andrews traders who registered with the North British to operate railway wagons were Cunningham, William Fairfoul and James Rutherford. Private owner coal wagons which were frequently seen on the Leuchars to Anstruther section included Fife Coal Company, Wemyss or other colliery-based wagons from outwith the area; the one exception was the Guard Bridge Paper Company's wagons which are dealt with separately.

Apart from the paper mill,† the main local industrial user of coal was the gas company in St Andrews. The St Andrews gas works, started up in 1835 and owned by the St Andrews Gas Light Company, was situated near to the harbour, and initially most of the coal required was brought by sea. In the late 19th century coal was brought by rail to the Links goods yard and transported

---

* Such wagons, known as Traders or Private Owner wagons because they were not owned by the railway companies themselves, were carried by them from consignor to consignee (usually coal pits to coal merchants) at pre-determined rates.

† The traffic from and to the Guardbridge mill, its private owner wagons and the mill's internal railway system are all dealt with in *Chapter Thirteen*.

BROWN & SONS,

Coal, Coke and Firewood Merchants, and Carting Contractors,

164, SOUTH STREET,

Telephone 177.   ST. ANDREWS.

Agents for all the principal Collieries.

Largest Retailers of Coal in the District.

Wagon loads delivered to any Station.

Shipping and Emigration Agents.

One of the Brown & Sons of St Andrews fleet of wagons built by the Motherwell Wagon Company.   *David Lyle Collection*

Rutherford Son & Grubb
(ALEXANDER GREIG)
Coal Merchants and Colliery Agents
109 MARKET STREET, ST. ANDREWS
Household, Steam, and Anthracite Fuels
always in stock

TELEPHONE
No. 18

CARTING CONTRACTORS — MOTOR HAULAGE
Carrying between St. Andrews and Dundee
OFFICE:
109 Market Street, St. Andrews

Shunting at Leuchars in the early 1920s - the first wagon has Great Central and North Eastern tarpaulins covering its load while the trader's wagon labelled 'J.N. & Co' belongs to the firm of James Nimmo & Co. Ltd, coalmasters who operated pits in the Falkirk area of Stirlingshire.
David Edwards/W. Hennigan Collection

NBR 'C' class 0-6-0 goods locomotive No. 776 on the branch passenger service at Leuchars, 1922.
S. Ellingworth/W. Hennigan Collection

by carts supplied by the local firm of Radleigh & Brown. From 1901 coal was again brought in by ship and then horse cart, the railway yard being too congested to deal properly with this traffic but this was short-lived and from 1920 onwards motor lorries replaced the horse. An interesting situation arose in the 1930s when the LNER changed the St Andrews passenger station illumination over from using coal-gas purchased from the local gas works to the relatively new illuminant of electricity. The manager of the gas works, annoyed by what he considered to be a deliberate slight, then arranged to have a consignment of coal delivered by sea and this was done by a vessel called the *Lochinver*. The last steamship to use the harbour for commercial purposes was the SS *Locksley* which, in 1936, delivered 120 tons of coal for the gasworks. Nationalised after the war, the St Andrews gas works were closed down in 1962, by which time all deliveries to it were by road.

Leuchars

The major freight handled at Leuchars (Old) was, in earlier years, of an agricultural nature and consisted mainly of barley, wheat, potatoes and livestock with linen and other woven goods handled. Over time, however, the yard became one of the busiest in the area and the limited siding space and high quantity of goods handled led to serious congestion which was only partially alleviated by a partial remodelling in 1927. At that time a survey of lorries and carts bringing goods into the yard for dispatch by rail showed that potatoes, grain, straw, wood and rye, together with livestock and coal were all being handled. In addition agricultural machinery, cattle feed, fertilisers and other similar products reflecting the largely rural hinterland served by the station were also to be found in large measure. The station served as a convenient railhead over a considerable area and those farmers and traders with motor lorries often found it more convenient to take or collect their goods from here rather than to use smaller yards such as Guardbridge or Mount Melville where goods were often delayed in awaiting onward transmission or delivery by the local train. Leuchars also handled traffic destined for the nearby RAF station. This traffic principally consisted of building materials in the early years and immediately prior to World War II (cement, bricks, timber, aggregates and steel), aviation fuel (in rail tank wagons), spare parts for aircraft, miscellaneous materials and coal and coke for the central boiler house which served the whole of the complex. In addition coal was also supplied to the local gasworks situated immediately to the north-east of the level crossing gates at the station. In contrast, Leuchars Junction handled only newspapers, parcels, mail and other small items sent by passenger train, which traffic was not dealt with at Leuchars (Old). The goods yard at Leuchars (Old) remained open until 1967 when the line leading to it was finally abandoned.

<u>LEUCHARS SHUNT ENGINE.</u>

<u>No. B.8⁰</u>

<u>Leuchars Pilot.</u>

<u>Class 2 F. (J.36) Engine.</u>

SX.   4-50am to 11- 0am
SX.   1-35pm to 7-40pm

<u>Locomen.</u>	On. a.m.	Off. a.m.
1st Shift	3-40	11-40
2nd Shift	12-25pm	8-25pm

<u>Guards.</u>		
1st Shift	4- 0am	12 Noon
2nd Shift	12-25pm	8-25pm
3rd Shift	3- 0pm	11- 0pm

	S.X. arr. a.m.	S.X. dep. a.m.
Dundee E.S.		4-30
Leuchars	4-50	5-40
Guardbridge	5-50	6- 5
St. Andrews	6-25	7-10
Leuchars	7-20	

Shunt and assist as required.
Make trips to Wormit, St. Fort and
Sand Siding as required.

Leuchars		9-55
Guardbridge	10- 5	10-35
Leuchars	10-45	11- 0 LE.
Dundee E.S.	11-20	1-15pm LE.
Leuchars	1-35pm	3-10
St. Andrews	3-25	5-15
Guardbridge	5-23	5-50
Leuchars	6- 0	

Shunt as required.

Leuchars		7-40LE.
Dundee E.S.	8- 0	

BR pilot and trip working arrangements, 1962.

Guardbridge

The goods yard here handled domestic coal and a small amount of agricultural produce and, in the early days, tiles and other clay products made by the several nearby brick works. Another regular source of revenue were the mussel beds of the Eden estuary and in the mussel season several wagonloads of mussels were dispatched each week from Guardbridge. The main traffic, however, was in connection with the single largest customer on the whole of the East Fife network, namely the Guardbridge paper mill but the small public goods yard at this station handled a fair variety of other goods including, when the new road crossing over the Eden was being built in the late 1930s, a great quantity of cement and concrete and some 145 tons of steel to be used as reinforcements for the bridge. Goods receipts from the yard and Seggie siding were aggregated and produced the highest freight figures for any station on the line, far outstripping not only its nearest rival, St Andrews but the combined total of all of the goods depots from St Andrews to Anstruther. The public goods yard was closed on 20th June, 1966, the same day as St Andrews yard was closed; thereafter Seggie siding was served by occasional trip workings from Leuchars until it was closed along with the rest of the St Andrews branch on 6th January, 1969. There were also, at differing times, private sidings serving Edenside brickworks and the Seafield tile and pottery works and these are more fully dealt with in *Chapter Sixteen*. Although there was at one time a Shell oil depot adjacent to Guardbridge station, this was not rail-served but supplied by road deliveries from Cupar.

St Andrews

Goods traffic at St Andrews was handled at the former passenger station at the Links and the main inward traffic consisted of coal. Other goods which arrived by rail included general building materials and a wide variety of other items such as wood for the manufacture of golf clubs, wines and spirits, tobacco, newspapers, yeast, flour, butter (with a regular supply from Aylesbury), sausages and other foodstuffs including fish (from Aberdeen and Montrose) for local traders and hotels. Wilson & Company, who occupied the Argyle Brewery, were a well-known local firm of manufacturers of aerated water who imported by rail both the bottles and the ingredients for their products; in addition they bottled Aitchison's Edinburgh beers and Tennent's lager from the Wellpark Brewery in Glasgow and accordingly these beverages were brought in bulk by train from those cities. There was also a considerable parcels traffic and in British Railways days this was delivered locally by a three-wheeled Scammell Scarab tractor and trailer unit which replaced the earlier horse-drawn floats; at the beginning and end of the University and St Leonards school terms a great volume of trunks and other luggage was handled at the Links station and this had to be collected from boarding houses and halls of residence. Outwards freight traffic included agricultural produce from the local area (mainly potatoes and grain) and occasional traffic in tar from the gasworks.

NBR Holmes 'C' class 0-6-0 No. 667 leaving the north end of St Andrews with a mixed array of stock on the 'Coast Goods' from Thornton to the Links, *c.*1920.

S. Ellingworth/W. Hennigan Collection

Holmes class 'C' 0-6-0 No. 794 passing St Andrews locomotive shed with a train of horse boxes, *c.*1920.   *W. Hennigan Collection*

St Andrews Links from the signal box with the shed on the left, the gables of the station master's house in the middle and the goods shed towards the right, 3rd November, 1958.

J.L. Stevenson

St Andrews slowing (*left to right*) the goods shed, engine shed, lines of coal wagons, the infamous 'black sheds' known to golfers and the station master's house, his car and greenhouse, 22nd August, 1956.

A.G. Ellis

NBR 'P' class No. 1325 with a train of cattle wagons at St Andrews Links, 1922.
H. Stirling Everard/W. Hennigan Collection

LNER 'J35' class 0-6-0 No. 9038 (ex-NBR 'B' class) on a train of empty cattle wagons in Leuchars Junction sidings; the third wagon has been washed down with lime, *c.*1924.
H. Stirling Everard/W. Hennigan Collection

There was also a traffic in hides and pelts from the local slaughterhouse; these were bound for a tannery in Dundee. However in the words of the *Third Statistical Account*:

> St Andrews must be virtually unique for a town of 10,000 inhabitants, in having no industrial establishments that employs more than a handful of workers - and very few, even of these.

Other miscellaneous traffic included motor fuel prior to World War I, petrol for cars was received at St Andrews goods yard in large tins, eight to a wooden crate there being, of course, no roadside filling stations then. The petrol mainly came from a London firm, Carless Caple and Leonard but, motoring then being only for the moneyed classes, the quantities received were modest. A highly unusual traffic was in connection with the occasional Bertram Mills' circuses held on the West Sands when special trains were run, the circus party together with all their props and animals being detrained at the goods station; the sight of the elephants alighting was, apparently, a memorable one!

Some traffic was also generated by the town gas and electricity works. The town's electricity generating station was located at Largo Road and was owned by a London company, the Electricity Supply Corporation Ltd.* Coal-fired, it was a small concern with a miniscule generating capacity in 1925/6 of some 290 kilowatts and supplied only direct current to local homes. Being inconveniently situated for the railway there was no private siding and instead coal was delivered via the goods yard and carted by road to the power station. There was also an auxiliary diesel-powered generator and diesel fuel for this was delivered by rail tanker to the goods yard and then discharged into a road tanker owned by Brown & Sons; from here it was taken to the power station. Once the national grid was established, St Andrews power station was closed and the town was supplied via the grid instead.

By 1960 the yard was still relatively busy and was open from 8 am to 5 pm. Outwards traffic was concentrated in the winter and consisted of sugar beet and potatoes as well as sundries in small lots which mainly consisted of beer kegs being returned to the brewers and empty chemical drums being returned by the Science Department laboratories of the University to the suppliers for re-use. Inwards traffic included coal for Thomas Muir, Sons & Patton, a Dundee firm who had by this time a depot at the goods station and a shop in Market Street and who supplied fuel for domestic purposes as well as schools, the hospital and the University; a second local coal merchant, Websters, also received coal by rail. Fruit and vegetables were sent to St Andrews goods station from the Glasgow Fruit Market for Patterson Brothers, who dealt with the retail trade, and William Smith Leslie, who dealt with hotels and commercial institutions. Other imports included 'Ever Ready' batteries which were collected daily by the local agent, miscellaneous traffic for the Woolworths shop in the town, mail order goods from Lancashire, ham-and-egg pies from Wiltshire, china and dishes for Piries, china merchants in the town, lemonade and cider in bottles and fruit syrup in casks and drums for Wilson Brothers, beer in casks from Scottish Brewers Ltd bound for local hotels, homing pigeons in wicker baskets

---

* Other power stations owned by this company included Dalkeith, Dollar, Jedburgh and Melrose in Scotland and Totnes and Chelmsford in England.

and miscellaneous other goods for the local shops and University. Occasionally Irish cattle were received for the local slaughterhouse and beet pulp was sent from the Cupar factory to a local landowner, Mr Cheape of Strathtyrum, to be used as cattlefood. No fuel oil or petrol, fertilisers or farm machinery came by rail at this time, the nearest rail-served oil depot being at Cupar. Fish was not a major traffic although on occasions fish was delivered by passenger train at the New station. On occasions tanks and other military vehicles were taken by rail on flat wagons to the summer camp of the University Officers' Training Corps. Goods facilities at St Andrews Links were finally withdrawn on 20th June, 1966, the same day as at Guardbridge and thereafter the only goods traffic on the line was related to the paper mill.

Goods Trains

The St Andrews Railway trains were initially mixed and called at the sidings *en route* from Leuchars to St Andrews. By 1883 there were still six mixed trains a day on the branch although only one goods-only service called at Seggie, Brickworks and Seafield sidings while another ran only as far as Seggie Siding and Guardbridge - the working timetable nevertheless contained the enigmatic entry 'the trains on the St Andrews branch will be available for Goods and Passenger traffic, but the former will be wrought by any particular Train, providing time can be kept'. The branch locomotives were responsible for carrying out shunting operations at Leuchars and St Andrews. The St Andrews to Leuchars section was served by a number of short workings, most of them carried out by the Leuchars No. 2 Pilot engine which began its duties by leaving Dundee shed at 4 am and, on three separate shift workings, carrying out shunting of goods and passenger vehicles at Leuchars, Seggie and St Andrews before finally returning to Dundee early the following morning. By 1962 goods services over the branch were operated by the Leuchars No. 1 pilot, a 'J36' which left Dundee Tay Bridge shed as a light engine at 3.30 am, arriving at Leuchars Junction at 3.50. The locomotive then shunted wagons at Leuchars (Old) and then set out for Guardbridge and St Andrews at 5.05, working the goods yards at Guardbridge and St Andrews and the Seggie siding, returning light engine to Leuchars at 7.02. The engine then shunted and worked the St Fort sand sidings on the main line 'as required' before returning making two morning trips to Guardbridge, with a trip to Dairise in between as required. There was further shunting at Leuchars and on Saturdays the locomotive then returned to Dundee at 5 pm; on weekday afternoons there was a further trip working over the branch serving both St Andrews (where the locomotive shunted between 3.22 and 5.12 pm) and Guardbridge before returning to Dundee at 9.50 pm. On weekdays there were three shifts of locomen and guards detailed to work the pilot workings and each crew travelled between Dundee and Leuchars by passenger train with the exception of the first outward and last inward working to Dundee which was run light engine with its crew. When St Andrews and Guardbridge were closed to goods, the Seggie siding traffic was worked as required by a Dundee pilot engine.

Chapter Thirteen

Rags and Reams:
The Chronicles of Seggie Siding

*'Off the St Andrews Railway is a siding which
goes into the works - a great advantage'*

Fifeshire Journal

In the Beginning

As time progressed the principal source of goods traffic on the St Andrews branch was the Guardbridge paper mill, served by the adjacent Seggie Siding, and this traffic remained until the end of the line, being the last freight to be carried south from Leuchars. Much of the early history of the St Andrews Railway Company and the Seggie Siding has already been recounted in Chapter Four of this book; this chapter is concerned with the history of the most northerly paper mill in Fife and its railway traffic.

The first mention of Seggie Siding was as far back as 1853 when it was opened to serve Robert Haig's Seggie Distillery but this business was short-lived and by 1860 the distillery had closed and the siding was lifted shortly thereafter. In 1867 Seggie Siding was re-laid when Haig's firm started to use the old distillery buildings as a maltings and brewery but, once again, the business failed to prosper and Seggie Siding found itself without traffic. The turning point, however, came soon and the reason for this was paper.

Traditionally paper had been manufactured mainly from rags which essentially consisted of off-cuts and end of rolls of materials and unused threads from mills and factories and from old household linen and discarded linen and cotton clothing, often obtained through the offices of the 'rag and bone' men in industrial cities. This material required to be sorted, stripped of extraneous items such as buttons and fastenings, and then cut up by hand into rags which could then be bleached and processed into paper and not only was this an extremely labour-intensive task, albeit one carried on by lowly-paid women, but the supply of material was also variable and the quantity of suitable rags that could be obtained did not always keep up with demand. During the 1860s both wood pulp and, importantly, esparto grass began to supplant rags and become the major factors in the rapid increase of the manufacture of paper. Then, in 1870, James Chalmers, a Tayport schoolmaster, in partnership with two of the sons of John Haig of Cameron Bridge, formed the firm of Chalmers & Company with the aim of setting up a wood-pulping works on land immediately adjacent to the abandoned Seggie Distillery. They aimed to meet the growing demand for paper fuelled by the introduction of compulsory primary school education in Britain and the growing literacy rates and by the abolition of the duties on newspapers and periodicals. The business of Chalmers & Co did not, however, prosper and the site was later advertised for sale with the added incentive that 'Seggie is situated on an arm of the ocean

Guardbridge mill from the east side of the estuary at low tide.

Guard Bridge Paper Mill Collection

Seggie Siding and the paper mill; note the shunting horse at work and the Guard Bridge Paper Company wagons in the foreground.   *Guard Bridge Paper Mill Collection*

which will carry off any quantity of refuse, a most important qualification in these days of River Purification'. Whether the works ever produced any wood pulp is debatable but, since the 1871 Census taken in April of that year lists 10 workmen engaged in building the new works and living temporarily in the village, the working life of the works cannot have been very long.

The Guard Bridge Paper Company

In April 1873 the Articles of Association of the Guard Bridge Paper Company were signed and the new company, whose £30,000 worth of share capital was owned by members of the Haig family and others, took possession of part of the site of the old Seggie Distillery including the existing pulp mill on the 15th of the following month. The main reason for the setting up of the paper mill was to make use of the Seggie site, for it had a number of great advantages like its proximity to a good supply of fresh water from the Motray burn, a proximity to the Fife coal fields, ready access to the ports of Tayport and Leven (and later Methil) and, perhaps most importantly of all, good rail access through Seggie Siding. The first cargo of Norwegian timber was imported through Tayport dock and taken to the mill by rail via the St Andrews branch in November 1873. By this time James Weir of the Strathendry Mills at Leslie was busy negotiating the purchase for the company of the necessary machinery and esparto preparation plant. In 1874 John Galloway, a former St Andrews bank clerk, was appointed as manager of the new mill and much of its future development and prosperity was due to his efforts.

In 1875 the mill made a profit of some £88 and the *Fifeshire Journal* of 22nd July of that year commented that:

> The duster, rag-cutter, water pumps &c. are driven by an old steam-engine which was there when the place was a distillery. The kinds of paper manufactured are fine printings and news paper, of which upwards of twenty tons are turned out weekly. Off the St Andrews Railway is a siding which goes into the works - a great advantage - and the loading goes on under a shed close to the finishing room. The number of hands employed, both male and female, is about one hundred, double the number employed when it was a pulp work ... The employees, for the most part, reside in the contiguous village of Leuchars, owing to the want of dwelling houses at Guardbridge; but a number of houses are in the course of building, which, besides giving a look of prosperity to the village, will add greatly to the comfort of the workers, who must be put to considerable inconvenience at present, more especially in wet weather.

The paper mill flourished and as production increased so did the need for raw materials brought in by rail and processed in the factory. By 1888 three paper-making machines were in use at the mill and about 125 tons of paper were being turned out every week while the products of the mill (principally fine printing, drawing, music, plate and chart, envelope and tinted papers and pulp boards) were also dispatched by rail via the busy Seggie Siding . By 1903 the traffic handled by rail amounted annually to some 70,000 tons, making the mill the single largest goods customer on the St Andrews branch. As the mill

Guardbridge paper mill from the air, 1968. Note the St Andrews branch and Seggie siding in the foreground and the Motray Burn and Eden estuary in the background. *W. McLeod Collection*

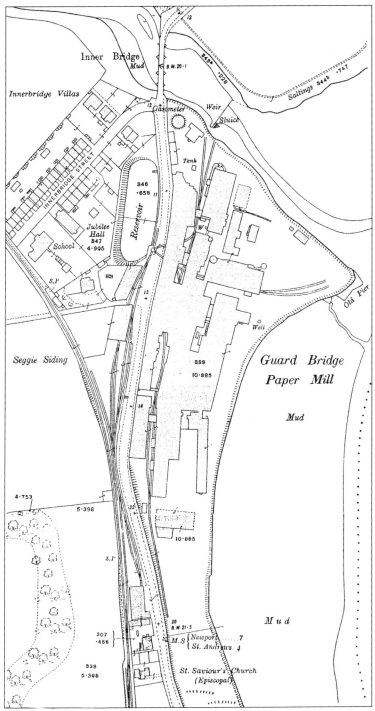

Seggie Siding and the Guardbridge paper mill, 1914.

Reproduced from the 1914, 25 in. Ordnance Survey Map

expanded, so did the village and good-quality housing was built at Inner Bridge Street and River Terrace and elsewhere to house the mill workers in what was to become very much a single-employer settlement.

By the turn of the century, the future of the Guardbridge papermill seemed to be secure and production continued unabated. The mill now specialised in those types of paper which it was felt there was a ready market for and up to 1914 trade was brisk. World War I resulted in the mill being kept short of raw materials and profits would have collapsed had it not been for the fact that the company won a contract to produce shell cases and parts for artillery pieces. The 1920s initially brought prosperity but in the economic slump that followed Guardbridge mill was lucky enough to ride out the storm and survive.

Steam Power

The manufacture of paper requires the use of large quantities of energy in the form of steam and heat and for most of the period during which the mill was rail served this energy came from the burning of coal; as a rough guide at the turn of the century it required the energy from four tons of coal to produce one ton of paper. Coal was therefore the biggest single import by rail and it came from a variety of sources, mainly in West Fife and also from the Wemyss pits of Michael, Wellesley, Rosie, Muiredge and Lochhead. Originally most of this coal was seaborne and unloaded at the railway pier adjacent to the works but by the end of the century this was mainly arriving by rail, the piers going out of use and gradually disappearing as the reclamation of the shores adjacent to the piers progressed. In the 1920s the coal was sourced from the West Fife colleries including the Jenny Gray Pit at Lochgelly (owned by the Lochgelly Iron & Coal Company), the Mary Pit at Lochore (owned by the Fife Coal Company) and the Wemyss colleries, this coming via their Denbeath washer.

All incoming coal by rail was deposited at Seggie Siding by the North British and its successors and the wagons which were left there were then taken across the Guardbridge to Leuchars main road level crossing and into the mill on a private line which penetrated and reached all parts of the site. By the 1950s coal was initially taken in the wagons in which it was delivered and deposited in the mill yard where it was then unloaded using a self-propelled Newton-Chambers grab crane and the resulting stock piles of coal were then taken by the same self-propelled crane and placed into internal user wagons which were then drawn to the entrance to the boiler house. From here wagons were hauled by means of electric capstans and wire hawsers up to the point under which an internal Strachan and Henshaw grab crane ran. This crane scooped up the contents of each wagon in turn and placed it into an overhead coal bunker which then gravity-fed the coal into the boilers. The internal railway layout within the mill yard also allowed full main line wagons to be taken directly to the mill boiler house coal lye to be unloaded. The mill yard was not the only place where coal was stored and there were subsidiary stores at the south end of the works and by the Motray Water. Coal consumption increased along with productivity and at the turn of the century there were 13 Lancashire Boilers powering the 18 steam engines driving the mills. With the advent of locomotive haulage on the internal railway system, the Lancashire Boilers were hand-fired from coal directly shovelled in through the hatches immediately alongside the tracks.

From the 1880s onwards the mill generated its own electricity and the works had steam engines with a total steampower of 1,000 hp, meeting their own requirement for electricity. Before World War I the whole system had been radically overhauled when an electric generating station powered by steam turbines was brought in use. The small weekend load for minimal mill lighting and village requirements was provided by a Howden high-speed engine driven generator until, after World War II, it was supplanted by a diesel engine. The mill also had a small gas works adjacent to its north-west corner and, until 1934, this was equipped with an Ashworth & Parker steam engine.

By the 1950s the mill's main steam boiler plant was equipped with three coal-fired mechanically-stoked water tube boilers built by John Thomson Ltd of Wolverhampton. Each of these huge boilers was rated as being capable of producing up to 55,000 lb. of steam per hour at a pressure of 450 lb./sq. in. and at a temperature of 775 degrees Fahrenheit superheat. These boilers burned a cheap type of coal called washed duff and coal consumption was, in 1960, about 35,000 tons per annum. The steam produced was passed through the turbines in the mill's electrical power station providing the electrical power required for the mill. The power station had an installed capacity of 8.5 megawatts although the mill's normal demand for electricity did not exceed 5 megawatts. During the 1950s the power station had two steam turbines: a British Thomson-Houston set and an older Metropolitan-Vickers set both of which were pass-out condensing types. The pass-out steam from the turbines sufficed for the steam needs of the various processes in the mill.

The mill was wholly dependent on its own electric power generation and did not import power from the national grid. In addition to the mill's own internal needs the power station also supplied electricity for streetlights in Guardbridge and power and lighting for the 200 or so houses in which the mill's employees lived. To put it into context, the mill's power station generated sufficient electricity to suffice for the needs of a small town and in the early 1960s it was reckoned that the mill produced about three times as much electricity as was required by the town of St Andrews.

A Mixed Bag

Esparto grass, which came from Spain but more often from North African countries, particularly Algeria and Morocco and exported via the port of Oran, was an important ingredient of the type of paper produced at Guardbridge and it was unloaded at the railway docks at Tayport and, latterly, at Methil. Here it was placed in open railway wagons with short sides which were then sheeted and worked in block trains to Seggie Siding, 9,000 tons alone being carried in this manner in 1894. A horse then drew the wagons into the grass storage shed and the esparto bales were unloaded by travelling overhead Morris-built cranes of the Telfer type to allow every part of the storage shed to be covered. The sheds could hold between 4,000 and 5,000 tons of grass. As an illustration, between June and December 1881 some 2,635 tons of esparto grass was imported by the mill and this accounted for nearly 96 per cent of the fibre requirements of the mill, the balance being made up of 2.5 per cent rags and 1.8 per cent wood pulp. By 1923, the mill was using some 20,000 tons of esparto grass annually but in later years the mill reduced its dependence on esparto grass, replacing it with wood pulp which by 1954-5 amounted to 17,500 tons of esparto (84.3 per cent of the total) to 3,240 tons of wood pulp (15.2 per cent). After this the percentage of the two materials used moved closer together because wood pulp was both a cheaper ingredient and less labour-intensive while the use of rags, essential for certain high quality rag papers, formed only a minute proportion of the total. The rags were by then no longer derived from discarded clothing but were principally cotton linters, i.e. waste offcuts of clothing or other fabric manufacturing processes. Wood pulp was imported from Scandinavia and was latterly received at Methil docks (and, on occasion at Grangemouth) where it was placed into short-sided open wagons covered with waterproof tarpaulins and worked to the mill.

Other items imported by rail included starch, which came in hessian sacks loaded into vans, size, rosin and various dyes. Lime was needed to make the bleaching powder required to whiten the paper and originally this came from Cults Lime Works, connected to the North British main line via a steeply-graded branch line which reached the main line between Ladybank and Springfield stations. The lime was delivered in sacks. Also used was soda ash, supplied in bags and manufactured by Imperial Chemical Industries, and chlorine, made by the same company and delivered in railway tank wagons - these were normally four-wheeled with a white-painted tank barrel surmounted by yellow-painted domes. As a war-time precaution taken to protect the chlorine tankers from aerial attack, a small brick and concrete shed was built across the headshunt at Seggie Siding. China clay, used to make coated papers, came by rail from the Cornish-based company of English China Clays Ltd. At one time china clay was packed into bags and loaded onto railway wagons which were worked directly to Seggie Siding.

The End of the Roll

By the 1950s the mill had a workforce of around 620 and had five paper-making machines. The factory occupied 24 acres of ground and there was about 12 million cubic feet of space occupied by buildings. In the early part of that decade traffic by rail was still such that anything between 75 and 100 full wagons per week were being dealt with at the siding, including about 10 wagons of coal a day but changes were in the air. Outward traffic from the mill consisted of finished paper which was dispatched to customers in covered railway vans but after the 1955 railway strike the company acquired five long-distance lorries and these were increasingly used to transport the paper and also to bring in certain of the raw materials. Coal was still rail-borne but, following the contemporary fashion, the coal-fired boilers were all converted to burn heavy fuel oil between 1967 and 1969, the fuel oil being wholly delivered in road tankers. Seggie Siding continued to be used on an intermittent basis after 1967 and there was still some occasional outward traffic handled by rail such as paper consignments to HM Stationery Office. The last rail traffic at the siding was in the latter half of December 1968 and Seggie Siding was officially closed along with the rest of the St Andrews branch line on 6th January, 1969.

After the withdrawal of rail services to the mill, the china clay used was still taken by rail from Cornwall but only as far as Mossend yard in Lanarkshire; from there it was transhipped to lorries for the cross-country journey to Guardbridge. So heavy and environmentally unfriendly was this road traffic deemed to be in a more ecologically minded age that, in the early 1990s, a proposal was made to provide a new siding at Leuchars station. The clay would then only be required to be taken the short distance from there to the mill by lorry but the paper company could not agree terms with British Rail and the proposal came to naught. The Guardbridge paper mill is still very much in existence and continues as a major local employer. At the time of writing the mill is owned by Curtis Fine Papers, an independent Scottish company, and it produces annually about 35,000 tons of paper.

'B1' No. 61180 on a weedkiller train passing Seggie Siding on 17th April, 1967 - note the yellow-painted chlorine tank wagon and the 16 ton steel mineral wagons in the siding.
Mike Jodeluk

'Guard Bridge Paper Coy. Limited, No. 1' - the battery locomotive in its original livery with its driver and engineers in the 1930s. *Mrs Janice Morton Collection*

No. 1 outside the mill in the mid-1950s. *Sandy Murdoch/The Transport Treasury*

The Battery Locomotive

Until 1925 the mill, in common with many similarly sized industrial concerns, used horses to pull all wagons on its standard gauge internal railway system and this was found to be both economical and an avoidance of the fire risks which a conventional steam locomotive might produce. In that year, however, it was felt that, with increasing loads and the extent of the damage done to the hooves of the horses by spillages of the lime used in the mill, the time had come to acquire a locomotive to replace them. Accordingly a four-wheeled battery electric shunting locomotive was acquired from the English Electric Company at a cost of £2,540 and this carried out the work required of it satisfactorily for the next 45 years. Built at the Dick, Kerr Works, Preston, in 1924 this was a No. 3 Standard locomotive (Works No. 684) and had a wheelbase of 7 feet and a tractive effort of some 4,200 lb. Having an overall length of 19 ft 1¼ in., the locomotive weighed 20 tons in working order. Since paper mills were full of highly inflammable materials conventional steam locomotives which produced sparks and hot gasses could not be used and some mills had, by then, already solved the problem by using 'fireless' locomotives, which had no firebox or chimney and which worked by means of being filled with high-pressure steam obtained from the mill's boiler house. Since the mill's high pressure steam was all fed directly into the steam turbines in the power station and the exhaust or pass-out from these turbines was low pressure steam at about 20-25 lb./sq. in. there was no ready source of high-pressure steam for a fireless locomotive. Accordingly the only real alternative was a battery one, an ideal choice given the significant generating capacity provided by the mill's own electric power station. The locomotive resembled in appearance the Fairfields shipyard engine

The Guard Bridge Paper Company's sole English Electric battery locomotive shunting at Seggie Siding - note the BR steel-bodied mineral wagons in the background. *George Bett*

FOR SALE

A standard gauge Battery Electric Shunting Locomotive (Type No. 3 standard), built 1925 by English Electric Co. Ltd., Dick Kerr Works, Preston. This is a twin axle locomotive with a tractive effort of 4,200 lb. Weight in working 20 tons, wheel base 7 ft., length 19 ft. $1\frac{1}{4}$ in.

Offers should be sent to:

THE GUARD BRIDGE PAPER CO. LTD.
GUARD BRIDGE
FIFE, SCOTLAND

No. 1 looks for a new owner, 1971 – alas! None was forthcoming and the locomotive was subsequently scrapped.

Authors' Collection

now preserved at the Bo'ness & Kinneil Railway and the two long-gone battery-electric locomotives used at Aberdeen power station. Originally bearing the legend 'Guard Bridge Paper Coy. Limited, No. 1', the locomotive was latterly painted in a light green colour with no number or other markings.

Details survive of this engine's acceptance tests, carried out at the mill on 29th May, 1925. These showed that, in a 7½ hour working period, the engine hauled 1,098 tons (excluding its own weight), travelled a total distance of 7.8 miles, and consumed electric power of approximately 60 kilowatts. The batteries at the start of the test showed a specific gravity of 1.280 and at the end of the day a specific gravity of 1.230.

After a day's use, the mill locomotive required to have its batteries recharged overnight and was therefore 'hooked up' to the battery charging apparatus from 5 pm until 6 am the following morning, there being no internal railway traffic during the night. The wheel sets on this locomotive required to be re-profiled and turned at intervals and as the mill did not have the specialised apparatus to carry this out (it would have needed a large wheel lathe), the wheel sets were sent during the 1960s by rail to the National Coal Board's Fife District Central Workshops at Cowdenbeath as this establishment had the machine tools and expertise to carry this out. The regular driver of the mill locomotive was at that time Alex Harvey. The mill locomotive was used for drawing rakes of wagons out of the exchange siding, across the Leuchars road at the ungated level crossing, and into the mill yard where the respective wagons would then be taken for discharge.

When the railway facilities were withdrawn at the mill, this useful little engine was redundant. The company then offered it for sale to enthusiasts through an advertisement in the *Railway Magazine* in both the May and June 1971 issues, but no suitable replies were received and instead it was sold to scrap merchants S. Dalton of Gogar, near Edinburgh and was subsequently broken up in about October 1973.

The Narrow Gauge System

In addition to the standard gauge system within the mill there was also a 2 ft gauge railway system in use for transporting spent lime from the mill to a dump in the mill yard. The spent lime was then used for land reclamation to extend the mill site out into the Eden estuary and, from 1947 onwards, the line crossed the Motray water on a slender concrete bridge to enable an area on the far side of the burn to be reclaimed. At one time it had been intended to store incoming coal on this site and the land was reclaimed for this purpose but the storage of coal there was not proceeded with, despite the Motray bridge having been designed to carry fully loaded standard gauge coal wagons. Two locomotives were known to have worked this system namely a four-wheeled petrol-mechanical Lister engine, Works No. 5913, built in 1934 and supplied new to the company and a four-wheeled diesel-mechanical locomotive, Lister No. 11221, supplied new in 1939. The diesel locomotive survived the closure of the system and went to the Leighton Buzzard Narrow Gauge Railway on 17th November, 1973.

One of a batch of 8 ton wagons built by Hurst Nelson for the Guard Bridge company and painted in a grey livery with white lettering. The plate on the right-hand side reads 'Empty to Cardenden Colliery'. *HMRS Collection*

One of the R.Y. Pickering-built batch of five 10 ton wagons built for the paper company. *HMRS Collection*

Private Owner Wagons

The Guardbridge Paper Company had, excluding the coal masters' fleets, one of the largest fleets of private owner coal wagons in the county, numbering 70 in total and these comprised of four batches, delivered between 1900 and 1905. The first batch, Nos. 1 to 20, were 8 ton solid buffer wagons from an unidentified source that was probably either R.Y. Pickering or Hurst Nelson, the two major Scottish builders of such wagons, and were put on to the line on 24th March, 1900. The second batch were Nos. 21 to 60, 8 ton spring-buffered wagons from Hurst Nelson and these were also placed on the line on the same date. The third batch were 10 ton spring buffer wagons Nos. 61 to 65, placed on the line on 10th March, 1904 and products of R.Y. Pickering. The fourth batch, Nos. 66 to 70, were similar to the third but manufactured by Hurst Nelson and these were placed on the line on 27th July, 1904.

The surviving records of R.Y. Pickering, give details of the livery used on the third batch (and, presumably, on all Guard Bridge Paper Company wagons) and the Card Order Book gives the following details:

> Order 27 February 1904. 5 x 10 ton sprung buffered, steel underframe wagons (NBR plates 17116 to 17120 inclusive). Colour of body: Slate. Lettering: White with Red shading. Nos. 61 to 65 inclusive. Deliver to Kelty Colliery.

These wagons were to be delivered to a pit which, at that time, supplied the mill with coal. Kelty is a former mining town in West Fife and there were at that time a number of pits in the immediate area such as the Aitken, Lindsay, Blairenbathie and Lassodie Mill, all owned by the Fife Coal Company who seemed to have supplied much of the coal to the mill. These wagons would be used for the conveyance of coal from the pit to the mill boiler house but at times would also have been used to carry raw materials such as esparto grass to the mill. The use of private owner coal wagons all but ceased in 1948 but whether any of the Guard Bridge examples survived to the end of the LNER period is unknown to the authors. Other Scottish paper mills that had their own wagons included Smith Anderson of Leslie (the Fettykil mills), Guthrie, Craig Peters at Brechin, Hill,Craig & Company's Balerno Bank mills, the Carrongrove mills at Denny and Henry Bruce & Sons' Kinleith Paper Mill at Currie but Guard Bridge had, by far, the biggest fleet of main line wagons of any Scottish mill.

At a later date (probably in the early 1960s) the mill had a number of standard gauge internal user wagons for use within the company's own area. So far as is known these wagons (number unknown) were ex-Great Western Railway rigid wheelbase 4-wheel steel-bodied open wagons of a capacity of (perhaps) 13 tons - Caldwells Paper Mill at Inverkeithing had a number of similar wagons which were also reserved for internal use. These Guardbridge wagons were used in taking coal from the coal storage piles in the yard at the south end of the mill up to the coal siding for the boiler house and also on general internal haulage and, following the cessation of rail traffic, were broken up for scrap around 1970.

NBR Holmes 'K' class 4-4-0 No. 321 near St Andrews Links; note the lawn roller in the foreground and the carriages passing in the loop behind the locomotive. This photograph was taken in about 1920 and the engine was withdrawn one month before the Grouping.

H. Stirling Everard/W. Hennigan Collection

NBR Holmes class 'P' 0-4-4T with an NB loco coal wagon at St Andrews Links, 1922.

H. Stirling Everard/W.Hennigan Collection

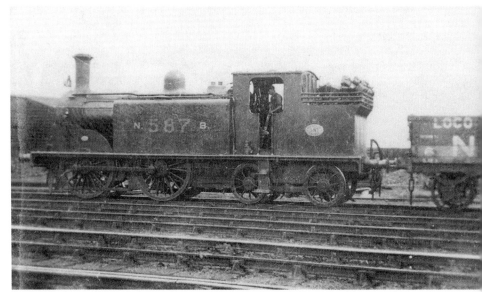

Chapter Fourteen

Working the Line:
Locomotives, Signalling and Staff

'Never better! I haven't been off the line for years'
Jack Burns

Locomotives

The St Andrews Railway

The locomotive history of the St Andrews Railway company, worked from the outset by the Edinburgh, Perth and Dundee is, of necessity, somewhat lacking in detail but for many years a single dedicated locomotive, shedded at St Andrews, was allocated to work all branch workings and rarely strayed off the line except when it required attention at the EP&D's Burntisland works. Given the fact that the Board of Trade sanctioned a single tank engine to work over the line and that the line was built to withstand only light loads, the initial locomotive used was likely to have been one of a pair of the 2-4-0 tank engines (EP&D Nos. 33 and 34) built by R. & W. Hawthorn in 1850. Early complaints about the lack of power of these locomotives resulted in trains being banked, on occasions, between Guardbridge and Leuchars, presumably by one of the Leuchars pilot engines. Within a few years larger tender engines were in use on the branch, running tender first in the down direction owing to the lack of a turntable at the terminus and these heavier engines began to cause havoc with the poorly engineered bridges and badly-laid track.

North British Railway

In North British days the St Andrews branch was worked by locomotives shedded at Dundee and the small sub-shed at St Andrews. These included a number of members of the small Drummond 0-6-0 tanks (which resembled the Brighton 'Terriers' and became LNER class 'J82') that bore names of places with which they were particularly associated, painted on the tank sides - *St Andrews* (No. 108, formerly *Hamilton* and afterwards No. 1356) and *Guardbridge* (No. 151, formerly *Dalmuir* and afterwards No. 1330) while another class, the Drummond 4-4-0Ts of LNER class 'D51' included *Anstruther* (No. 1010, which later became No. 1426). Among other locomotives known to have worked the line regularly was Drummond 0-4-4T (LNER 'D50') No. 495 which had been originally built to haul fast heavy trains between Glasgow and Helensburgh and was, between 1913 and 1916, put out to grass on the banks of the Eden. Other locomotives included Drummond 0-4-4Ts (LNER 'G8') Nos. 88 (1326), 89 (1327), 157 (1320), 167 (1334), 314 (1338) and 480 (1325). The Reid-built 'G9 'class,

NBR Holmes 'C' class 0-6-0 No. 250 on southbound train leaving St Andrews Links *c.*1920; note the original footbridge. The engine was rebuilt in 1923 and was withdrawn in 1947.

S. Ellingworth/W. Hennigan Collection

NBR Holmes class 'M' 4-4-0 No. 735 approaching Leuchars Junction with a Fife Coast train from Edinburgh to Dundee, 1925. Note the Fife Coal Company wagon on the right.

W. Hennigan Collection

similar but larger engines, also worked the branch until the 'C15' class ('Yorkies', on account of them having been built by the Yorkshire Engine Company of Sheffield) and the similar but superheated 'C16' 4-4-2T locomotives took over these duties after World War I. Regular visitors to the line then included the Reid class 'D30' 4-4-0s (the 'Scotts', since they were all named after characters in the Scott's Waverley novels or his poem 'The Lady of the Lake') and the 'D34' 4-4-0s ('Glens', named after glens adjacent to the West Highland line). Freight services became the mainstay of 0-6-0 locomotives and, in the immediate pre-Grouping period, the 'Coast Goods' was often in the hands of a 'J34' class. Wheatley 'J31' locomotives were often employed on Leuchars pilot duties and thus strayed on to the St Andrews branch on trip workings.

LNER

The Grouping brought new locomotives the branch line and these included some members of the Great Northern 'N2' class of 0-6-2 tanks which were tried out on both the Tayport and the St Andrews branches but, apparently, without much success. It was said that the main difficulty encountered with the 'N2s' appeared to revolve around the lack of a leading pony truck or bogie which had a tendency to foul the branch line's tight curves. Otherwise ex-North British 4-4-0 locomotives of classes 'D29', 'D30', 'D32', 'D33' and 'D34' and 0-6-0s of the 'J35' and 'J37' classes still held sway with only a few LNER interlopers making any inroads into the traffic, the most notable of which were the 'D11/2' 'Scottish Directors'. These were an LNER development of a Great Central 4-4-0 design named after Directors of that company, the LNER Scottish examples being named after characters in the Waverley novels. Occasionally Eastfield shed would roster a 'K2' and, in the words of C.W.R. Bowman 'its throaty GNR note would contrast with the sharper bark of the Scotts and Glens and the deep boom of the Directors'. Towards the end of the period, the LNER 'B1' class 4-6-0s began to arrive on the scene and became a familiar sight on through trains from Dundee and Thornton, replacing the older NBR classes of 'D29', 'D33' and 'D36', which disappeared for scrapping at Cowlairs or Kilmarnock.

British Railways

Known to have been seen at St Andrews during the period between 1948 and 1968 were members of the following classes - ex-LNER 'B1', 'C16', 'D11', 'D29', 'D30', 'D33', 'D34', 'J24', 'J35', 'J36', 'J37', 'J39', 'K2', 'K4' and 'V4'; ex-LMS Fowler '3P' 2-6-2T, Fairburn '4MT' 2-6-4T, Stanier '5MT' 4-6-0, Pickersgill '3F' 0-6-0, Hughes/Fowler 'Crab' 2-6-0, Ivatt '2MT' and '4MT' 2-6-0; and BR Standard locomotives '5MT' 4-6-0, '4MT' 2-6-0 and '4MT' 2-6-4T. Trainspotting activities at Guardbridge between March 1954 and March 1955 saw 'B1s' Nos. 61293, 61184 and 61117 in evidence together with 'D11/2' No. 62677 *Edie Ochiltree*, 'D30' No. 62434 *Kettledrummle*, 'D34' Nos. 62478 *Glen Quoich* and 62485 *Glen Murran* , 'J36' Nos. 65309, 65330 and 65331, 'J37' Nos. 64581, 64620 and 64631,

NBR Reid 4-4-2T No. 15 taking water at the south end of the up platform at Leuchars Junction while working a horse box special to St Andrews and the Fife Coast line, 1923.

H. Sirling Everard/W. Hennigan Collection

Ex-NBR Reid 'M' class 4-4-2T, LNER 'C15' No. 9043 taking water at the north end of St Andrews station, 31st July, 1939.

J.L. Stevenson

Reid 0-4-4T, LNER No. 9355, on a Dundee to St Andrews local service at Leuchars Junction, 4th September, 1925.   *H. Stirling Everard; W. Hennigan Collection*

LNER 'G7' 0-4-4T (NBR Holmes class 'P') at Leuchars Junction, 1st August, 1925.
H. Stirling Everard/W. Hennigan Collection

Drummond 'D' class 0-6-0 No. 1421 with the early 'L & N E R' form of lettering but still bearing an NBR number in 1924 at St Andrews Links; this engine was withdrawn barely two years later.
H. Stirling Everard/W.Hennigan Collection

NBR Drummond 'D' class 0-6-0 No. 1421 on the 'coast goods' at St Andrews Links, 1923.
H. Stirling Everard/W. Hennigan Collection

Holmes 'J36' class 0-6-0 No. 9781 on a goods train returning from St Andrews passing the Golfers' bridge just a month after World War II ended in Europe, 11th June, 1945.

J.L. Stevenson

'J38' No. 65901, 'J39' Nos. 64790 and 64950, 'K3' No. 61931 and an interloper in the form of Caledonian 0-6-0 No. 57578. Through services between Tayport and Leuchars were in the hands of 'Director's or 'B1s' and from the mid-1950s, class '4MTs' worked some services as well as making regular appearances on the St Andrews to Leuchars line. Goods services were in the hands of 'J35s', 'J36s' and 'B1s'.

After the introduction of the diesel multiple units in 1959 steam-hauled locals were few with only a couple of daily runs undertaken by the Leuchars pilot; the occasional excursion train continued to be steam-hauled although by 1962 these had gone and the only regular steam workings seen at St Andrews were on trains bound for, or from, Crail, Anstruther and the South. The Leuchars pilot, which worked the trip workings to Seggie, Guardbridge and St Andrews sidings was a 'J36' (often No. 65330). The route availability (i.e. the categories of locomotive permitted over a line and based upon axle loads) of the section from East Fife Central Junction (between Cameron Bridge and Leven) to Leuchars via St Andrews was 6, but locomotives of classes 'J37', 'J38' and 'L1' were additionally permitted to run over the section.

Between St Andrews and Leuchars class '101' Metro-Cammell two-car sets allocated to Dundee were seen on local workings, with occasional three-car

'D30' class 4-4-0 No. 62434 *Kettledrummle* on the 6.45 pm Leuchars to St Andrews leaving Guardbridge on 28th May, 1955 and crossing over the Eden viaduct - the coach visible is a post-war LNER composite third No. SC82765E built by BR in 1950. The locomotive was withdrawn from Dundee shed in April 1958.   *J.L. Stevenson*

Fellow 'D30' class 4-4-0 No. 62419 *Meg Dodds* on the 2.18 pm Dundee to Edinburgh via Crail service passing St Andrews Links on 16th April, 1949 - note the painted BR number on the buffer beam.   *J.L. Stevenson*

Thompson 'B1' class 4-6-0 No. 61132 on the 12.47 pm St Andrews to Leuchars local passing the Links station with the town in the background.   *J.L. Stevenson*

units of the same type also employed. Other dmu classes included, infrequently, class '100' Gloucester units and, rarely, Cravens twin sets. There were no passenger or goods services over any part of the line which were scheduled to be hauled by diesel locomotives although excursion trains hauled by English Electric type '1' Bo-Bos (class '20') were occasionally seen on summer extras from Glasgow. Other visitors included Birmingham type '2' (Sulzers, later class '26'/'27'), Derby type '2' (Sulzers, class '24'/'25') and NBL type '2s' (class '21'/'29').

The last steam locomotives to travel over the St Andrews Railway on passenger workings were on 12th October, 1966 when 'Black Five' No. 44722 hauled a train from St Andrews to Dundee on a special working for the University and 'B1' No. 61278 brought it back again - both locomotives were shedded at Dundee Tay Bridge and both were withdrawn for scrapping in April 1967. In that same month and barely a couple of weeks before the end of steam in Scotland a pair of 'B1s' had the honour of being the last steam locomotives of all to traverse the St Andrews branch.* The last passenger service on the St Andrews branch was provided by a Metro Cammell two-car diesel multiple unit.

---

* For details of this and other enthusiasts' reminiscences, see Chapter Seventeen.

The signal box at St Andrews Links during the latter part of he NBR era with the signalman posing at the top of the stairs. *NBRSG Collection*

Taking the token at Milton Junction for the last train through from Dundee to Edinburgh via Crail, Saturday 4th September, 1965. *Norman Turnbull*

Signalling

Little is known about the early signalling on the St Andrews Railway, although it seems probable that since the line was originally worked by one locomotive only at a time it is possible that it was worked without signals. The Railway Inspectorate report of Captain Laffan confirmed that it was, indeed, worked on the 'one engine in steam' principle. The sidings were worked by a system similar to the Annett's key system, i.e. the guard of the train working the line had a key with which the points on the line could be released and it is likely that the driver would be in possession of such a staff permitting him to enter the section from Milton Junction to St Andrews. Upon the extension of the St Andrews & Anstruther Railway to St Andrews additional signal boxes were provided at St Andrews (New) and St Andrews (Links); all signals and boxes were to the design of the contractors, the Railway Signalling Company of Fazakerly, Liverpool.

The North British era saw many changes to signalling including the installation of fully interlocked points and signals (made compulsory by the Regulation of Railways Act 1889), the installation of semaphore signalling along the line and the installation by the late 1890s of the Tyer's electric tablet instruments at each signal cabin; this replaced the older train staff system for controlling single lines. Most of the signals were of a pattern supplied by Stevens & Sons of Glasgow and London and the signal box at Guardbridge was of their design. Among the alterations carried out towards the end of the century was the construction of a new box at Guardbridge. In 1920 a new signal box was erected at Leuchars North. The NBR General Appendix of 1922 lists the method of working the various sections of the line as follows: Tayport to Leuchars Old worked by electric key token; Leuchars Old to Leuchars South Junction by (double-line) block telegraph; Leuchars South Junction to St Andrews Links by converted tablet and St Andrews Links to St Andrews by tablet No. 6; the St Andrews to Leuchars South section was reduced to 'one engine in steam' working in September 1967.

The block sections travelling south were Leuchars (Old) to Leuchars North Junction (0 m. 32 ch.), Leuchars North Junction to Leuchars South Junction (0 m. 30 ch.), Leuchars South Junction to Guardbridge (1 m. 2 ch.), Guardbridge to St Andrews Links (2 m. 71 ch.) and St Andrews Links to St Andrews station (0 m. 39 ch.) A chronology of opening and closing dates of the signal boxes between Leuchars (Old) and St Andrews station appears in *Appendix One*.

In 1926 the weekday opening hours of the relevant signal boxes were as follows: Leuchars (Old) 7.45 am to 2.55 pm, 3.55 to 5.30 and 7.00 to 8.30 pm; Leuchars North continuously; Leuchars South 5.25 am to 10.00 pm (Saturdays 10.40 pm), Guardbridge 5.25 am to 10.15 pm (Saturdays 10.45 pm); St Andrews Links 5.30 am to 10.15 pm (Saturdays 11.00 pm) and St Andrews Station 6.50 am to 10.15 pm (Saturdays 11.00 pm) On Sundays all boxes were closed with the exception of Leuchars North which was open from 7.00 am to midnight.

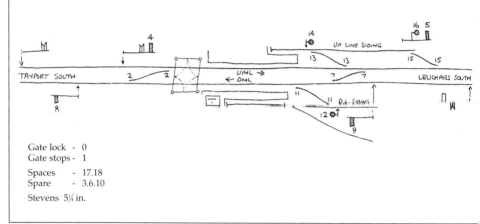

Signalling diagram of Leuchars (Old), November 1927.   *Ed Nicholls Collection*

Signalling diagram of Guardbridge, 1967.   *Ed Nicholls Collection*

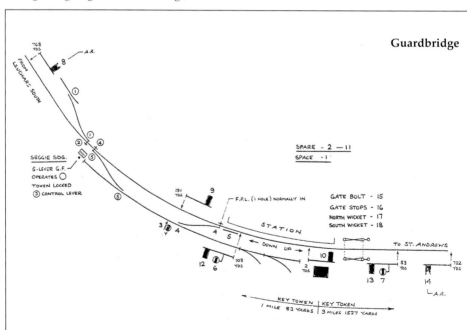

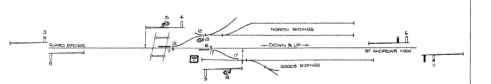

St Andrews Links

Signalling diagram of St Andrews Links, *c.1950*.   *Ed Nicholls Collection*

Signalling diagram of St Andrews (New), *c.1950*.   *Ed Nicholls Collection*

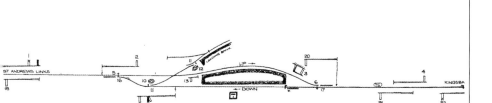

St Andrews (New)

Spotlight on St. Andrews

When ST. ANDREWS is mentioned thoughts turn to golf and present day publicity has made it so. Although ST. ANDREWS is the " Home of Golf " that game alone has not been the reason for the town's popularity as a holiday resort.

On the extremity of the East Neuk o' Fife the resort is a healthy bracing one with many and varied attractions. These bring thousands of visitors of all tastes to ST. ANDREWS year after year.

The University and many buildings connected therewith, the Cathedral and Priory founded in 1160, along with the ruined Castle, all give ample scope for the interest of the scholar and the historian.

There are four golf courses and as they are the property of the Townspeople there is no necessity to be a member of a club before playing. Tennis, bowls, horse riding, swimming, boating, angling and walking are all sports of ST. ANDREWS.

At the railway station the principal freight handling is sundry traffic, but a very large number of passengers both season ticket holders and holidaymakers travel by train.

ST. ANDREWS station won a premier award in the Station Gardens Competition and our photograph was taken this year when the flowers were in full bloom.

The photo-strip shows : C. Davidson, stationmaster ; D. Pringle, station foreman ; M. Borland, clerkess ; and W. Paul, signalman.

Spotlight on St Andrews. *From the 1959 BR Staff Magazine, Scottish Region*

Staff

Railway Careers

The essence of the Victorian railway was to be found in its staff who, loyal to the company they worked for by a combination of incentives and discipline, were prepared to travel anywhere on its system to obtain promotion. On the line between Leuchars and St Andrews there were about 70 employees of the railway, with a great number of others whose livelihood depended, however directly or indirectly, on the company. Highest in the local railway hierarchy were the locomotive men, drivers and firemen, although there were only a handful of crews who lived locally and who were employed at the small sub-sheds at Anstruther and St Andrews; the majority of crews who worked over the line came from Dundee, Thornton and Glasgow. The largest category of employees living locally were the station and goods staff, ranging from station masters to clerks, porters and shunters. Other staff employed locally included signalmen and crossing keepers, permanent way men who usually worked in a small squad dedicated to a particular stretch of line, carriage and locomotive cleaners, carters and lorrymen. In addition canvassers and agents were employed to secure further business.

Although employees could rise up the ranks from, say, porter to station master or locomotive cleaner to driver, the fact that the area which the line served was somewhat remote from any major industrial areas combined with the relatively small size of local railway installations, meant that staff often had to move considerable distances over the North British system (and, later on, the LNER and BR empire) in order to secure promotion. Local newspapers carried many accounts of well-liked local railwaymen moving in or out of the East Neuk. One example was William Docherty, who started his railway career as a porter at Mount Melville in 1927, became relief clerk at Crail in 1928, was transferred to Leven in 1939 and, after war service, recommenced work with the railway at St Andrews in 1946, being transferred to Dundee in 1948 and his last position was as cashier in the goods yard at Kirkcaldy. There was, however, little difficulty in recruiting staff due to the agricultural nature of the area, particularly when farming was undergoing one of its regular setbacks and when local trade was suffering from a depression. Wages paid compared favourably to what one could earn from most local employment and subsidised housing and coal, free and discounted travel and a continuity and security of service made a railway job popular.

With the rapid run-down of the railway from the 1950s onward the position began to change dramatically. As wages fell in comparative terms and redundancies occurred it became harder to recruit staff and those who did continue to work on the railway tended to be ageing and were often somewhat dispirited. The area still contains some railway employees, but they now commute by car to Leuchars, Kirkcaldy or Dundee.

The driver looks on as 'J37' class 0-6-0 No. 64569 waits to depart from St Andrews with the RCTS special on 28th August, 1965. *S. Rankin*

Stanier class '5' No. 44954 in the hands of driver Selby awaits the 'right away' from
Leuchars on a St Andrews train, 16th March, 1954.   *Dr Edward M. Patterson*

Station Masters

The duties of the station master (known in North British parlance as 'station
agents'), were wide and varied and much depended on the importance of the
station. Regarded as something of a breed apart and revered for their
knowledge of business and railway matters they were often regarded as the
fount of local knowledge.

The status, and pay, of the station master, and the nature of his duties, was
defined by the grading of the station. Locally St Andrews was classified by the
North British and LNER as a class '1' station, while Leuchars Junction/Leuchars
(Old) being a joint appointment was class '2', and Guardbridge class '3'. In BR
days class '5' was deleted as a category and, in ascending order of seniority,
station masters' appointments were classified from 4 to 1 followed by 'Special
A' and 'Special B' - by the mid-1950s St Andrews was a 'Special A' appointment
and Dundee (Tay Bridge) a 'Special B'.

An important duty of the station master was, at the smaller stations, to sell
domestic coal on commission and in general to drum up business for the
railway company by seeking and arranging excursion and special traffic, by
distributing and promoting publicity and by, in all respects, being the local face
of the North British Railway and its successors. In 1922 John Currie was the
station master at St Andrews while Walter Douglas occupied a similar position
at Guardbridge.

Other Grades

The number of station staff employed locally varied with St Andrews passenger station having the largest staff of 18 employees excluding the refreshment room and bookstall staff while the Links goods station, even in the early 1960s, still had a staff of six, namely chief clerk, a clerkess, a goods lorry driver, two goods porter and an additional porter who covered general duties; by 1966 this had dwindled to two porters and a booking clerk; Guardbridge had a staff complement of five. Clerks were employed to undertake a number of duties including selling tickets in the booking office and keeping records, the latter often being a complicated task which involved book keeping, calculation of rates including, prior to 1948, through rates to other railway companies.

Crossing Keepers

Level crossings were often manned by the wives and families of surfacemen who were allowed to live in the adjacent houses free of rent in exchange for carrying out their duties. Crossing gates operated by signalmen were normally kept open for road traffic when no trains were running but the reverse was the rule in relation to those operated by crossing keepers. Where gates were to remain open the NBR rules stated that:

> In each case the gate-keepers must also, before leaving off duty at night, see that the lamps upon the level-crossing gates are trimmed and burning so as to show a red light in each direction to the line of railway.

From north to south the level crossings were situated at Leuchars (Old) worked by the signalmen there; Seggie worked by a gate keeper and Guardbridge originally worked by the station staff from a hut and, from 1894, by the signalman. All other gated crossings were occupation crossings worked by the user.

Some Notable Staff

Over the years there were many well-known railwaymen working on the lines. A famous early example was Jack Burns, who managed to combine railways and golf in a unique way. A plasterer by trade and native of St Andrews, Burns won the 1888 St Andrews Open in somewhat controversial circumstances. He was then greenkeeper and professional at Warwick Golf Club but, wishing to return to his native town, he took up employment with the North British as a platelayer on the St Andrews branch line. Always one with a ready sense of humour he was asked in his later years how his golf was getting on and, using a golfing phrase, replied 'Never better - I haven't been off the line for years!' A Victorian station master at Leuchars, Thomas Robertson, born in Edinburgh and who rose through the ranks to become station master at Haymarket and then Waverley, has his reminiscences of the night that the Tay Bridge fell featured in the last chapter of this book.

St Andrews station staff posing on the down platform, *c*.1910.   *BR Staff Magazine*

A previous station master at Leuchars was William Anderson, previously station master at Kingskettle. Appointed in 1849 at a salary of £70 per annum, he wore, in an era when uniforms were apparently not required, a light suit and straw hat and his duties do not appear to have been too onerous. A memoir written by his son Martin, a local artist who produced humorous postcards under the 'Cynicus' name, contains much local detail and recounts how Anderson abruptly left the railway service and became a shipping agent at Guardbridge.*

According to the late Jo Grimond, leader of the Liberal Party and a native of St Andrews, the railway officials at St Andrews in his childhood 'were well-known and respected local figures: the station master, Lees; the guard Haddow; and Docherty the foreman porter'. He likened Haddow 'to a rather stout Sir Walter Scott' and Docherty 'more of Stevenson's build and colouring'. 'Both were men of standing and authority.'

At St Andrews John Bennett was appointed station master in the early 1950s and in 1955 was promoted to one of three 'Special Class A' relief station masters in the Burntisland District - among relief tasks he carried out were station master and yardmaster at Dundee and station master at Leuchars and St Andrews. In May 1966 he became freight depot assistant at Dundee West, from which duty he retired as an employee of National Carriers Ltd. In retirement he

* The memoirs of Cynicus were published in 12 instalments by the *Glasgow Evening News* between 24th February and 11th March, 1930; a biography *The Fortunes of Cynicus* by Elspeth Reid and Flora Davidson was published in 1995.

'Last Train for St Andrews', a cartoon by Martin Anderson (1854-1932), who published humorous postcards under the name of 'Cynicus'. Anderson was born in the station house at Leuchars, where his father was station master.   *Authors' Collection*

wrote a local classic named *Random Reflections of a Roving Railwayman* - he also gave generously of his time to contribute to the present work. The last incumbent of the post of station master at St Andrews was Charles Davidson, who began his railway career at the age of 19 with a position with the North British Railway at Kinross Junction in 1920. Promoted to relief station master for the Burntisland area in 1940, he was, 15 years later, appointed to full-time station master at St Andrews in 1955. On 25th April, 1966 the post of station master at St Andrews was abolished when the station came under the control of Dundee and Mr Davidson was transferred to Kirkcaldy where he served out his last six months in a clerical capacity prior to his retirement from the railway.

At Leuchars the last station master was Alan Reid, previously station master at Ladybank, who, when the post was abolished, was appointed as a staff training officer with the divisional manager in Edinburgh. The last station master at Guardbridge was Ernest Cant, who previously had the distinction of being last station master at Dundee East until closure of that station in 1959. Mr Cant, after the closure of Guardbridge station, became a class '1' relief station master in the Burntisland District.

Chapter Fifteen

Five Memorable Miles:
The Line Described

*'The sea came up so far that it almost touched the low embankments
as we wound our way across the flatland towards the links.'*

Mike Jodeluk

Chains, Furlongs and Metres

This chapter describes the principal features, both geographical and railway, of the St Andrews Railway southwards from the original junction station at Leuchars (Old) to the 'new' station at St Andrews. Not all of the features listed would, of course, have necessarily have been seen at the same time but unless otherwise specified the descriptions are typical of the North British period immediately prior to World War I. The figures in brackets are the distances in miles and chains from Leuchars Junction station and, for the benefit of those too young to have travelled on the line, one mile equals 1,609 metres and, approximately, eight kilometres equals five miles. Miles are divided into 1,760 yards and each yard is divided into three feet. Surveyors used the measure of 22 yards or one chain (20.11 metres) and chains are particularly associated with the construction of canals and railways and still survive as the 'official' mileage unit for railways; 10 chains or one-eighth of a mile (201 metres) equals one furlong (the distance that a horse could plough in a day and a measure which is still used in horse-racing) and 80 chains or 8 furlongs equal 1 mile - thus 20 chains equal a quarter-mile and 40 equal half a mile. Following normal railway conventions, measurements for through passenger stations are taken from the mid-point of the platforms while sidings are taken from the point where they diverge from the main line. The directions up and down refer, respectively, to the lines running from Leuchars (Old) to St Andrews and vice versa.

Leuchars Old and New

The journey starts at the station which formed the original exchange point for passengers transferring to the St Andrews branch from the North British main line from Burntisland to Tayport. The main line here was double from the outset and Leuchars station (00.45) (known from 1879 as Leuchars (Old)) had platforms on the up and down lines, the outer face of each having a south-facing bay. The down platform, constructed in 1858 to replace the original decayed wooden structure of 1850, was later extended to 210 feet in length - the change in height between the old and new being clearly visible right up until closure; a bay, capable of holding three bogie carriages, was provided but the platform was devoid of buildings apart from at its north end where Leuchars (Old) signal box was situated. This rather gaunt brick structure, dating from the resignalling

Gradient Profile

S? *ANDREWS, NEW*

S? *ANDREWS LINKS*

Gradient post between St Andrews Links and St Andrews (New).

S. Rankin

GUARDBRIDGE

leaves Main Line

LEUCHARS JUNCTION

for the opening of the Tay Bridge in 1879, was tall enough to enable the signalman to see over the footbridge to the level crossing and beyond. The box controlled the long single line section between Leuchars North Junction and Tayport and wooden token exchange platforms were provided on each side of the line. The up platform, slightly longer than the down at 270 feet, had a similar extension and change of height and a bay similar to but shorter than the down bay, contained a plain single-storey brick building with the waiting room and station offices. Originally a flat-roofed awning was provided on the rail side of the building but this was removed some time after 1921 when, after the closure of the station to passengers, the building was converted for use as a goods office.

To the north of the platforms was an iron lattice footbridge and the level crossing over Main Street (part of the A919 Guardbridge to St Michaels road). In LNER days the Tayport trains used to slow to walking pace through Leuchars (Old) in order to pick up the tablet and according to one correspondent 'the station looked a curious old structure with its very low platforms'. Beyond the level crossing lay, on the up side, the two-storey station master's house which dated from 1854 and which continued in use as such for the Leuchars (Old)/Junction station master (a joint appointment) until the mid-1960s. The section of the former main line between Leuchars (Old) and Tayport was singled in 1929 and abandoned in 1956. South of the station and parallel to the running lines there were a number of sidings, the access to which was altered in 1927 to alleviate traffic delays at the level crossing and on the down side was a goods crane with a maximum handling capacity of two tons.

The line from Leuchars (Old) to Leuchars Junction was singled in 1959 and continued in existence until 1967 when Leuchars (Old) was abandoned and the track was then lifted from there to the junction with the **Leuchars Aerodrome Siding** (00.28), also known as **HM Aerodrome Station Siding**, which dated from 1912 and trailed off on the up side, crossing the adjacent public road over a gated crossing before entering MOD property. At **Leuchars Junction** (00.13) the double track main line from the Tay Bridge and St Fort joined the Tayport line at a trailing junction on the down side. On the up side was situated the signal box known as **Leuchars North**, erected in 1878 and replaced by the present (surviving) box in 1920, a brick and wooden structure 33 feet in length which was renamed Leuchars in June 1970 and refurbished in 1994-95. The original box, some 18 feet in length, was situated on the site of the up shunting siding opened in 1920.

Leuchars Junction station (00.00) lay immediately to the south of the junction. Opened in 1878 in connection with the new Tay Bridge line, this station was constructed by contractor George Bruce of St Andrews and had an exceptionally long and wide island platform some 890 feet in length and 25 feet in width. There were two internal bays, the north-facing one being 360 ft-long and known as the Tayport dock while the south-facing bay was 410 ft-long and known as the St Andrews dock. A water column was situated at the south end of the platform between the up platform and St Andrews dock. This column was fed from a cast-iron tank mounted on a stone base on the down side of the luine and the tank was supplied with water from a local spring by means of a gas-driven pump. The station building, situated in the gap between the bays,

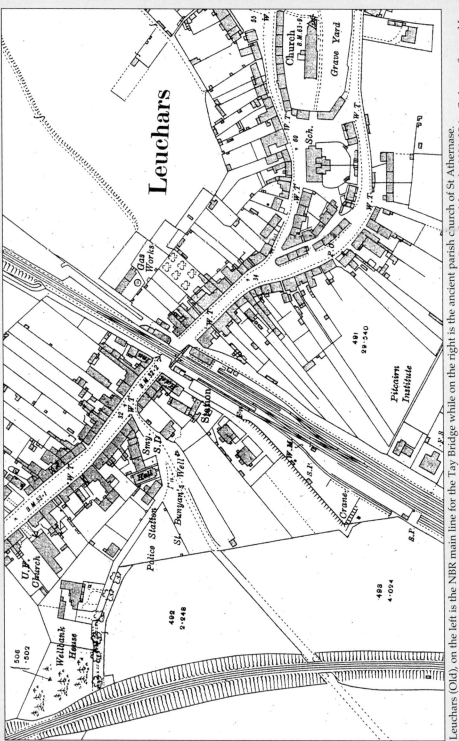

Leuchars (Old), on the left is the NBR main line for the Tay Bridge while on the right is the ancient parish church of St Athernase. *Reproduced from the 1894, 25 in. Ordnance Survey Map*

North British Railway
Drawing of Signal Box
Leuchars North

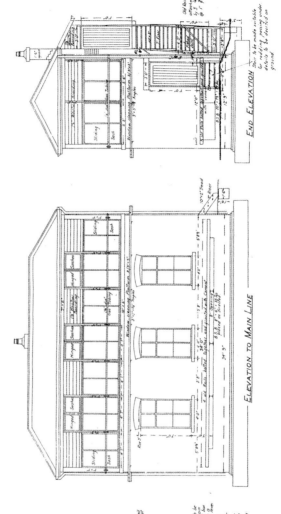

ELEVATION TO MAIN LINE

END ELEVATION

SECTION

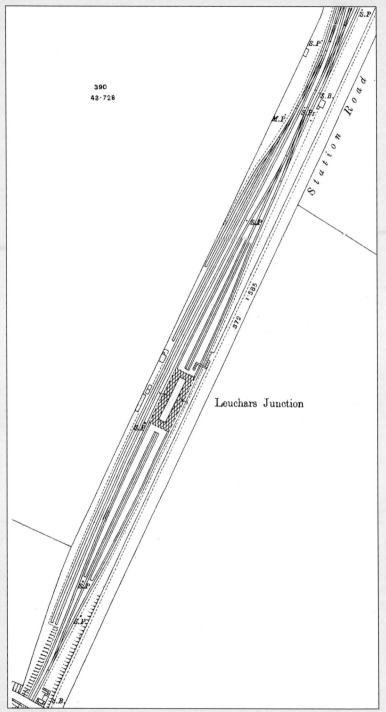

Leuchars Junction, with at bottom left Leuchars South signal box and, at top right, Leuchars North. *Reproduced from the 1910, 25 in. Ordnance Survey Map*

was built of brick and 110 feet in length, housed the main station offices and waiting rooms with the toilets at the south end and on the up side a cast-iron NBR drinking fountain was placed next to the booking hall entrance. The building was surrounded on all sides by a hipped-roof glazed wrought-iron canopy which had an all-round overhang of 12 feet, giving a meagre degree of protection to the hapless passengers waiting for the often-late connecting services. After a disastrous fire in 1913 the station buildings were rebuilt in brick and wood to the same layout and incorporating the gables, chimney stacks and part of the walls of the earlier station but with better appointed waiting rooms and booking hall and a refreshment room and with a wider canopy; it survives to this day little altered apart from some modernization carried out in the 1960s. The unsatisfactory access to the station from the public road over a narrow lattice footbridge with steep stairs remained, despite frequent requests for a subway, until 1997. In that year and in the spirit of new disability discrimination legislation, a wider ramped footbridge was substituted and the original bridge was donated to the Kingdom of Fife Railway Preservation Society who hope to re-erect it at their railway heritage centre at Kirkland. The station survives as 'Leuchars for St Andrews', the only remaining intermediate stop between Dundee and Cupar. Still manned, the station is comparatively little changed apart from the filling in of the bays and still retains semaphore signals and the former Leuchars North signal box. A number of sidings lay parallel to and west of the station.

Milton to Seggie

South of Leuchars Junction and on the up side lay **Leuchars South** signal box, again dating from 1878 and closed along with the St Andrews branch in 1969. This was a tall structure located immediately south of the brick bridge which carried the Guardbridge to Balmullo road over the line with a brick base and a wooden upper store at a height such that the signalman could see the line in both directions. On the up side, was a wooden token exchange platform for the branch trains. Nearby on the up side was a tall lattice junction signal and crossover on the main line immediately north of **Milton Junction** (00.17), named after the nearby Milton Farm and the physical point at which the single-track St Andrews branch diverged at a facing junction on the up side. Until this point the main line from Leuchars (Old) had been entirely on the level but the branch now descended on a gentle downwards gradient of 1 in 209 which, although nominally slight, had proved extremely troublesome in the opposite direction to the underpowered steam locomotives of the Victorian era. As the line fell it swung away in a gentle arc to the south-east across a stretch of wet pasture land and, passing a platelayer's hut on the down side and running over a short embankment, then crossed the Motray Burn on the **Motray viaduct** (00.34). This was a single-span plate girder structure some 140 feet in length carried on three cylindrical stone piers linked by iron cross braces; it was a replacement for Bouch's original wooden structure bearing the same name.

A short incline of 1 in 232 was followed by a quarter mile of level track which passed, on the up side, the mill reservoir and housing in River Terrace and

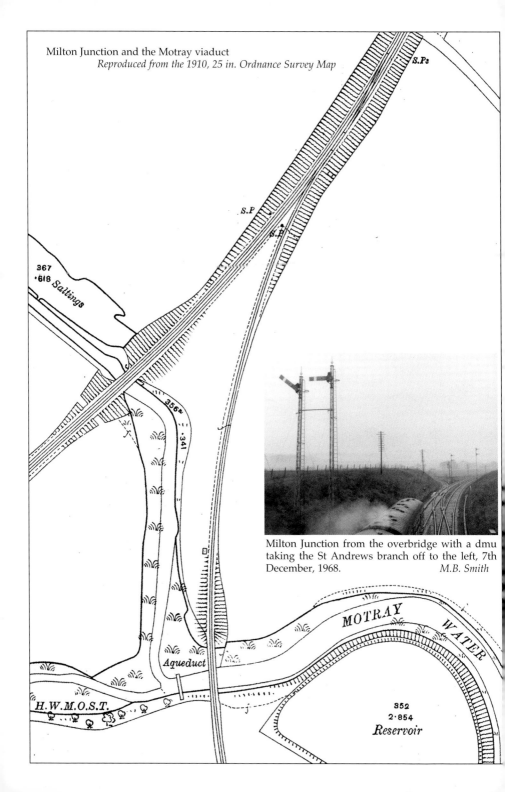

Milton Junction and the Motray viaduct
Reproduced from the 1910, 25 in. Ordnance Survey Map

S.Ps

S.P

S.P

367
·618 *Saltings*

356ᵃ

·341

Aqueduct

H.W.M.O.S.T.

MOTRAY

WATER

352
2·854
Reservoir

Milton Junction from the overbridge with a dmu taking the St Andrews branch off to the left, 7th December, 1968.   *M.B. Smith*

Innerbridge Street, all of which had been built by the Guard Bridge Paper Company and then Fife County Council's Guardbridge Primary School. At **Seggie level crossing** (00.66) the line crossed over the Seggie to Guardbridge by-road on a manned gated crossing with a keeper's cottage built in 1910; because of the curvature of the line at this point a whistle board for down trains was situated 360 feet before this crossing. A hundred yards or so to the south of the crossing lay **Seggie Siding** (00.72), a private siding originally provided for the distillery and later used for the paper mill. Closed along with the branch in 1969, Seggie Siding was both the busiest and the last-surviving goods facility on the whole branch line.

Seggie to Seafield

The mill dominated the views on the up side as the line continued almost due south and on a downward gradient of 1 in 128 to **Guardbridge station** (01.16) which had a curved platform 360 feet in length situated on the up side of the line. Midway along the platform was a typical NBR brick and wood single-storey building of the 1890s with gables, canopy, barge-boards and decorative valancing. The original St Andrews Railway station building, built out of local freestone, was situated at the south end of the platform and at right angles to the line; entered from the platform through a wooden porch, the older building served as the station's booking office and station master's house. The platform had a wooden picket fence, flowerbed and rockery and the station was well cared-for until its closure in 1965. To the north of the station lay a passing loop controlled at its northern end by a ground frame controlled by tablet lock. Opposite the passenger platform was a small goods yard with two (later increased to three) sidings and a 2 ton crane; the goods yard was closed in 1966. In the early days the yard was connected by a horse-worked tramway to the Seggie Brick and Tile Works. Immediately beyond the passenger platform and on the down side was Guardbridge signal box, opened in 1894 and reduced in status to a gate box in 1967; the box controlled the busy **Guardbridge level crossing** over the A919 Leuchars to Guardbridge road. A token exchange platform was placed next to the signal box and, until the end, was illuminated by an ornate Victorian oil lamp.

Beyond the level crossing the line now ran due east before reaching the **Eden viaduct** (01.21), the major engineering feature on the line. The original wooden structure was some 300 feet in length but was later replaced by a plate girder structure of nine spans supported on eight sets of cylindrical stone piers linked by iron cross braces and simlar in style to the contemporaneous Motray viaduct. From the down side could be seen Bishop Wardlaw's original stone bridge along with, from 1937, the ferro-concrete road bridge replacement. Emerging from the bridge, the line then crossed behind the Guard Bridge Hotel on the seaward side before passing, on the down side, the facing **Brickworks Siding** (01.27) which served the adjacent Eden Brick and Tile Works. Opened in 1873 at the expense of Messrs McLean & Cunningham, the siding fell out of use at a later stage but was rebuilt and reopened in 1897 before permanent closure and

Guardbridge and the Eden viaduct.

Reproduced from the 1914, 25 in. Ordnance Survey Map

Guardbridge, looking towards Leuchars. The booking office is the original St Andrews Railway booking office while on the platform is the NBR waiting room. The *Daily Record* billboards clearly date this photograph to 26th September, 1934. *Jim Page Collection*

Guardbridge level crossing with a Ford 'Zephyr', Morris 1100 and Co-op van all waiting to cross, 7th December, 1968. *M.B. Smith*

Leaving the Eden viaduct for Guardbridge, January 1969.   *Hamish Stevenson*

The Eden viaduct seen through the cab of a dmu in 1960. Note the Guard Bridge Hotel on the left and Bishop Wardlaw's bridge on the right.   *John Hurst*

The Eden viaduct at high tide with 'J37' class 0-6-0 No. 64619 working tender first on the 4.05 pm from St Andrews on 13th September, 1958.   *J.L. Stevenson*

Following the Eden estuary - the 11.59 from St Andrews service near Seafield, 13th December, 1968.   *Hamish Stevenson*

The Golfers' bridge, Eden course, St Andrews. The bridge allowed golfers playing on that course to cross between the 2nd and 3rd tees and the 16th and 17th.   *Nigel Dyckhoff*

Platelayers' hut on the Guardbridge to St Andrews section, 1955.   *Nigel Dyckhoff*

lifting in 1906. From the brickworks, the line followed the south shore of the Eden estuary, taking a gently undulating course over a series of short gradients and declines which, though not presenting an undue difficulty to the locomotives working the line, did cause the carriages to rock and sway in a manner which delighted youthful passengers as the crews of late-running trains attempted to make-up lost time. At **Coble Shore crossing** (02.25), a gated occupation crossing carried a lane leading to the shore over the line. From the crossing the line turned south-eastwards reaching **Seafield Siding** (02.47), a short siding on the down side which was linked by a horse-worked tramway to the Seafield Brick and Tile Works a quarter of a mile to the south. Seafield Siding was opened in 1853 and closed by the end of the century.

Crossing the Links

At Balgove Links an occupation crossing was passed and about half a mile further on a path crossed the line over the Golfers' bridge, a wooden footbridge with steep stairs which was a very distinctive part of the scene. Skirting the Old Course, and passing over another gated occupation crossing, the line reached **St Andrews Links station** (04.56). This was the original terminus of the St Andrews Railway and served as the town's passenger and goods station until the extension southwards to the new station was opened in 1887; from then onwards the Links station served as the town's good station until its eventual closure in 1966. On the down side of the line was placed St Andrews Links signal box, a rather squat brick building dating from 1887; according to J.M. Bennett, the box afforded 'a convenient and cosy grandstand to observe golfers holing out on the first green of the Eden course, the 16th of the Old Course and also driving from the 17th Old tee to the famous Round Hole'. The box was closed in 1957 and thereafter the sidings were controlled from a ground frame. Almost opposite was the single-line dead-end wooden engine shed, 50 feet in length, in which the branch engine was kept until 1960. South of the engine shed was the coal yard with its four sidings and coal stances, next to which were situated the rambling buildings known as the Black Sheds, once used for the storage and seasoning of wood for making golf clubs; according to Mr Bennett 'many a brave golfer taking the direct line incurred a penalty when he failed to clear them'.* The Old Course Hotel ('Ugly, graceless and out of scale', according to Jo Grimmond) was built on the site of the coal yard but the small gabled station master's house with its gabled porch and dormer windows continued in use after the opening of the new station and survives to the present day. On the down side was the original terminus building which, as far back as 1868, was described as 'a tumble-down erection … neither ornamental nor adequate'. Built as an open-ended train shed, it was said that the station buildings 'was full of goods placed everywhere' and that there were 'yawning imperfections of the cob-webbed and unpainted pile'. Constructed of wood planking and with a slated roof, the station building was 40 ft-long and 25 ft in width and survived until the fire of 1901 when it was replaced by a large brick-built covered goods shed some 110 ft in length and capable of holding five wagons at a time under

* For an account of playing over the Black Sheds see *Chapter Seventeen*.

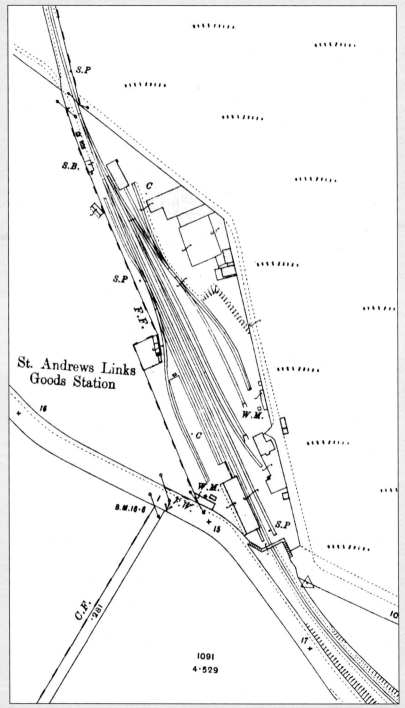

The Old or Links station at St Andrews.   *Reproduced from the 1914, 25 in. Ordnance Survey Map*

cover. The goods station was succinctly described by Jo Grimmond as 'not a thing of beauty perhaps, but to small boys a joy forever'. The yard crane had a capacity of 5 tons, the greatest of any on the line. South of the goods shed the line was spanned by a wooden footbridge, later replaced by a standard NBR lattice example; this kept open the right of way for pedestrians over Old Station Road which was closed to vehicular traffic when the public road was realigned.

Because of the constraints imposed by the lay-out of the goods sidings at the Links station, a somewhat unusual method of working was employed and this was described by the late Douglas Brown in the following terms:

> The entrance to the goods station forms a facing junction to trains arriving from Leuchars Junction and it is desirable that the engine should not be trapped by its train in the arrival siding. The train stops a short distance from the entrance to the yard to allow the guard to walk up to the engine. The train then restarts and when it has gained sufficient momentum, the guard uncouples the leading wagon from the engine. The latter immediately accelerates and takes refuge in one of the sidings, while the guard makes his way back to the brake van in order to control the braking of the engineless train, for which the signalman meanwhile has reset the road into an adjacent siding.

The Junction Line and New Station

The next section of line, known as the Junction Line and opened in 1887, provided the link between the original St Andrews Railway and the Anstruther & St Andrews Railway. Crossing the diverted St Andrews to Guardbridge A91 road by the single-span girder **Petheram bridge**, the line began an ascent at a gradient of 1 in 60 for quarter of a mile over an embankment which was built to double-line standards although only the up line was ever laid. In the 1940s the unused part of the embankment was grassed over and planted with ornamental shrubs. **St Andrews (New) station**, (05.04), was now reached. This station, by far the busiest on the entire East Fife coastal section, was the 1902 replacement for the original Anstruther & St Andrews Railway structure destroyed in a wilful fire-raising attack the preceding year. Handling only passenger traffic, the station was situated in a deep cutting with stone retaining walls (later replaced, in part, by a less attractive brick retaining wall with concrete coping) and had an island platform 400 feet in length with iron water columns at each end. The main building, 120 ft long, was constructed from brick and wood with a glazed canopy supported on decorated iron piers, had a narrower southern extension which contained the toilets. Other facilities included first and third class waiting rooms, a refreshment room, booking and left luggage offices and a bookstall - the refreshment room was later closed and the bookstall relocated to the bus depot. At the northern end of the platform a covered footbridge gave access to the station approach road and taxi rank; in 1954 a bus depot and garage owned by Alexanders was built next to this road and provided a transport interchange. A small wooden signal box was perched upon the down side retaining wall; known as St Andrews Station box it adjoined the footbridge and was the only substantial remnant of the original station. A projecting wooden tower next to the footbridge signified the presence of a hydraulic

St Andrews with the goods shed, looking towards the city. The station master's house can be seen on the left and the branch set is seen in the foreground *c.*1950.   *John Hurst Collection*

St Andrews Links goods shed showing the loading platform, crane, office building and the ubiquitous Scammell 'Scarab' goods lorry, 1955. *Nigel Dyckhoff*

St Andrews Links looking north, *c.*1955, with, *from left to right*, the goods shed, signal box and the station master's house - the latter, built for the St Andrews Railway in 1854, survives to the present day as the Jigger Inn. *Nigel Dyckhoff*

'J35' class 0-6-0 No. 64482 leaves St Andrews for Leuchars and travels along the Junction Line embankment in 1954 - note the tidy track and newly-planted shrubs.

T.G. Hepburn/W. Hennigan Collection

St Andrews, looking towards Leuchars, with the down track removed and the branch under a death sentence.   *M.B. Smith*

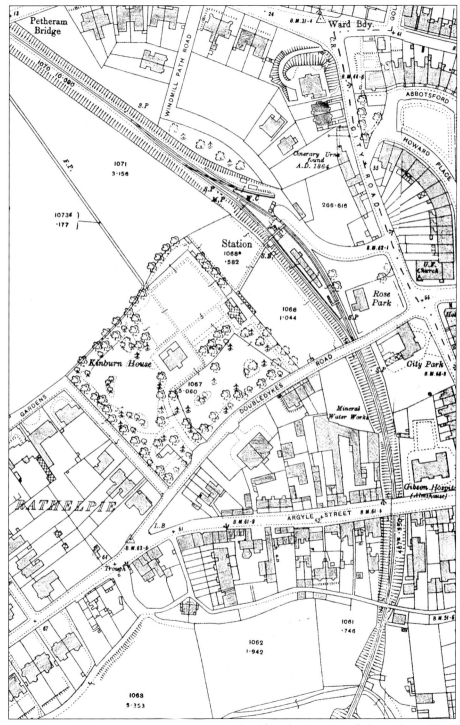

St Andrews station. *Reproduced from the 1914, 25 in. Ordnance Survey Map*

luggage lift. At the southern end of the platform was a small lattice footbridge giving access to a footpath leading to Doubledykes Road. In 1967, two years after the closure of the line to Crail, the rails serving the down face of the platform were removed and the signal box closed. A small carriage dock was situated on the up side to the north of the station; latterly this was used for the temporary storage of camping coaches prior to their being sent to St Rollox works; in winter to store a camping coach. At the head of the dock was a rectangular stone and iron water tank similar to that at Kingsbarns on the line to Anstruther.

A special feature of St Andrews station was the hanging flower baskets under the canopy. These were a source of pride to the staff and, in LNER and BR days, the station was regularly awarded First Prize in the annual 'Best Kept Stations' competitions. In addition the adjoining embankments were regularly tended with fine flower displays provided with the assistance of gardeners from the Town Council, St Leonard's School and the University. According to Mr Bennett:

> The embankments were on a high level overlooking the platforms and being on a steep slope made for difficult working conditions but provided an ideal stage for display. Much 'spade work' was necessary behind the scenes as the pattern of layout of the various sections was different each year and involved a great deal of scheming, keeping in mind the height and colour of the various species of flowers to achieve the best end result. The stationmaster attended to this aspect and also to the provision of necessary plants along with the greater part of the planting work, which was done in May and June. Many thousands of plants were needed which meant literally hundreds of boxes of bedding plants had to be available.

St Andrews (New) from the north, *c.*1955, showing part of the gardens, the footbridge, luggage hoist and (*on the right*) the signal box.   *Nigel Dyckhoff*

Chapter Sixteen

Tramways, Planes and Miniatures: Some Minor Local Railways

'Attack and Protect'
Motto of RAF Leuchars

Apart from the St Andrews and Anstruther & St Andrews lines and the Seggie paper mill there were a number of other railways and tramways which operated in the area and these fell into four distinct categories, namely (a) the horse-drawn tramways serving the Seggie and Seafield brick works, (b) the RAF railway at Leuchars, (c) the Cameron waterworks line and (d) the miniature railways at Craigtoun Park and these are dealt with below in the same order.

The Horse-drawn Tramways

The Seggie Tramway

In the 19th century it was common for short lengths of tramway to be laid to serve industrial concerns both to facilitate movements within the factory (much as forklift trucks would be used today) and as a link to the outside world where transhipment points would be provided to the railway sidings serving the works. Two of these tramways existed locally and both served brickworks. The Seggie Brick and Tile Works seemed to have pre-dated the St Andrews Railway but a short siding just to the south of Guardbridge station was laid out in 1852 to serve the works. This siding was never connected to the adjacent works but a short tramway, some 32 chains in length, was laid between the works and a clay pit to the west, the pit being situated immediately to the south of Seggie House. The gauge and method of working of this line is unknown, but it is presumed that it would have been worked by a horse as there is no evidence of a locomotive having been used - in any event steam power would have been highly uneconomic over so short a line. The works had closed and the tramway abandoned before the end of the 19th century and no trace remains today.

The Seafield Tramway

The Seafield Brick and Tile Works, situated to the south of the St Andrews to Guard Bridge main road had a tramway link from the works to the Seafield Siding, 1 mile 21 chains east of Guardbridge station. This tramway, which was of an unspecified gauge but most probably 2 ft, left the siding and ran southwards and at right angles to the St Andrews branch before crossing the main road on an ungated crossing and entering the yard on the east side of the brickworks. Having a total length of about 44 chains (i.e. just over half a mile)

249

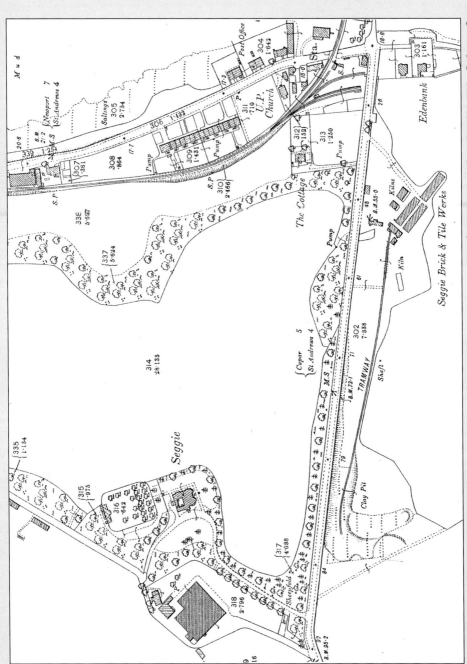

The Seggie Brick and Tile Works Tramway. Note Guardbridge station in its original form, to the right. *Reproduced from the 1894, 25 in. Ordnance Survey Map*

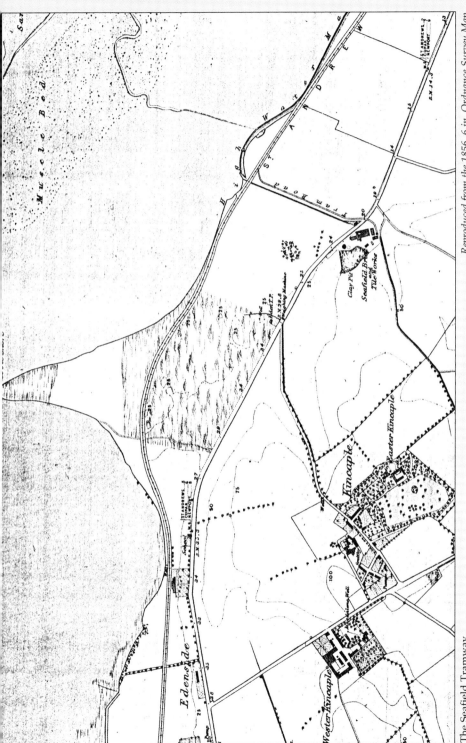

The Seafield Tramway.

Reproduced from the 1856, 6 in. Ordnance Survey Map

the tramway was used for two quite distinct and separate purposes. Inward traffic consisted of coal for the four coal-fired kilns in operation here while outward traffic consisted of the finished products of the works, namely tiles, field drains and bricks. The flat wagons (known as 'bogies') were pulled either by a horse or, on certain occasions when the horse was otherwise occupied, by two men and there is no evidence to suggest that the tramway was ever converted for locomotive haulage. Both siding and tramway were noted as being removed by August 1898 but one suspects that they had gone out of use long before this as most of the products of the works were designed to be sold locally rather than exported great distances. There was, however, a second tramway which was apparently independent of the main one and this was a line some 12 chains in length, connecting the works with a clay pit lying to the west. It is not clear whether this second tramway was of the same gauge or connected with the principal tramway and whether it not it was worked manually or by horse. It is still shown as being in existence on the 1919 Ordnance Survey map and may well have survived in use right up to the closure of the works themselves in 1942.

The Eden Works

There is no objective evidence of there ever having been a tramway at the nearby Eden Brick and Tile Works although the clay pit for the works was situated on the south side of the approach to the road bridge. An unsubstantiated report, however, suggested that a tramway had once run between the pit and works but this seems unlikely and such a line is not shown on any map.

The RAF Leuchars Railway

The Airfield

Although not strictly an adjunct to the St Andrews branch, the RAF railway system at Leuchars is, nevertheless, of interest. The first use of the flat site by the Eden for aviation purposes appears to have been by the Army in 1908 to test out the possibilities of man-lifting kites and in 1911 a squadron of Royal Engineers, who had set up a training camp at Tentsmuir, were joined by the embryonic Royal Flying Corps with their primitive 'string and sealing-wax' aircraft. Fuelled by the stimulus of war with Germany, a site at Reres Farm was acquired for the Royal Naval Air Services and work began in 1916 on levelling and construction work for the airfield. Designated as a 'Temporary Mobilisation Station', the building of the landing strips had not been completed before the Armistice was signed in November 1918 although the base was in use before then and airmen were trained in all duties from initial flying to fleet co-operation work and a total of some 900 staff were stationed there.

Retaining its nautical links, whereby because of the position of the airfield the aircraft's principal use had been to act as the aerial eyes of the Royal Navy, the installation became known as RAF Leuchars in March 1920 and remained in active use throughout the inter-war period. In 1935 it became home to the No. 1 Flying Training School and practice bombing ranges were established at Tentsmuir but by 1938, with the threat of imminent war, the airfield became operational in nature rather than merely training, and 224 and 233 Squadrons were then based at Leuchars. On the second day of the war a Hudson of 224 Squadron attacked a Dornier flying over the North Sea and thereby became the first British aircraft to engage with a Luftwaffe plane. Leuchars remained a highly active and strategically important airfield for the whole of the war, attracting some enemy bombing and in 1950 entered the jet era with a transfer from Coastal Command to Fighter Command. Continuing to play a strategic role in the Cold War and up to the present day RAF Leuchars looks like it will survive into the future despite the general defence cutbacks of recent years.

Early Days

In about 1912 a short siding known as HM Aeroplane Station Siding, was laid with a junction parallel to the former main line track on its up side between Leuchars Junction and Leuchars (Old) stations. This was used on an intermittent basis and from 1916 to 1918 made connection with a 2 ft gauge line which conveyed materials in connection with the building of the aerodrome and its runways. Similar to aerodrome construction lines elsewhere (e.g. at West Fenton),* the motive power was provided by a War Department 0-4-0 outside cylinder saddle tank, built by Wm Bagnall of Stafford No. 1725, which was delivered new by its makers to Leuchars and which bore the name *Concrete*. The narrow-gauge line was closed in the spring of 1918 and the locomotive was returned to its makers in June of that year, being subsequently sold to J.F.Wake of Darlington.

Standard Gauge

The 2 ft gauge line was, at the end of the war, replaced by a standard gauge line operated by the Air Ministry Works Department. The line was used to convey materials, stores, petroleum and aviation fuel to the air base and saw increasing use from 1937 onwards as the desire to equip the base to deal with the perceived air threat from Germany intensified. The line connected up with the LNER siding, crossed the Milton to Leuchars (Old) by-road that passed by Leuchars Junction station and ran at first in an north-eastwards direction where it passed a Works Department store, a contractor's store and the engine shed, all served by a short siding. The line then continued eastwards and crossing the main Leuchars Village to Guardbridge road, before entering the airfield itself. A siding then led to a fuel store while the line itself curved southwards and terminated in two sidings with a gantry and loading platform. The airfield and its associated railway were extensively rebuilt to cope with the demands of

* See A. Hajducki, *The North Berwick & Gullane Branch Lines*, Appendix One (Oakwood Press, 1992).

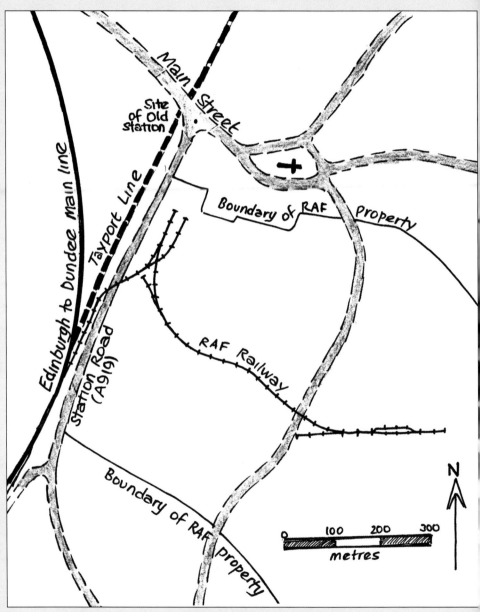

Sketch plan of the RAF Leuchars railway, *c.*1983.

World War II when two parallel reception sidings were laid at the junction with the Leuchars to Tayport line and a gated level crossing was provided over the by-road. Two sidings then diverged in a northerly direction to serve the stores area beside the power house and also the locomotive shed, the main line continuing past the married quarters and across the main road, where there was an open crossing protected by traffic lights, and into the airfield behind the new hangars and served a loading bank with a run-round loop and headshunt.

The line was, from 1920 onwards, the responsibility of the Air Ministry and later the Ministry of Defence. In 1963 the running of the line became the responsibility of the Ministry of Public Building and Works, later renamed the Department of the Environment (Property Services Agency (PSA)) until in December 1984 supply and servicing of stock came under control of the Army with track maintenance and similar matters remaining under the auspices of the PSA.

Locomotives

Motive power on the standard gauge line initially seems to have been provided by the North British but at a later date Admiralty No. 1024, an outside cylinder 0-4-2 saddle tank built by Kerr, Stuart (No. 3127 of 1918) appeared to commence service on the line. This engine was originally supplied to work at Longside (otherwise Lenabo) Airship station next to and connected with the Great North of Scotland Railway Peterhead line and was transferred to work the Leuchars internal line in about 1919, following the run-down of the Longside installation. It then remained at Leuchars and seems to have been the only regular locomotive in steam until 1939 when the line was dieselised. No. 1024 was then retained at Leuchars for strategic reasons (i.e. the fact that it used a non-imported fuel) until 1948 before being sold to Arnott Youngs for use in their Dalmuir shipbreaking yard; transferred to their Old Kilpatrick Yard, the locomotive was scrapped in August 1956.

In January 1939 Air Ministry No. 147, an 0-4-0 diesel mechanical locomotive was delivered direct from its makers Hudswell, Clarke of Leeds (Works No. D613) to Leuchars and remained there until 1962, when it was sold to Connells and moved to another Fife location, Caldwell's Paper Mill at Inverkeithing. No. 147 appears to have been the sole engine in regular use until, in January 1951, Air Ministry No. 212, another 0-4-0 diesel-mechanical shunter, but this time a Fowler product (22959 of 1941 but subsequently rebuilt by Fowler), was transferred to Leuchars from the RAF at Stafford. But its arrival may well have been delayed or its operation found faulty for a Special Traffic Notice of the period stated that BR 0-4-0 saddle-tank No. 68114 (ex-LNER/North British class 'Y9') had spent a six-week period from the end of March 1951 on the line; a further loan was that of BR 'Y9' No. 68095 which was stationed at RAF Leuchars from November 1952 until January 1953. No. 212 was replaced by a similar locomotive No. 217 (Fowler 22964 of 1941) which was transferred from the RAF at Handforth Cheshire in 1953; this locomotive was sold for scrap in June 1984. Sister locomotive No. 218 (Fowler 22965 of 1941) was transferred to Leuchars from Stafford in about May 1976 and had a similar fate. Two more Fowler diesel-mechanical 0-4-0 locomotives were seen at Leuchars, namely No. 243

A view of the RAF railway showing both locomotives, *River Eden* in the foreground and *River Tay* in the background, October 1987.   *Jim Page*

River Tay on shed at RAF Leuchars airbase, October 1987.   *Jim Page*

River Eden at the Village level crossing on the RAF Leuchars railway, October 1987.   *Jim Page*

(No. 23000 of 1943), rebuilt by Fowler and transferred from Handforth in May 1976 and transferred to Burtonwood in Lancashire in June 1964 and Army No. 243 (No. 22890 of 1939) spending a brief period at Leuchars between Armistice Day 1969 and October 1970 before being transferred to Bicester.

In 1971 a Drewry 0-4-0 diesel-mechanical locomotive No. 228 (2182 of 1945) was transferred from the Ministry of Defence, Army Department at Bicester to Leuchars but was again transferred to the MOD at Chilwell, Nottinghamshire in February 1972 being replaced by another Bicester locomotive, No. 427 (Ruston Hornsby 0-6-0 diesel-hydraulic No. 466616 of 1961). This stayed on the line until being transferred to Donnington four years later. In January of that year a diesel-hydraulic 0-4-0 appeared, No. 405 (North British Locomotive Co. No. 27426 of 1955), followed in January 1984 by another North British diesel-hydraulic locomotive, No. 400, this time an 0-6-0 (NBL No. 27421 of 1955) and, in something of an innovation, they acquired names carried on neat nameplates on their sides - No. 400 being *River Tay* , while 405 carried the name *River Eden*. These two venerable locomotives worked the line until 1987 when, with increasing age and prone to mechanical faults, they were replaced within a few years and both were presented by the Army to the Lochty Private Railway in June 1989. Their replacements were No. 425, *River Tay*, (Ruston & Hornsby No. 45919 of 1961) and No. 440, *River Eden*, (R&H No. 468041 of 1962). These 0-6-0 diesel-hydraulic locomotives had both come from the Ministry of Defence depot at Longtown near Carlisle (in August 1987 and March 1989 respectively) and were the last two engines to work the line, remaining at Leuchars until October 1994. The two Lochty locomotives passed into the ownership of the Fife Railway Preservation Group who, subsequently disposed of No. 400; No. 405 is at the Kingdom of Fife Railway Preservation Society's depot at Kirkland near Leven and is currently is in working order. No. 427, which formerly worked at Leuchars, is now at the East Kent Light Railway Society's depot at Shepherdswell in Kent. A preserved locomotive seen at Leuchars, but in a rather different category than the small locomotives listed above, is No. 60009. The LNER 'A4' Pacific *Union of South Africa* made guest appearances at the railway during the annual September Airshow and, although in steam, was taken in and out by one of the diesel locomotives.

Later Operations

The engines were shedded in a small brick shed with an arched corrugated iron roof, the back wall of which showed signs of repair where a locomotive had been inadvertently reversed into it. By 1987 there were two full-time staff in charge of the line and both staff were qualified drivers although usually only one locomotive was in use at the time and the other staff member would spend his time as a shunter/porter. The railway was still in use on at least two days per week and a fitter from the Longmoor Military Railway in Hampshire would call once a month in order to carry out any maintenance work required on *River Eden* or *River Tay* and he would usually require to spend three to four days at a time on this duty. The track, some of which had been in poor condition with rotted sleepers and chairs of Caledonian Railway origin, was completely relaid to a good standard in 1987. Traffic noted then included two large flat wagons which had been previously used to convey machinery and a khaki-painted bulldozer loaded on to a well wagon. The most common usage of the line was, from 1945 onwards, to bring in aviation fuel to the large bulk storage installations at the end of the line and in later years this was brought in by large bogie tanks of either 8,500 or 17,000 gallon capacity.

The line was already under threat in the late 1980s as some fuel was being delivered by road and a new pipe line was in the course of being laid into the airfield from the railway sidings at Linkswood near St Fort and situated on the main line between Leuchars Junction and the Tay Bridge. Although the railway operating staff had been told that the new pipeline installation was merely to complement the railway workings from the base and not to replace them, their fears were well-founded for in October 1994 the internal line was, without notice, closed to all traffic and subsequently lifted, thus ending the 80 year association between the airfield and the railway and, incidentally, also providing a conclusion to the services on the last extant RAF internal railway in the United Kingdom. The main line siding remains, overgrown and disconected, but retained no doubt for some possible future national emergency.

The Cameron Waterworks Railway

A major construction work carried out just before World War I consisted of the Cameron Reservoir and waterworks at Cameron mid-way between Largoward and St Andrews and, in common with many such works of the period, a contractor's line was laid down in order to assist with the construction works. Little is known about the line itself, which was built to 3 ft gauge and the motive power was apparently a Barclay tank engine (possibly No.1633/01). The contractors were the well-known firm of James Kinniburgh Ltd of Great Western Road, Glasgow and the contract for the Cameron scheme was let out in January 1911, the works all being completed prior to the outbreak of war in August 1914. No trace of the line now remains.

'Off to Fairyland' - the 'Deltic' locomotive at work, c.1970. *Alan Brotchie Collection*

The Craigtoun Park Miniature Railway

Craigtoun Park, situated a couple of miles to the south of St Andrews and which was acquired by Fife County Council after the war, consists of the major part of the grounds of Mount Melville house whose earlier inhabitants played a part in the story of the Anstruther & St Andrews Railway. The mansion house, which replaced an earlier rather more antique structure, is described in the *Buildings of Scotland; Fife* as a 'huge pink sandstone Jacobean chateau of 1902 designed by Paul Waterhouse for the brewer James Younger' and with an 'asymmetrical entrance front, the detail surprisingly small-scale and flat, perhaps to avoid the suspicion of *nouveau riche* taste'. The house became a maternity hospital in 1949 and the grounds were opened to the public as a pleasure park, described in a contemporary guidebook as 'completely charming in its various beauties'; such beauties included a rose garden, the Cypress Walk and a Dutch Village, together with a boating lake, sports facilities and, last but not least, a miniature passenger-carrying railway.

The original line, known as the 'Fairyland Railway' was opened in about 1958 and was of 5½ inch gauge and the stock consisted of a petrol-driven locomotive which loosely resembled a 'Deltic' diesel and a number of flat wagons with seats arranged across the track. In about 1975 the line was reconstructed to 7¼ inch gauge and an 0-6-0 petrol-driven locomotive, which formerly ran on the Silver Sands Miniature Railway at Aberdour, was employed. This reincarnation was short-lived and appears to have been abandoned by 1976.[*]

[*] *A Survey of Seaside Miniature Railways*, D.J. Croft (Oakwood Press).

The line was, again, completely reconstructed in the late 1970s and now consists of a 15 inch gauge single line which encircles the lake over a route of some 400 yards and with an average journey time for the complete trip of about five minutes. Originally there was a siding on which the locomotive and carriage shed was situated but these were later rebuilt on to the main line and the siding abolished. There are now no points or signals on the line and facilities consist of a platform, an ungated level crossing and a shed through which the line runs and in which the stock is stabled overnight.

The sole motive power consists of a 2-8-0 tender engine of vaguely US steam locomotive appearance enhanced by 'Rio Grande' being emblazoned on the tender. Bearing the fictional number 278, the locomotive wears a black livery with polished brass fittings and the smokebox, chimney, coupling rods and cowcatcher are all painted red. Weighing two tons and powered by a 1600 cc Ford Sierra Cosworth car engine, the locomotive was built by Severn Lamb Engineering of Stratford-upon-Avon (Works No. R8/76) and has been at Craigtoun since new. Rolling stock consists of three coaches, two open and one roofed; each coach weighs about 1 ton and is capable of holding a maximum of 16 passengers.

At one time there was a 'road-train' bearing the name *Puffing Billy* and consisting of an agricultural tractor hauling several roofed trailers with open sides along the internal road system in the park. The future of the miniature railway may be in some doubt as in the spring of 2005 Fife Council, as part of a strategy to increase the popularity of the park and arrest the declining numbers of those resorting to it, identified the need to spend some £43,846 on the refurbishment of the 'Rio Grande Railway' or provide for its complete replacement at a cost of £70,000.

The Craigtoun Park 'Rio Grande' 2-8-0 petrol locomotive with train, April 2007; note the train shed and station platform in the background. *Alan Simpson*

Chapter Seventeen

On and Off the Rails:
A St Andrews Railway Miscellany

'Just at that moment, he heard the approach of the
7.26 am Leuchars to St Andrews diesel train and his engine stalled'
St Andrews Citizen, 1966

The Night the Tay Bridge Fell

The following formed part of an article which appeared in the *Edinburgh Evening Dispatch* of Tuesday, 9th May, 1905 and was written by Thomas Robertson, one-time station master at Leuchars Junction, on the occasion of his retirement from railway service. Born in the Guildford Arms Hotel, Edinburgh in 1840, where his father was the landlord, Robertson entered the employment of the North British Railway first as a boat inspector on the Burntisland ferries and then as clerk on the North British vessel *Gareloch* operating from Helensburgh. In 1874 he became station master at Guardbridge and was promoted to Leuchars Junction in 1878; eventually he became station master at Haymarket followed by the same position at Edinburgh Waverley. This was his description of how he came to hear of the Tay Bridge Disaster on Sunday 29th December, 1879.

I was appointed to Leuchars Junction only five months after the opening of the bridge. It was a big undertaking and naturally enough there was a great deal of talk about it. It fell on a Sunday night. It was a terrible night. I had experienced some rough weather at sea, but never anything such as we had on that fateful evening.

We were kept busy at Leuchars making everything as safe as we possibly could. The hurricane increased in strength every minute and the few hands about the station had a rough time indeed. When we found that there was nothing more that we could do, we knocked off and I got to my house at Old Leuchars shortly after eleven o'clock. Even inside things were bad enough and my wife and I had, for safety, to remove the children from their room in the west wing of the house to another on the east side. I sat down at the fireside after this had been done and was just taking off my boots when a rap came at the door.

I went to the door and opened it. I could see nothing for the darkness. Straining my eyes as I might, I could see nothing, but through the shrieking of the wind I thought I heard a coarse voice murmuring something. Then I caught the sound of 'The Tay Bridge' and shouted 'Come inside!' There lurching forward into the light the figure of a man; when I saw him I recognised the foreman surfaceman of the length of railway leading up to and on the Tay Bridge. He had tramped through the fearful night the six miles that lay between his post and my house. He was in a particularly agitated state of mind and I saw at once that he had sustained some great shock. 'What brings you, man?' I said. He looked at me queerly for a moment and then said in a halting kind of way 'Oh, man, the brig's doon!'

I thought there was something wrong with the man, in fact I began to have a suspicion that he was not quite right in the head, but I drew him into the room and made him sit down by the fire and got my wife to give him a glass of brandy. Then I said 'Now tell me all about it'. This is the story he told me.

'As the night drew on and the storm showed no sign of tacking off, I began to have an uneasy feeling about the bridge and when the Newport train came up I watched her going over. As she crossed, I saw the sparks flying from her wheels and then the signalman got her clear, proving that she had crossed safely. When the Edinburgh train appeared, I was standing at the end of the bridge and saw her pass on to it. She passed quite close to me. As she drew out over the bridge the three tail lamps - two at the side and one near the centre of the tail carriage - were quite visible. They got closer and closer together as the train went farther away and all at once a cloud of sparks flew up and the lamps disappeared. It struck me at once that there was something wrong and in a fright I ran down the bank. The moon came out and then I saw the gap.'

The story was a terrible one. He told it correctly enough, but broke down when he had finished it. I slipped round to the doctor's and I asked him to come and look at the man. To the doctor, however, he repeated his story and the doctor, turning to me, said 'I'm afraid he's right; there's something in it'.

I borrowed the doctor's gig and drove into St Andrews. It was now early in the morning. The storm died away with an extraordinary rapidity and the scarcely full moon shone out from an almost cloudless sky. I shall never forget the impressiveness of the scene as we neared St Andrews. The old city lay quiet and peaceful, with the bright lights of the moon shining down on it the sodden road over which we were travelling and the trunks of the trees blown down by the gale an hour or two before and the knowledge I had of the ghastly tragedy that had happened a few miles away - the incongruity of it gave rise to some very queer thoughts.

We gave the alarm at St Andrews and returned to Leuchars, there to await the arrival of the special train from Edinburgh, with the heads of departments; Mr Walker, the general manager, was there and so was Sir Thomas Bouch, the engineer of the bridge, accompanied by his son. He was in a pitiable state of mind. That was all I had to do with the Tay Bridge disaster. Curiously enough my wife went over on the train the Friday before the bridge fell and when she returned she said 'Now Tom, I'll never cross that bridge again as long as I live, for just as we got to the centre I felt the bridge swing'.

The 1950s Remembered

On 31st January, 1953 widespread damage was done in the district by a severe gale which blew all day and resulted in part of the signal box roof at St Andrews being blown off and landing on the glass canopy over the platform, causing a considerable amount of damage; temporary repairs were carried out the following day. In 1955 at St Andrews a two-coach local train had arrived at St Andrews at the up platform and the locomotive then intended to run-round the train via the down platform in order to take it back to Leuchars but owing apparently to a misunderstanding the engine travelled back on the up line and collided with the carriages, causing them to ride up and damage the valancing on the platform canopy.

A handful of passengers had entered the carriages while the running-round was taking place and two were taken to the St Andrews cottage hospital with bruises and shock; both were discharged the following day. No disciplinary action was taken, it not being found possible to apportion the blame between the train crew and signalman. In February 1958 a one-day snowstorm caused the telegraph wires to collapse near to Leuchars with the result that services had to be suspended when the branch engine arrived there with the wires and other debris draped around its chimney.

Changing at Leuchars

A lady who lived in Errol and travelled by train to and from St Andrews as an undergraduate in the 1920s told the authors that, after changing stations at Dundee between the LMS West and LNER Tay Bridge stations she met up with friends at Leuchars where they awaited the St Andrews branch service:

> We put up our suitcases, put a travelling rug over them and made up a four at Bridge (Auction then, not Contract as now!). We could get in quite a few rubbers before the train to St Andrews came in. Fortunately the weather seemed to be good enough to sit out on the platform and thus encourage spectators!

Another correspondent related that towards the end of the railway era, many University students would travel to Edinburgh on a Sunday, using the connecting bus service from Leuchars (there being, of course, no rail service on that day) and he leaves a vivid picture of a somewhat bleak Scottish Sabbath evening in the village:

> You got off the train at Leuchars some 400 yards from the village centre. The timing of the train and the switching off of the town lights were such that you reached the main - let's be fair, only - street in Leuchars at the exact moment when all the lights went off and you were plunged into instant, chilling, midnight darkness. It was eerie. If you were doing it for the first time and didn't know that there was a friendly fish-and-chippie out of sight round the corner where the driver of the last bus to St Andrews would be sure to call, it was just ever so marginally frightening.

A Narrow Escape

The last reported accident to take place on the St Andrews Railways took place shortly before Christmas 1966 when a car and train were in collision on the Coble Crossing (otherwise known as the Shelley Crossing). The *St Andrews Citizen* of 24th December takes up the story:

> Two men had a narrow escape last Saturday when their car was wrecked by a train at Shelley Level Crossing. The crossing at Edenside is an access path to the estuary of the River Eden, where considerable duck shooting takes place at this time of year. Lawrence Gibb, a 20-year old electrician, 22 Almond Place, Kirkcaldy was driving the car, and Robert Ross, a 43-year old shot firer, 36 Main Street, West Wemyss was his passenger. One of the crossing gates was open and while Ross was opening the other, Gibb moved the car forward on to the line. Just at that moment, he heard the approach of the 7.26 am Leuchars to St Andrews diesel train and his engine stalled. He had just time to scramble clear before the train hit the car. No one was hurt, but the line was blocked for more than two hours while wreckage was cleared away. During this period, rail passengers between St Andrews and Leuchars were conveyed by bus.

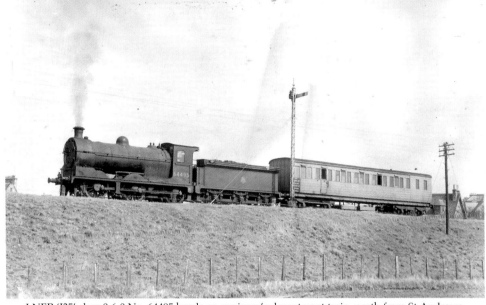

LNER 'J35' class 0-6-0 No. 64495 heads an engineer's department train north from St Andrews, 22nd April, 1959; the locomotive was withdrawn from service in the following year.

J.L. Stevenson

'J38' class 0-6-0 No. 65902 on a down ballast train from Thornton heading north from St Andrews, *c.*1961. *Mike McDonald*

Footplate Hurls and Unexpected Visitors

Douglas Paul, now resident in Kilconquhar, had an early interest in railways and wrote that:

My family moved to St Andrews in 1952 from Ilford in Essex when I was nine years of age. It was a huge culture shock to move from the London suburbs, where almost every schoolboy revelled in the abundance of steam on the main line to East Anglia, to an environment which was almost steam-free. Fortunately I did find one friend, Alan Meade, who shared my passion and together we spent many hours at St Andrews station getting hurls on the footplate of *Kettledrummie, Peter Poundtext, Dumbiedykes* and the like. The motive power on show was generally predictable but occasionally a really unexpected engine would turn up. On a dark night in March 1953, imagine our surprise when the 8.30 pm arrival from the Fife Coast loomed into view, not with the usual 'B1' in charge but 'Crab' 42708 of Newton Heath, Manchester which had apparently been allocated to Thornton Junction for a month before returning south. We would regularly cycle to Leuchars Junction where there were many more variety of classes to see and it was a particular thrill to watch the London-bound fish trains hurtling round the sharp curve with coal flying off the tenders of the Pacifics and 'V2s' hauling them. Most Sundays we cycled to Anstruther to see what was 'on shed' and that introduced me to exotic names such as *Luckie Mucklebackit* and *Jingling Geordie.*

On schooldays I used to go to St Andrews station at lunchtime for a footplate hurl and one day, to my shock and horror, the engine continued on towards Leuchars. I protested to the driver in vain and finally arrived back at the Burgh School about 3 pm covered in grime and fearful as to how Mrs Roche, our teacher, would react. When I entered the class she had a face like thunder but she and the class collapsed into laughter when I spluttered out my excuse for being late.

We lived on the Largo Road overlooking the Canongate and I had a grandstand view of trains battling up the 1 in 49 gradient to Mount Melville. There was very little going up and down the line between 1953 and 1961 that escaped my attention and I still have vivid recollections of the sights and sounds being played out every day on the line across the field. Summer Saturdays were particularly exciting when a Glasgow Queen Street to St Andrews holiday train would come rolling down the hill from Mount Melville about lunchtime with a pair of Eastfield 4-4-0 'Directors' in charge. The coaches remained in the platform, returning to Glasgow at 4.13 pm, usually behind a St Rollox 'Black Five' which was sometimes parked in the short siding at the Leuchars end of the station. On 20th June 1953, for example, 'D11s' 62684 *Wizard of the Moor* and 62688 *Ellen Douglas* and 'Black Five' 45115 were the engines involved. Ocasionally locomotives from further afield were seen storming up the hill on the return train to Glasgow, e.g. Carlisle Kingmoor 'Crab' 42830 on 12th July, 1958, Kirkby Stephen BR Standard 2-6-0 76051 the following Saturday and Motherwell 'Hiker' 44969 on 27th August, 1960.

One memorable day, the 4.13 started up the hill with more coaches than usual (about ten from memory) and the 'Black Five' couldn't cope with the gradient. The locomotive ground to a halt half-way to Mount Melville and, after several attempts to restart the train, the fireman ran back to St Andrews for help. Eventually 'K4' *McLeod of McLeod* appeared, sprinting up the hill to give banking assistance. This was the only time I saw a 'K4' on the line although the Dunfermline 'K2s' did make the odd appearance. On 4th April, 1955, for example, the 9.35 am arrival from Dunfermline appeared behind 61770 in place of 'B1' 61101 which for years was the regular performer on this working. Likewise, Dundee 'B1' 61118 was invariably in charge of the train which departed Dundee at 2.17 pm for Edinburgh via Tayport and the Fife Coast (3.18 from St Andrews). Thornton 'B1' 61103 was the stalwart of the 12.12 arrival from Glasgow.

A wartime view of NBR 'Scott' class 4-4-0 No. 9497 *Peter Poundtext* on the 2.15 pm Dundee to Edinburgh via Crail service climbing the bank to Mount Melville on 17th January, 1945 - note the burnt smokebox door and the check rail.   *J.L. Stevenson*

Peter Poundtext in early BR livery on the 12.01 pm St Andrews to Leuchars service with the A91 to Guardbridge on the right, 24th May, 1949. The locomotive was finally withdrawn from Dundee in October 1957.   *J.L. Stevenson*

On a wet cold evening around February 1959, 62487 *Glen Arklet* from St Margarets shed, Edinburgh made an unexpected appearance on the 5.30 pm train to Edinburgh in place of the usual 'B1'. By this time NBR 4-4-0s had become extremely rare over the line and 62487 was in a dreadful state. It ground to a halt half-way up the hill to Mount Melville in the rain with steam issuing from everywhere it should not have. After a while the crew detached the first two coaches from the last two and 62487 ran forward to Mount Melville where the two coaches were deposited in a siding while the engine ran back for the two coaches abandoned on the gradient. This was perhaps the last duty performed by this locomotive. Another notable visitor to St Andrews was Fowler 2-6-2T 40069 which appeared on a St Andrews local on 26th April, 1958, freshly transferred to Dundee from Nuneaton. Another of the same class, 40011, was allocated to Keith shed from Carnforth at the same time and these were probably the first of the class to be allocated to Scotland.

Sunday trains were not permitted at St Andrews and this was breached only once to my knowledge when Dundee Caledonian 0-6-0 57653 headed out light engine to Mount Melville one Sunday afternoon in the mid-1950s shortly before its transfer to Carlisle Kingmoor. This was the only Caledonian locomotive I ever saw at St Andrews, so it was a rare siting on both accounts.

Douglas Paul was a keen golfer and contributed the following tale of the Black Sheds next to St Andrews Links station:

The Black Sheds helped to make the 17th hole of the Old Course one of the most feared in the world of Championship golf. They rose in front of the 17th tee and had to be driven over to reach the fairway on the other side of this dog-leg hole. The line to aim for was a telegraph pole behind the Sheds and any ball that struck to the right of it was likely to end up out of bounds on the railway. On one occasion in the late 1950s, I was playing with my father in the semi-finals of the Family Foursomes, a popular competition in St Andrews. We were one down with two to play when we arrived at the 17th tee. It was my turn to drive and the ball soared away to the right of the telegraph pole. It was touch and go if it would make the fairway. When we walked round the Sheds we found the ball in bounds, having just cleared them. It was my Father's turn to play the next shot and when he did so, the ball fizzed bizarrely away to the right and on to the railway. On inspecting the ball afterwards we found a great gash in it - it had obviously hit the guttering of the Sheds on its descent from my drive. The Black Sheds had cost us the match.

Varied Routes, the Ghost Train and a Locomotive called Peter

One of the co-authors of this book, Mike Jodeluk, recalled that:

My earliest reminiscence of the Fife Coast line dates back to the early 1950s. My grandfather was a railway employee who had worked for the Caledonian and subsequently the LMS companies and, latterly, the nationalised British Railways. He used his railway pass/privilege tickets to take us to St Andrews every year for our summer holiday. The route taken from our home in Stirling was firstly to Dundee West station from where we walked next door and down the stairs to the equally draughty Tay Bridge station to catch the train to Leuchars Junction to change once again. The family had taken various routes over the years including, in the earlier years of the century, the Stirling and Dunfermline (S&D) line to Alloa and on via the single-track Devon Valley Railway changing at Kinross Junction for the equally rural single-track

Peter Poundtext approaches St Andrews Links signal box - note the kissing gate in the foreground and the Golfers' bridge just visible in the background, 18th April, 1953.

J.L. Stevenson

line via Auchtermuchty to Ladybank. Changing here a main-line train was taken to Leuchars, where a change was made for the last section to St Andrews. Occasionally a variation of route was to travel via the S&D through Dunfermline to Inverkeithing where a main-line train was taken via Kirkcaldy and Leuchars. Motive power on the rural line varied, but was often an ex-NBR 4-4-0 and non-corridor coaches. However a Sentinel steam railcar was often used on the Devon Valley Section and the family nicknamed it the 'ghost train' as it didn't have a locomotive at the front. When it was slowly climbing the steep gradient from Tillicoultry to Devon Siding the guard used to show off to the passengers by unloading his bicycle and cycling along the cess at the side of the track to show that he could cycle faster than the railcar.

Often on arrival at St Andrews my grandfather would conform to my wishes and take me forward to inspect the engine while he would exchange pleasantries with the footplate crew. With my grandmother observing from afar, I never managed to prevail on my grandfather to arrange a trip up onto the footplate but we did get close and I can remember leaning over to look at the valve gear between the frames under the boiler. A further recollection was that the locomotive was often a 'Scott' class 4-4-0 by the name of 'Peter', but I couldn't recall the surname. It was a few years later that I found it was No. 62438 *Peter Poundtext*.

Lunchtime Escapades and Wind, Snow and Steam

Trainspotters were once a common feature on Britain's railways and St Andrews station was no exception as Mike goes on to relate:

In the 1950s it was common to see young boys hanging around stations, although they were usually large stations where the bigger locomotives could be seen. These were the legendary 'trainspotters' who would shout with joy when a long sought-after locomotive appeared and its number could legitimately be underlined in their Ian Allan *abc* booklet in which all the locomotive numbers were listed. Not many locomotives were seen at St Andrews and those seen were usually regular performers so trainspotting was hardly a keen sport there. However, the writer and a friend used to leave Madras College primary school and race along to the railway station during their lunchbreak, eschewing the delights of the shore, harbour or cathedral grounds favoured by other pupils.

We became quite friendly with the locomotive crew and guard of the lunch-time train which would have arrived before us in the up platform. The loco would run round and haul the train out of the up platform and propel it back into the down platform for departure to Leuchars or Dundee. The station master being away for lunch, we occasionally managed to get a 'hurl' in the guard's compartment of the brake coach during these operations. Ambition drove us further and, following suitable admiration of the loco from the platform, we were occasionally invited onto the footplate during shunting operations. This had a higher status than 'trainspotting' and was classified as 'cabbing' the locomotive. While on the footplate the driver would kindly answer our questions about the various brass wheels and dials and the firemen would be putting in the odd shovelful of coal from the tender into the firebox to keep the fire going and the boiler pressure up for the imminent departure. We occasionally got to do the honours with the shovel as well but we found it very long, heavy and unwieldy and would sometimes 'scart' our knuckles on the lubricator below the driver's or the fireman's bench-like seat and we could feel the heat from the firebox on our hands and through the sleeves of our dark navy blue blazers. It was refreshing after such exertion to sit on the fireman's seat and lean out of the single cab window to enjoy the cool sea breeze. It was often an ex-NBR 'D30' 'Scott' class that we met with such as 62427 *Dumbiedykes*, 62434 *Kettledrummle*, 62436 *Lord Glenvarloch* or, my favourite, the aforementioned 62438 *Peter Poundtext*. Other appearances were put in by ex-LNER 'D34' 62485 *Glen Murran* , one of a number of ex-NBR 'J37s' including 64575, 64538 and 64620, and the occasional LNER 'J39' such as 64786. The standard train formation was three or four non-corridor coaches.

The train would then be taken out of the up platform to clear the points along the embankment leading to the Petheram Bridge. Looking out of the fireman's window or the spectacle window on the right hand side, I could see the wall at the top of the brae with its doorway leading from Kinburn Park and the steep path known as 'Jacob's Ladder' leading down towards Petheram Bridge on the far side of Mr Maronski's market garden - I knew the ownership of this field as his daughter, Felicja, was in my class at school. Once the train was clear of the points at the north end of the station the driver sounded the whistle, with an extra couple of 'pops' pulled on it by ourselves. The loco then propelled the train back into the down platform to await the departure time. Meanwhile it was time to make ourselves scarce after a quick wash in the fireman's shovel courtesy of the use of soap and some not very hot water from the slacker pipe.

School authority, as with railway authority, frowned on our lunch-time activities so we had to be clear of the station before the station master appeared as we were obviously not bona fide passengers and we daren't be after the bell into school or appear in grimy disorder. But what memories!

Again in the 1950s, I recall a winter afternoon that was bitterly cold due to an icy wind from the north-east. We were supposed to be playing rugby but despite the run along the street from the school and through Kinburn Park we were all chilled to the bone. Our teacher led us enthusiastically through the door at the top of 'Jacob's Ladder' and over the fence onto the playing fields (now built up with modern University buildings). We were more interested in keeping warm than listening to the teacher who was trying to coax the unwilling majority into action. Within a few minutes the wind brought flurries of snow; that quickly turned into a blizzard. Just at that moment a 'J36', No. 65330, appeared from the station in its deep cutting next to Kinburn Park heading down the gradient towards Petheram Bridge. After a quick 'pop' on the whistle as it cleared the points, the engine then took up the strain to push its three coaches back into the station emitting, as it did so, huge clouds of white steam that scudded across Mr Maronski's market garden and on to us in the playing fields amid the thickening flakes of snow. Meanwhile our teacher had decided

The Eden at low tide with 'J37' class 0-6-0 No. 64615 heading across the viaduct with a local from
St Andrews to Leuchars on the last day of June 1958.   *W.S. Sellar*

Ex-NBR No. 62412 *Dirk Hatteraick* on shed at St Andrews, 29th May, 1949; this engine was
withdrawn from service at Dunfermline Upper in September 1950.   *J.L. Stevenson*

to abandon the rugby training due to the worsening weather, but couldn't understand our change of mind as we dashed towards the clouds of steam trying to envelop ourselves in them as we reckoned they were warmer than the flurries of snow while others of us simply stopped to watch the progress of the train as it was very much still an age when self-respecting boys still wanted to be an engine driver when they grew up. We then walked down the Doubledykes overbridge to see the tail end of the train in the down platform of the station before dragging our way reluctantly back to school.

Sun, Sea and Sheds

A journey on the St Andrews branch was something to savour, with the spirited start from the bay platform at Leuchars, the descent down across the Motray Burn into Guardbridge, the busy level crossing there, the views out of the train window over the muddy Eden estuary to the Tentsmuir shore and the entry into St Andrews past the golfers who, anxious not to be distracted, did not even look up at the passing trains. Mike Jodeluk recounts here a memorable journey that he made on a Saturday morning in July 1965:

It was a warm, sunny day and I decided to make one of my regular trips from Cupar to St Andrews. Preferring the train to the bus I caught the Edinburgh-Aberdeen diesel-hauled train and, after struggling to find a window seat, I was just in time to see lines of wagons on the left-hand side at the Cupar beet factory, painted grey with BSC (British Sugar Corporation) in large white lettering - these wagons were for internal use only. There was a speed restriction for bridge repairs at Dairsie, but arrival was on time at Leuchars where I changed into the two-car metro Cammell dmu sitting in the south bay and awaiting the arrival of a train from Aberdeen. While waiting my mind drifted back 10 years to when I was waiting in the same place for a member of my family to arrive on a similar up train and the train duly arrived behind 'A4' Pacific No. 60004 *William Whitelaw*. I was quickly returned from my memories by two American 'Phantoms' and two French 'Mysteres' flashing overhead with a roar and my attention was drawn to the wreck of another French jet which had crashed only a few days before on the edge of Leuchars aerodrome. Meanwhile a diesel goods train had rumbled by northwards and the packed train from Aberdeen had arrived behind an English Electric type '4', No. D263, and was in the process of departing for Edinburgh.

Now it was our turn and the dmu, with a dozen or so passengers, sauntered out of the bay at 11.45, the driver picking up the single-line token at Leuchars South signal box. The guard came round to check our tickets as we passed the rusting rails of Seggie Siding where some of the black-painted wagons with white lettering still resided. There were a few mineral wagons waiting for the local coal merchant in Guardbridge station yard as we drew level with the signal box to exchange tokens and we then passed over the crossing and the Eden viaduct. I stood at one of the south-facing droplights and felt the sunshine and warm breeze brush my face as I breathed in the smell of the seaweed exposed by the low tide. We continued up the short gradient past the Guardbridge home and distant semaphore signals. There were weeds growing up through the track and the sea came up so far that it almost touched the low embankments as we wound our way across the flat land towards the links. Through the golf courses we passed and under the distinctive wooden footbridge and on through the jumble of sheds that marked the goods station at St Andrews. Then we crossed the Petheram Bridge and climbed up the bank passing the new university buildings then under construction on our right before entering the station in its deep cutting. Here the waiting room, kiosk and station buffet were all in the course of being modernised - was this an omen of something yet to happen?

'B1' class 4-6-0 No. 61102 in the dock at St Andrews with a motor boat which has just been unloaded from its train - a single BR full brake, 17th April, 1967.   *Mike Jodeluk*

The last steam locomotives at St Andrews, 17th April, 1967. 'B1' No. 61180 running round the weedkilling train - note the branch dmu in the dock and the Gresley coach No. DE320946, a 1935 York-built example. Within two weeks both locomotives had been withdrawn and all steam workings had ended in Scotland.   *Mike Jodeluk*

Steam, Weeds and a Gresley Coach

In a final contribution, Mike recounts the story of the final steam working on the St Andrews branch at the very end of steam in Scotland and not all that long before the branch itself was completely abandoned:

It was 17th April, 1967 and we all knew that the end of steam was nigh.* With hardly a fortnight to go in Scotland one couldn't afford to miss an opportunity to get a few final photographs before it became all but a memory. At Dundee Tay Bridge MPD an ex-NBR 'J37', No. 64576, was sitting outside the engine shed door in the spring sunshine while ex-LNER 'B1' No. 61072 was working as yard pilot in Tay Bridge goods yard. After taking a few photographs of both I had a chat with one of the shed fitters who informed me that there were two steam locos busy at work across in Fife and that he thought that it would be worth my while to go and see them - apparently a 'B1' was working as goods pilot at Leuchars and another of the same class was on a weed killer train at St Andrews. I was lucky enough to find an immediate bus connection to St Andrews (the next train would have arrived too late) and when I arrived there I found the weed killer train consisting of a brake van, a single goods van, six tankers and two ex-LNER teak Gresley coaches in the down platform with 61180 still connected to the brake van tender-first at the south end of the train. Painted details on the sides of the coaches stated that this was the 'Eastern Region Weedkilling Train - Civil Engineers Dept - To be returned to Leeman Road, York'. The yellow painted 'spray coach' was numbered DE320995 and had originally been built at York in 1935. The grey-painted 'lodging van' was numbered DE320946 and was of the same origin as the spray coach. I was astonished to find the Leuchars pilot engine. No. 61102, also there and sitting in the dock platform just below the bus station.

No. 61102 had arrived tender-first only a short time before, hauling a BG (brake gangwayed or full parcels brake coach) from which a small motor boat had been unloaded onto the dock platform. At 1.08 pm the loco left for Leuchars, propelling the BG. Meantime 61180 was being detached from the south end of the weedkilling train and was run round for the next part of its duties. I managed to race along the cutting on the west side of the station to get into position to photograph the loco as it completed its run round when I was surprised to find the branch twin-car Metro Cammell dmu, one coach in BR green livery, the other in the new Rail Blue, sitting in the dock platform at 1.21 pm, only 13 minutes after 61102 had left with its single coach.

After a brief conversation with the inspector on the weed killing train, I found out that it was going to Tay Bridge South, reversing to Newport-on-Tay East† and then travelling via Stannergate, Dundee to the terminus of the Kingsmuir goods branch in Angus. I received permission to board the train provided that I touched nothing and we set off at 1.23 pm. After a brief stop on the way, we passed Guardbridge box and, after barking up the steep gradient past the paper mill we were given a straight run through to Leuchars Junction at 1.39 and so left the St Andrews Railway. A final bit of excitement with steam only days before it was finally banned in Scotland.

---

* The actual date for the cessation of steam in Scotland was 30th April, 1967 but the standard gauge steam locomotive on BR lasted at a few outposts in the North West of England, until 11th August, 1968.
† The terminus of the Tayport branch after the line had been truncated beyond that station on 22nd May, 1966 to allow the Tay road bridge approach roads to be built; a bus service linked Tayport station with Newport-on-Tay East for a brief period until 18th December, 1968; the final closure of the branch between Wormit and Newport took place on 5th May, 1969.

The tablet is exchanged at Guardbridge on the last steam working over the branch, 17th
April, 1967.   *Mike Jodeluk*

Reminiscences of a Relief Clerk

The following reminiscences were contributed by Michael B. Smith who was
employed on the St Andrews branch in the mid-1960s:

'Chute Leuchars Junction vice ... Monday first' or 'Chute St Andrews vice ...
Wednesday to ...' were amongst the contents of telegrams that I received periodically
by means of the railway telegraph system, when I was relief clerk on the district 'spare'
based at BR's District Commercial Manager's Office at Dundee during the years 1963-5.
In long used railway telegraph terminology, this was translated as 'Take duty at
Leuchars Junction or St Andrews in place of ... from ...' The area of the district covered
meant that, while my home station was Dundee, I was available to be posted to any
point requiring office staffing on the former LNER and Dundee & Arbroath Joint Line
section between Montrose and Inverkeithing and branches. The enticement of a 10 per
cent aggregational allowance attached to the post salary was intended to cover
incidental inconveniences such as making one's way to and from work, by whatever
means were at hand, which did not include necessarily travelling by train.
    At that time, travelling to and from Fife seemed a considerable adventure for, whilst
long connected by rail, somehow from the Angus side of the estuary it still seemed to be
a place apart, to be ventured into with some caution, or so it was hinted darkly in
various of the Dundee offices - Fifers were then seen to be very different, almost insular
people, although I never found this to be so! Relief work required the undertaking of the
duties of the person whose post was to be covered - including the appropriate shift. For
work in Fife, this meant the prospect of travelling by the first available train, usually the

06.20 Dundee Tay Bridge to Edinburgh Waverley, having first made judicious enquiries (if working at Leuchars Junction) as to whether or not it would be possible to arrive by that train to take up duty. Occasionally such bookings as were the case at that early hour could be covered by the Leading Porter on duty, but this could not be guaranteed and the 'exigencies of the service' decreed that it was entirely up to the 'spare man' to appear on duty at least some 20 minutes before the first train of the day, especially if he were unfamiliar with the workings of that office. This could mean that, on occasions, travel the previous evening was necessary, with appropriate sleeping arrangements in a porter's bothy or convenient coach being required especially when taking up early duty at Tayport station.

My recollections of working at Leuchars Junction and St Andrews remain fairly clear, even now, and so now it may be convenient to provide a few vignettes of work at each station.

The various turns of duty which I undertook at Leuchars Junction booking office consisted mainly of late shifts beginning at 13.00. The station master of the time, Alan Reid (who had been promoted to that post from Ladybank) was a charming man and railwayman of the old school and a stickler for keeping the daily balance books correct. Accordingly he was liable to appear, without warning, as part of his summer evening walk from the Station House in Leuchars village, red pencil flashing, to check through my entries in the account books after the evening balance had been taken and ensure that everything was in order. Fortunately, they were so! RAF warrant traffic from the adjoining air base constituted the major part of booking office duties although there was also a constant but lesser flow of passengers and parcels traffic which emanated from the nearby villages of Balmullo and Leuchars itself. Work in the office could often be a social event with plenty of conversation (if time permitted) on the topics of the day, the weather or the location of a missing parcel. Train services at the station were, primarily, the Edinburgh to Aberdeen main-line trains with some through St Andrews to Dundee services. Supplementing the latter were the branch line services proper, a two-car Metro-Cammell dmu set, which used the bay platform at the south end of the station. The north bay, effectively out of use since the closure of the Tayport link in 1956, was used periodically for storage and the occasional extra northbound local train; its removal came later.

The use of the branch line service brought even greater meaning to the term 'Junction' at various times of the year when, for instance, the University and St Leonards terms started or finished or, as in 1964, when the Open was held at the Old Course. At these times, the deluge of passengers detraining from a main line arrival blackened the platform considerably, at least until everyone was shoehorned into the branch dmu. Whilst, periodically, complaints about overcrowding found their way back to the booking office, I know from my own experience of travelling on the branch service in such conditions, that these were largely assuaged by the unrivalled views of the Eden estuary and the approach to St Andrews and, most importantly for many, of the Old Course, which greeted the traveller as the train threaded its way across such hallowed ground. I remember the panorama reducing one of two passengers from far away Oklahoma, previously and loudly vocal, to a hushed 'Gee, Mildred, and this train takes us *through* what we came *all this way* to see!' Transfer to and from the branch service on these occasions involved also considerable amounts of luggage, arriving from and distributed to all points of the railway system. This was loaded into, or removed from, the capacious van accommodation on the dmu, largely by means of the ubiquitous but elderly three-wheeled barrows. It demanded from the platform staff expert handling at some speed, coupled with, so often, considerable physical and often verbal efforts, some of the more choice of the latter on occasions being heard as far as the booking office!

On the RAF base 'Open Day', usually held in September each year, incoming traffic, primarily by train, resulted in a complete overload on local services, with extra trains being provided from Dundee Tay Bridge, Edinburgh Waverley and elsewhere. In the case of the Dundee trains, at that time, these were usually powered by whatever motive power Tay Bridge shed could provide - usually 'B1' 4-6-0s - with non-corridor stock in rakes of six having been exhumed from carriage siding storage at Dundee West. I recollect that some of these workings would 'lie over' at Leuchars Junction, whereas others travelled on to Thornton Junction, to await the return workings later in the day.

As far as I can recollect, delivery of the parcels and goods traffic into the village and the RAF quarters was dealt with by road motor lorry from St Andrews, and did not normally concern the parcels office at the Junction unless, of course, the item concerned arrived 'to be called for'. This meant additional, and continuing transfer at the station of a considerable amount of parcels traffic, which would vary from day to day, in addition to the peaks mentioned earlier. I was able to observe, from the booking office window, the periodic arrival and departure of the rail oil tanker vehicles which served the air base planes and the steam hauled freight workings on the St Andrews branch line. My recollections of working at Leuchars Junction, during those years, are of constant action, main line and branch, considerable passenger and parcels bookings, never knowing what kind of enquiry might come next. This was all challenging work against the backcloth, for the most part, of a golden evening sun - prophetic, perhaps, in view of the imminent disappearance of the St Andrews branch.

Memories of St Andrews station leads me conveniently to mention some aspects of work there. Office staffing at the station was split between the Booking Office and Parcels Office with, I remember, two members of staff on each of early and late shifts at the former, one senior to the other, and double-shifted clerical and porter Parcels Office staffing, with assistance as required at peak periods, which is why and where I was launched into periodic maelstroms of activity, all under the benign but expert supervision of Charles Davidson, station master. By 1964 St Andrews station had been freshly repainted (the more cynical of railwaymen were wont to remark that this was usually the first step towards closure) with some improvements having been effected to make it more 'user friendly' for the public. The results of these works became apparent immediately upon descending the stairs from the overbridge leading from the bus station. The intending passenger now faced the booking office windows, with the parcels office being located further south towards the Crail end of the island platform, a vista bordered by attractive hanging flower baskets.

The summer of 1964 was a particularly busy one, with the Open being held on the Old Course, as well as the normal movement of University and school traffic. Being sent to St Andrews, however, meant that I was suddenly at the 'sharp end' insofar as all the requests for trunks to be uplifted from St Salvator, Chalmers or other halls, as well as the local hotels and board residences (well before the era of wheeled cases!) were channelled through the parcels office - so, a busy phone line! In addition, originating incoming traffic loaded off the branch trains, from either direction, required to be sorted into geographical areas, prior to being loaded on road motor lorries for delivery. Before any deliveries could take place, the long, often wearisome business of sheeting the parcels* had to be undertaken.

When the 1964 Open was at its height and the station already was filled to capacity, a notable appearance was that of the Scottish Region General Manager's saloon, complete with the then incumbent of that post, William Geoffrey Thorpe (a larger than life former LNER Manager who scrutinised employees over the top of his half-moon glasses), accompanied by his chief assistants. The saloon was hauled by a BRCW type '2' locomotive complete with an advertisement for a well-known brand of Scotch whisky which then, as now, was 'still going strong'. It had long been the practice for the GM to make periodic visits around his fiefdom to keep in touch with staff and provide a degree of 'hands on' management but the presence of the headboard was inexplicable.

---

* Listing the parcels on to delivery sheets so that the lorry driver could obtain a signature for each item.

Whilst my duties at St Andrews were confined to the parcels office, from time to time I required to visit the adjacent booking office. Originating passenger traffic was extensive with a certain amount of commuter traffic to Dundee as well as longer distance traffic, much of which originated from the University and schools 'peaks'. Considerable efforts were demanded of the staff and the consistent thump of the Edmondson ticket dating machine testified to the traffic passing through combined with the handling of a wide variety of enquiries and 'out of the way' bookings to relatively unusual destinations which demanded considerable mental agility while using the BR regional timetables. If passengers (not 'customers') intended to travel by the nightly London sleeper services calling at the station then the staff had to telephone Dundee and, when the line was busy, much patience was required on the part of booking clerks and passengers alike - how different from the instant computer booking system of today.

Whilst recently standing on the site of the eastern platform edge at St Andrews it was not difficult to cast my mind back these forty, and more, years to remember the periodic crowds, the smell of the Parcels Office gum, hear the Edmondson being 'gi'ed laldy' (i.e. considerably overworked) during busy times and to reflect specifically upon an answer given there to a persistent lady who, having requested the time of the next train to Dundee and being given the relevant information inquired further 'Aye, but is there no one afore that?' The unanswerable response of the booking clerk was 'Madam, the company *never* runs a train before the next one!'

Birmingham RC&W Bo-Bo type '2' (class '27') with the General Manager's Special at St Andrews, 11th July, 1964. *M.B. Smith*

Appendix One

A Brief Chronology

All opening and closing dates are the 'with effect from' dates; the actual date upon which the last train ran may be one or two days before if the closure date was a Monday. In the case of signal boxes closure dates given are when use of box was discontinued.

Sections of line

Leuchars (Old) to Leuchars North Junction - opened (Passengers & Goods) 17.05.1848 EP&DR, closed (P) 09.01.1956 BR, singled 08.06.1959, closed (G) 06.11.1967 BR.

Leuchars North Junction to Milton Junction - opened (P & G) 17.05.1848 EP&DR; remains open for all traffic.

Milton Junction to St Andrews Links – opened (P & G) 01.07.1852 StAR, closed (G) [excepting Seggie Siding] 20.06.1966 BR, closed (P & Seggie Siding) 06.01.1969 BR.

St Andrews Links to St Andrews (New) – opened (P&G) 01.07.1887 A&StAR, closed (P&G) 06.01.1969 BR.

Passenger Stations

	Company	Opened	Closed	Notes
Guardbridge	StAR	01.07.1852	06.09.1965	
Leuchars Junction	NBR	01.06.1878	-	
Leuchars (Old)	EP&DR	17.05.1848	01.06.1878	
		01.12.1878	03.10.1921	
St Andrews (Links)	StAR	01.07.1852	01.07.1887	a
St Andrews (New)	A&StAR	01.07.1887	06.01.1969	

Notes: a – Replaced by St Andrews (New) from that date.

Goods Stations, Sidings, etc.

	Company	Opened	Closed	Notes
Brickworks Siding	StAR	27.09.1873	07.1906	a
Guardbridge	StAR	01.07.1852	20.06.1966	
Leuchars (Old)	EP&DR	17.05.1848	06.11.1967	
Leuchars Airplane Station Siding	NBR	c.1912	01.10.1994	
St Andrews Links	StAR	01.07.1852	20.06.1966	
Seafield Siding	StAR	1852	10.08.1898	b
Seggie Siding	StAR	06.1853	06.01.1969	c

Notes: a – Lifted c.1880, reinstated 05.07.1897; b – siding out of use prior to this date; c - lifted c.1861 and reinstated Summer 1867.

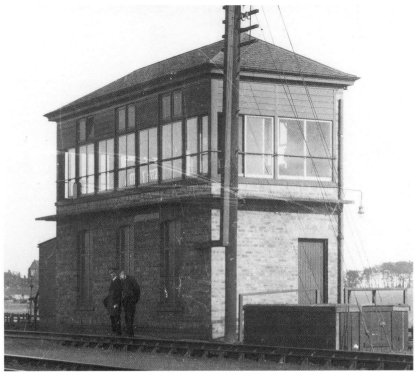

The NBR 1920 Leuchars North signal box, *c.*1930 - this box, now modernised and renamed plain Leuchars, still remains in use today. *Authors' Collection*

Signal Boxes

	Company	Opened	Closed	Notes
Guardbridge	NBR	19.03.1894	05.01.1969	a
Leuchars North (first)	NBR	01.06.1878	12.09.1920	b
Leuchars North (second)	NBR	12.09.1920	-	c
Leuchars (Old)	NBR	01.06.1878	05.06.1959	
Leuchars South	NBR	01.06.1878	05.01.1969	
St Andrews Links	A&StAR	01.07.1887	10.02.1957	d
St Andrews Station	A&StAR	01.07.1887	03.09.1967	

Notes: a – Reduced to gate box 03.09.1967; b – replaced by second box; c – renamed Leuchars 15.02.1970, still open; d – replaced by ground frame released by token.

Appendix Two

Station Traffic Statistics 1900-1934

	Passengers Booked (No.)	Receipts inc. parcels £	Merchandise & Minerals (tons)	Coal (tons)	Livestock (no.)	Goods £ (A)
St Andrews (Links) and (New)						
1900	131,319	13,389	16,851	17,934	7,537	3,601
1901	118,856	17,706	15,369	17,314	6,458	3,231
1902	115,383	13,628	16,811	18,916	4,508	3,225
1903	126,979	14,090	18,438	18,713	5,637	3,347
1904	140,456	15,174	21,279	19,922	6,809	3,525
1905	141,419	14,908	23,995	19,618	6,571	3,583
1906	134,985	14,507	25,012	20,640	8,089	3,275
1907	137,781	14,906	20,676	21,291	8,127	3,463
1908	132,774	15,626	24,082	20,514	8,207	3,982
1909	129,378	15,484	21,096	21,828	6,708	3,743
1910	131,995	15,268	21,431	21,054	6,998	3,318
1911	133,009	16,251	21,054	20,515	7,707	3,250
1912	128,011	15,767	21,423	21,498	7,392	3,224
1913	133,519	15,068	19,230	21,566	7,996	3,056
1914	133,650	15,103	19,281	21,094	5,951	3,056
1915	112,943	13,838	12,978	21,772	5,232	1,997
1916	114,588	14,824	12,285	21,274	4,675	2,638
1917	74,029	14,401	12,684	22,587	6,133	2,851
1918	94,291	17,646	12,630	21,206	3,272	2,661
1919	130,481	24,399	14,749	20,643	3,495	3,495
1920	141,437	30,014	19,230	23,310	3,679	6,871
1921	128,548	31,909	20,405	19,836	5,449	7,080
1922	145,947	31,213	18,563	22,723	4,231	6,490
1923	168,760	28,979	18,320	23,508	5,580	5,555
1924	169,175	29,851	18,918	24,087	6,009	4,713
1925	176,884	28,547	18,003	24,076	5,866	4,684
1926	161,846	27,668	28,058	17,744	5,851	5,422
1927	176,100	29,524	19,194	23,743	5,120	4,888
1928	165,599	28,761	16,996	25,063	5,344	4,558
1929	172,770	26,760	24,191	26,276	5,673	4,515
1930	162,007	25,682	15,469	27,222	5,661	4,527
1931	147,810	23,240	25,656	25,415	6,656	4,417
1932	139,686	20,999	12,302	25,656	5,545	2,081
1933	137,344	21,082	12,153	24,664	3,555	3,567
1934	36,360	20,581	13,481	25,282	4,064	3,736
Guardbridge						
1900	27,071	723	37,160	33,509	2,287	6,185
1901	28,887	791	36,408	31,847	1,909	6,156
1902	28,228	827	35,323	32,576	2,540	6,054
1903	30,823	736	38,913	36,005	2,248	6,311
1904	31,254	833	40,583	35,694	2,387	6,823
1905	30,084	839	41,392	33,030	2,875	6,874
1906	29,151	807	36,959	32,870	2,401	6,206
1907	29,530	868	32,345	39,551	3,274	6,615
1908	29,199	879	39,217	34,828	2,188	6,513
1909	27,682	870	38,234	34,372	2,312	6,383
1910	26,226	801	38,261	35,458	3,130	6,525
1911	28,844	895	41,470	34,906	3,462	6,825
1912	23,343	785	39,914	39,914	2,729	6,611
1913	50,513	1,334	46,918	36,767	3,326	6,357

	Passengers Booked (No.)	Receipts inc. parcels £	Merchandise & Minerals (tons)	Coal (tons)	Livestock (no.)	Goods £ (A)
Guardbridge (continued)						
1914	37,241	1,047	38,471	37,002	2,787	6,167
1915	23,930	734	29,406	35,330	2,568	6,160
1916	25,189	754	27,083	29,921	3,546	5,402
1917	14,946	656	21,624	27,987	3,735	8,266
1918	22,668	880	19,559	22,926	2,775	6,938
1919	31,679	1,196	24,510	26,835	2,643	7,691
1920	41,889	1,381	33,534	32,317	2,201	18,115
1921	29,305	1,307	18,016	20,800	2,444	9,918
1922	29,977	1,422	31,177	36,505	2,124	14,040
1923	33,011	1,431	44,006	42,932	3,641	17,959
1924	31,453	1,418	52,799	48,050	2,730	19,576
1925	33,454	1,406	45,597	43,644	2,281	21,046
1926	31,981	1,315	56,803	36,979	4,179	16,724
1927	33,806	1,407	53,937	50,506	3,489	18,385
1928	27,768	1,332	53,045	49,648	2,351	18,460
1929	31,896	1,099	53,633	48,535	2,822	17,203
1930	25,873	921	42,939	38,860	1,497	15,222
1931	26,742	889	38,112	25,418	6,656	4,417
1932	39,927	1,058	12,302	25,656	5,545	3,817
1933	41,416	1,086	12,153	24,664	3,555	3,570
1934	41,176	1,062	13,481	25,282	4,064	3,736
Leuchars Junction						
1900	33,124	1,483	-	-	-	-
1901	34,595	1,678	-	-	-	-
1902	34,334	1,690	-	-	-	-
1903	38,062	2,003	-	-	-	-
1904	37,758	2,042	-	-	-	-
1905	38,319	1,815	-	-	-	-
1906	35,717	1,744	-	-	-	-
1907	35,719	1,717	-	-	-	-
1908	33,504	1,847	-	-	-	-
1909	35,078	1,716	-	-	-	-
1910	34,376	1,908	-	-	-	-
1911	34,757	1,943	-	-	-	-
1912	35,245	1,788	-	-	-	-
1913	34,773	2,120	-	-	-	-
1914	36,418	1,812	-	-	-	-
1915	29,615	1,581	-	-	-	-
1916	30,616	1,470	-	-	-	-
1917	25,523	1,710	-	-	-	-
1918	88,819	3,172	-	-	-	-
1919	303,829	8,680	-	-	-	-
1920	68,497	5,981	-	-	-	-
1921	70,866	8,670	-	-	-	-
1922	74,738	10,466	-	-	-	-
1923	79,904	9,280	-	-	-	-
1924	89,345	9,221	-	-	-	-
1925	91,719	9,490	-	-	-	-
1926	78,914	8,608	-	-	-	-
1927	79,258	8,448	-	-	-	-
1928	71,154	8,510	-	-	-	-
1929	75,375	8,304	-	-	-	-
1930	66,027	7,598	-	-	-	-
1931	60,671	7,350	-	-	-	-
1932	55,712	6,499	-	-	-	-
1933	59,417	6,390	-	-	-	-
1934	62,043	6,217	-	-	-	-

	Passengers Booked (No.)	Receipts inc. parcels £	Merchandise & Minerals (tons)	Coal (tons)	Livestock (no.)	Goods £ (A)
Leuchars (Old)						
1900	13,190	337	5,678	3,069	4,614	463
1901	13,717	347	6,926	4,167	5,167	404
1902	14,319	344	6,046	2,863	6,274	423
1903	13,337	331	7,222	2,882	6,734	445
1904	13,888	338	6,771	2,900	6,434	473
1905	13,934	332	7,071	2,887	7,440	427
1906	13,035	321	8,210	3,048	6,754	373
1907	13,833	340	9,543	2,783	5,914	410
1908	12,482	328	8,289	1,828	6,262	432
1909	9,749	265	7,810	1,939	6,564	416
1910	10,066	270	7,339	7,777	6,944	351
1911	9,520	251	7,726	2,320	5,535	83
1912	7,231	402	6,752	1,705	4,564	498
1913	10,213	255	5,640	1,886	6,970	503
1914	9,911	265	8,419	1,928	5,165	420
1915	9,784	370	8,376	1,968	6,531	454
1916	9,195	438	8,119	1,890	8,223	412
1917	3,992	349	5,715	1,950	5,352	949
1918	5,435	459	44,190	2,261	8,551	1,816
1919	5,436	492	8,833	2,603	8,654	1,252
1920	7,458	723	9,290	2,656	6,779	1,208
1921	5,362	535	11,217	2,139	6,651	3,017
1922	-	-	11,517	2,946	5,890	2,761
1923	-	-	10,658	3,026	8,672	2,662
1924	-	-	10,897	3,169	8,953	2,002
1925	-	-	12,058	3,161	8,118	793
1926	-	-	10,687	2,407	9,165	705
1927	-	-	10,885	2,946	12,150	610
1928	-	-	8,863	3,119	11,890	768
1929	-	-	8,365	3,276	13,055	600
1930	-	-	7,280	3,507	11,247	559
1931	-	-	7,838	3,183	10,819	575
1932	-	-	6,042	3,128	7,469	609
1933	-	-	5,874	2,895	4,206	663
1934	-	-	5,762	2,946	4,263	415

General Note: All figures for years up to 1912 are the addition of six-month periods ending 31st July and 31st January of the following years. Owing to a change in the way figures were kept, the year 1912 comprises only of the statistics from 1st February, 1912 to 31st December, 1912. Thereafter figures relate to the actual calendar years.
(A) Cash remitted.

Appendix Three

St Leonards School
Christmas 1931 Travel Arrangements

The following special arrangements were provided to enable the girls of St Leonards to spend the Christmas holidays with their families and is taken from the LNER Southern Scottish Area *Supplementary Advice of Special Trains and Other Arrangements*, 17th December, 1931 (E. 66-113).

Tuesday, 22nd December

St Leonards School Pupils from St Andrews

90 Passengers for Glasgow About 4½ tons luggage	Passengers by 8.0 am train St Andrews to Leuchars Junction, Junction, accommodation to be reserved from Leuchars Junction by 6.10 am ex-Aberdeen. Two vestibule bogie thirds to be attached at Dundee to Glasgow portion and labelled for use of this party. Luggage to be attached on 21st and Van sent Leuchars Junction to be attached to 6.18 pm ex-Dundee for Thornton Junction, thence by 7.57 pm Thornton Junction to Glasgow.
7 Passengers for Perth About 7 cwts luggage	To St Fort by 8.40 a.m. St Andrews to Dundee train, thence Perth by 9.1 am ex-Dundee. Accommodation to be reserved in both trains.
14 Passengers for Dundee 8 Passengers for Aberdeen About 1 ton luggage	By 8.40 am St Andrews to Dundee train, Aberdeen passengers going orward from Dundee by 7.35 am ex-Edinburgh. Accommodation to be reserved in both trains.

No. 15 Special Express Train – St Andrews to Edinburgh

		am	Composition (leaving Leuchars Junction)	
Leuchars Junction (Empty)	*d.*	6.10	**Engine**	
St Andrews	*d.*	7.30	2 Thirds	King's Cross
Leuchars Junction	*a.*	7.40	1 Brake Van	Leeds
Do.	*d.*	7.48	1 Third	Leeds
Ladybank	*pass*	8.10	1 Brake Third	Liverpool
Thornton Junction	"	8.22	1 Third	Liverpool
Cowdenbeath Sth Jct	"	8.39	1 Third	Carlisle
Townhill Junction	"	8.43	1 Brake Third	Carlisle
Dunfermline (Lower)	"	8.46	2 Thirds	Edinburgh
Inverkeithing Cent Jct	"	8.51	Train to be double-headed. Express Passenger	
Forth Bridge North	"	8.56	Engines to be provided. It is important that the	
Dalmeny	"	8.59	train be worked punctually. District Operating	
Haymarket	"	9. 9	Superintendent, Burntisland, to make necessary	
Edinburgh	*arrive*	9.12	arrangements.	

Conveys passengers for destinations as follows:

70 for Edinburgh.
20 for Newcastle
3 for Darlington
6 for York
5 for Grantham and Peterborough
50 for King's Cross

a 25 for Manchester (Victoria)
a 15 for Liverpool (Exchange)

To go forward from Edinburgh by 10.0 am Express

a 20 for Preston
a 4 for Bolton
b 26 for Leeds and Sheffield.   To go forward by No. 16 *below*
c 10 for Crewe
d 14 for Birmingham
e 6 for Hellifield
e 2 for Skipton
   30 for Carlisle

a To connect with LMS 11.55 am from Carlisle, *via* Preston. Bolton and Manchester passengers change at Preston.
b To connect with LMS 12.5 pm from Carlisle, *via* Hellifield
c To connect with LMS 12.20 pm from Carlisle, *via* Preston. Passengers change at Carlisle.
d To connect with LMS 12.30 pm from Carlisle, *via* Preston. Passengers change at Carlisle.
e To connect with LMS 12.44 pm from Carlisle, *via* Hellifield. Passengers change at Carlisle.

The necessary accommodation to be reserved from Edinburgh.

Luggage for Newcastle, Darlington, York, Grantham, Peterborough and King's Cross to be loaded on 21st and despatched on 4.8 pm ex-Dundee, to get 7.45 pm Edinburgh to King's Cross. Brake Van to be provided, which must be labelled 'St Leonards School Pupils' Luggage for Newcastle, Darlington, York, Grantham, Peterborough and King's Cross', and wired accordingly by Station-Master, Edinburgh, instead of being included in total number of vehicles for King's Cross.

Luggage for Edinburgh to be loaded on the 21st, and despatched by 4.8 pm ex-Dundee. To be kept on hand at Waverley until passengers arrive following morning.

Luggage for Bolton and Manchester to be loaded on 21st, and despatched by 4.8 pm ex-Dundee, to get 9.55 pm Edinburgh to Carlisle. Six-wheeled Van to be provided and to be labled Bolton and Manchester (Victoria), *via* Carlisle and Preston.

Luggage for Preston and Liverpool to be loaded in Brake Third from Liverpool.

Luggage for Leeds and Sheffield to be loaded in Brake Van for Leeds.

Luggage for Crewe and Birmingham to be loaded in Brake Van for Carlisle, for transfer at Carlisle to LMS Company's 12.20 pm and 12.30 pm trains respectively ex-Carlisle.

Luggage for Hellifield and Skipton to be loaded on the 21st and despatched by 4.8 pm ex-Dundee. To be kept on hand at Edinburgh and sent forward in Guard's Van of 10.3 am Edinburgh to Carlisle following day.

Luggage for Carlisle to be loaded in Brake Van for Carlisle.

No. 16 Special Express Train – Edinburgh to Carlisle

		am	
Edinburgh (MU Plat)	dep.	9 18	**Conveys** St Leonards School Pupils for LMS Line, *via* Carlisle, arriving Waverley by No. 15
Portobello	pass	9 24	**Composition**
Hardengreen Junction	"	9 31	1 Brake Van Leeds
Falahill	"	9 51	1 Third Leeds
Galashiels	"	10 8	1 Brake Third Liverpool
St Boswells	"	10 17	1 Third Liverpool
Hawick	"	10 32	1 Third Carlisle
Riccarton Junction	"	10 57	1 Brake Third Carlisle
Newcastleton	"	11 7	It is important that the train be worked
Longtown	"	11 23	punctually. District Operating Superintendant,
Canal Junction	"	11 31	Edinburgh, to make necessary arrangements.
Carlisle (Citadel)	arrive	11 35	

Sources, Bibliography and Acknowledgements

This book has been compiled wherever possible from primary resources which are to be found in the National Archives of Scotland, the National Archives in Kew, the St Andrews University Archives and numerous private collections. Of chief interest were the Minute Books, accounts, cash books and journals and other records of the St Andrews Railway (NAS reference BR/SNR), the Anstruther & St Andrews Railway (BR/AST), the Edinburgh, Perth & Dundee Railway (BR/EPD) and the North British, LNER and British Railways Scottish Region and British Transport Hotels, together with timetables (public and working), General Appendices, special traffic notices, Board of Trade inspection and accident reports and a variety of other official documents together with advertising and other materials. In addition much help was derived from the Minute Books of the St Andrews Council and from local newspapers dating back to 1839 including:

The Scotsman, The Fifeshire Journal, The Fifeshire Advertiser, The Dundee Courier, The East of Fife Record, The St Andrews Citizen, The Fife News & Coast Chronicle, The Coastal Burghs Observer/East Fife Observer, The Dundee Evening Telegraph, The Edinburgh Evening Despatch and *The Edinburgh Evening News*. Other publications consulted included the *Railway Magazine, LNER and BR Scottish Region Magazines, North British Railway Study Group Journal* and *Railway World*.

Perhaps the most interesting sources of all were the personal reminiscences of those who worked on, used as passengers or merchants or trainspotted on the lines and special thanks are given for their most valuable contributions which helped this book to come to life.

The following works may prove of interest to those who wish to know more about St Andrews, Leuchars and Guardbridge or particular aspects of the line and its workings:

Local Topography

Farnie, H., *Handbook of St Andrews*, (1861); Geddie, J., *The Fringes of Fife*, (1907); Gifford, J., *The Buildings of Scotland: Fife*,(1988); Groome, F.H., *Ordnance Gazetteer of Scotland*,(1892); Lamont-Brown, R., *The Life and Times of St Andrews*, (1989); Leighton, J., *History of the County of Fife*, (1840); Lenman, B., *From Esk to Tweed*, (1975); Smith, A. (ed) *Third Statistical Account of Scotland: Fife*, (1952); Proudfoot & Brown, *Seafield Pottery, Brick and Tile Works*, (St Andrews Preservation Trust Year Book, 1991); Russell, K., *St Andrews*, (1954), Weatherill, L., *One Hundred Years of Papermaking: An Illustrated History of the Guard Bridge Paper Company*, (1973).

Local Railways

Batchelor, R., *East Fife Railway Album* (1984); Bennett, J.M., *Random Reflections of a Roving Railwayman*, (1976); Brotchie, A., *Fife Trains and Buses*, (1990); Corser,W.J.L., *Wings on Rails*, (2003); Corstorphine, J.K., *East of Thornton Junction*, (1995); Hamilton Ellis, C., *The North British Railway*,(1955); Macleod, W.M., *Across the Years by Rail*, (1996); Railway Correspondence & Travel Society, *Locomotives of the LNER* (various); Scott Bruce, W., *Railways of Fife*, (1980); Smith, D.J. *Action Stations No. 7: Military Airfields of Scotland, etc.* (1993); Stephenson Locomotive Society, *Locomotives of the NBR (1846-1882*; Thomas, J., *North British Railway*, 2 vols (1969, 1975).

Articles on the line which have appeared in railway journals include:

Anderson, D., *The Fife Coast Line*, (Steam Days, Feb. 1997); Bowman, C.W.R., *Souvenir of a North British Branch, Pt. II*, (Rly. World, Aug. 1964); Gairns, J.F., *The Fife Coast Lines of the LNER*, (Rly Mag., Apr. 1923); Mullay, A.J., *No Way to Close a Railway*, (Back Track, Sept. 2006); Patterson, E.M., *Souvenir of a North British Branch, Pt. I*, (Rly World, July 1964); Robertson, C.J.A., *The Cheap Railway Movement*, (Transport History, Spring 1974); Simpson, A., *East Neuk of Fife Line*, (NBRSG Journal 50 and 73); Simpson, A. *Rail Traffic to Guardbridge Paper Mills*, (NBRSG Journal 80); Simpson, A., *Traders Wagons on the East Fife Line*, (NBRSG Journal 95); Smith, W.A.C. and Anderson, P., *The Fife Coast Line : To Thornton the Long Way*, (British Rlys Ilustrated, July to Sept. 1994); Vallance, H.A., *The Fife Coast Line*, (Rly. Mag., Nov. 1953).

This book could not have been written without the assistance of the many persons who have, over the years, helped us and in particular Ian Addison, Richard Batchelor, the late J.M. Bennett, Tom Bigley, Alan Brotchie, Donald Cattanach, B. Chinn, Gordon Christie, Jim Corstorphine, the late William Docherty, John Gillespie, L.A.C. Horne, Douglas Hume, J. Hunter, Jeff Hurst, John Hurst, Matthew Jarron and the St Andrews Preservation Trust, John Langford, Brian Malaws, D. Mackay, Jim Mackie, Brian Macdonald, Alison MacKenzie, Sandy Maclean, Will McLeod, Ray Montgomery, the late Ed. Nicoll, Archie Noble, Jim Page, Douglas Paul, the late Roger Pedrick, Dr Madsen Pirie, John Purvis, Bill Rear, D.P. Rowland, Robert Smart, Martin Smith, Michael B. Smith, David Stirling, Douglas Sutherland, Isobel White, W. Whyte, D. Woodcock and Douglas Yuill. We would also wish to thank the staff of the Advocates' Library; British Rail Scottish Region headquarters, Glasgow; Cupar Public Library; Edinburgh Central Library; Glasgow Museum of Transport; Kirkcaldy Public Library; Glasgow University Business Archives; Leven Public Library; Methil Public Library; National Archives of Scotland; National Archives at Kew; National Library of Scotland including its Map Room; St Andrews Public Library and St Andrews University Library and Archive. Thanks is also given to many of the foregoing and to the following for kindly allowing us to reproduce photographs from their collections: the family of the late Gerald Baxter, George Bett, Nigel Dyckhoff, Bruce Ellis (for his late father's photographs), the late Roy Hamilton, Bill Lynn, the North British Railway Study Group for its comprehensive collections including that of the late Willie Hennigan, Stuart Rankin, Stuart Sellar, Hamish Stevenson (for his own and his late father's photographs), Anna Singer (for photographs by her late father, Dr E.M. Patterson), W.A.C. Smith, Nicholas Walker and, especially, Pete Westwater. Despite their efforts to trace the original photographers, the provenance of some of the illustrations is unknown to the authors, and apologies are tendered for any omissions. Particular thanks are given to Kate Hajducka for her hospitality and the meals that kept us going and for putting up with the clutter of documents, books, maps and other ephemera that lay on the dining room table for so long - perhaps, as an enthusiast for all things Fife, she will feel that the resulting book justifies her, and our, efforts!

Finally, any reader who is especially interested in the North British Railway, its predecessors and successors, is invited to join the North British Railway Study Group, the Group have a readily accessible website.

Index

A classic pose of *Peter Poundtext* waiting in the St Andrews dock at Leuchars Junction with a train of post-war BR-built non-corridor stock in the mid-1950s. *J.L. Stevenson*